DATE DUE

		MAR 2 4 2015
OCT 0 5 2006		
OCT 1 7 2006		
OCT 2 7 2006		
JUL 2 5 2007		
JUL 2 5 2007		
FEB 2 2 2011		
SEP 0 8 2011		
APR 0 9 2012		
MAY 1 7 2013		

The Power of Prayer

Make a Joyful Noise

BY PAMELA BRODE

Bahá'í
PUBLISHING

WILMETTE, ILLINOIS

Bahá'í Publishing, Wilmette, Illinois 60091-2844
Copyright © 2006 by the National Spiritual Assembly
of the Bahá'ís of the United States
All rights reserved. Published 2006
Printed in the United States of America on acid-free paper ∞

09 08 07 06   4 3 2 1

Library of Congress Cataloging-in-Publication Data

Brode, Pamela, 1948–
     The power of prayer : make a joyful noise / by Pamela Brode.
        p. cm.
     Includes bibliographical references (p.) and index.
     ISBN-13: 978-1-931847-10-0 (alk. paper)
     ISBN-10: 1-931847-10-X (alk. paper)
      1. Prayer. 2. Bahai Faith—Doctrines. I. Title.

  BP380.B76 2006
  297.9'343—dc22
                                                                2005057234

Cover design by Robert A. Reddy
Book design by Patrick J. Falso

Dedicated to
the three precious pearls of my heart,
my beloved sons
Justin, Alex, and Ben

Make a joyful noise unto God, all ye lands:
Sing forth the honor of his name:
make his praise glorious.

—Psalms 66:1–2

Contents

Author's Note

Dear Readers,

Because prayer has played such a vital role in my own life, I was motivated to seek out and interview individuals of diverse backgrounds who were willing to share personal, inspirational stories that testify to the awesome power of prayer. I threw in quite a lot of my own stories and also shared the illuminating perspective of prayer from the sacred writings of the Bahá'í Faith. But it was an especially thrilling and enlightening adventure to compile and write other people's testimonials of wondrous happenings that occurred in their lives as a result of prayer and faith. Hopefully, you will find these stories moving, intriguing, and inspiring—and joyous affirmations of the power of prayer as a sacred bestowal of God.

While all the narrations in this book are accounts of real people, they are presented anecdotally, with the exception of stories about the central figures of the Bahá'í Faith: Bahá'u'lláh, the Báb, and 'Abdu'l-Bahá; and the Bábí heroine Ṭáhirih, which have carefully been researched and referenced. Also, certain people have requested anonymity, and some of the names in the contemporary stories have been changed.

Regarding the use of pronouns: Bahá'í scripture was written in the Persian and Arabic languages. The translation of these writings into English frequently requires the use of the masculine pronouns "he" and "his" and words such as "man" and "men" in a generic, rather than gender-specific, sense. Bahá'í scripture explains, "Man is a generic term applying to all humanity. . . . In Persian and Arabic there are two distinct words translated into English as man: one meaning man and woman collectively, the other distinguishing man as male from woman the female. The first word and its pronoun are generic, collective; the other is restricted to the male."*

Enjoy, dear readers! Hopefully you will find reading this book as much an adventure as it was for me to write it.

—PAMELA BRODE

---

* 'Abdu'l-Bahá, *The Promulgation of Universal Peace,* p. 76.

Acknowledgments

First I offer my heartfelt thanks to Senior Editor Terry Cassiday for her generous and tireless outpouring of encouragement, support, and friendship. It has been a joy and blessing to collaborate with this very dear, talented, special person. I am also deeply grateful to Alex McGee for his outstanding editing, and I wish to extend loving kudos and appreciation to the General Manager, Lee Minnerly, as well as to all the excellent staff at Bahá'í Publishing for their prayers and support: Tim Moore, Suni Hannan, Christopher Martin, Bahhaj Taherzadeh, and Gini Adamo.

Loving gratitude and appreciation also go to all those precious souls who allowed me to interview them and graciously shared their wondrously inspiring stories of prayer and faith: Ann Bauer, Isik Cotton, Robert Crookall, Catherine Davis, Dilsey Davis, Eric Dozier, Ray Phlueger Estes, Rodney and Gwen Ferguson, Kathy Lee, Kevin Locke, Harvey McMurray, Jean Scales, Tangela Stanley, Cindy Thompson, Nat and Joan West, Cara Williams, and Ramine Yazhari. This note of appreciation is most warmly extended to the individuals who requested anonymity and are not acknowledged here by name.

It is amazing how profoundly the sweet words of encouragement can affect the spirit when they are offered sincerely and selflessly—which is why I most lovingly acknowledge Ruḥíyyih Khánum, who not only personally encouraged me to use the arts to serve humanity, but also helped me to open my eyes to the beauty of man's spiritual reality and purpose. I also thank three selfless souls who encouraged me to be a spiritual writer many years ago: Juana C. Conrad, Robert H. Stockman, and Kenneth E. Bowers; and I am extremely grateful for the encourage-

ment and support of Jeanette Hedayati, Mahyar Modifi, James Sturdi-
vant, and the Regional Bahá'í Council of the Southern States.

Finally, I wish to express my love and gratitude to my parents in the
next world, who always encouraged me to pursue artistic endeavors, and,
last but never least, to my dearest Roger, devoted husband and extraordinary father whose support, patience, and spiritual heart have helped
make our marriage "a fortress of well-being and salvation."

Introduction

When I was a little girl, it baffled me when I heard children at school ask each other, "Which god do you believe in? Do you believe in the Christian god, the Jewish god, or the Muslim god?" My parents had taught me that there is only one God—the Divine Creator of the Universe. He was the God I talked to every night before I went to sleep—and the God I talked to when I was sad or upset and called on for help any time of the day. He was the God of everyone. I loved God and I loved praying to Him.

I found it disconcerting that just because people practiced different religions it was assumed that they worshipped different gods. The idea seemed ludicrous to me even as a young child. I cannot remember at any time in my life, not even once, thinking of God as Jewish, Muslim, Christian, Buddhist, Hindu, or Bahá'í. When I think of God, I just think of God, our Creator—Omnipotent, Omniscient, and All-Loving.

The importance of a name, however, apparently still prevails. Very recently, a woman I know who was concerned about terrorists and ongoing violence in the Middle East remarked, "All these problems over religion. I can't understand it. The Muslims believe in Allah. Who is Allah? Do they even believe in God?"

"Well," I responded, "'Allah' is the Arabic word for God. So, yes, of course they believe in God."

"I'm sorry. I can't buy that," she said. "Either you believe in God or you don't. Muslims say they believe in Allah. Well, I believe in God and there is only one God! God is God! Who is Allah? If they believe in God, why don't they say they believe in God? Why do they say they believe in Allah?"

Just as when I was a child, I had difficulty comprehending her logic. I explained, "Allah means God—Allah is the Arabic word for God."

The woman insisted, "God is God! I believe in God, not 'Allah.' I don't know what god they believe in, but they believe in a different god from the rest of us."

I extracted my words slowly and gingerly, in my best effort to be understood. "All over the world people speak in different languages—right? So, isn't it only natural that people who speak in a different language will also call God by a different name? We live in a society where we speak English, and because the English word for God is 'God,' we call Him by such. But God is also referred to by other words in English, such as 'Lord,' 'Heavenly Father,' and 'the Creator.' If we all believe that there is one God, Who created all of the universe and all of humanity—then regardless of the name a particular culture of people calls Him, isn't He still God?"

Confident that I had gotten through to the woman, I was jolted when she responded vehemently, "All I know is that I believe in God. And if there are people who call their god something else, well, then they don't believe in the same god that I do."

I gave up. She was too fixated on the name of God to recognize what was behind the name. Yet, unlike when I was a child, I can now somewhat understand and sympathize with the woman's convictions. I have come to realize that it can be very difficult and even painful for people to accept change in their pattern of thought and behavior when they have long grown accustomed to believing certain ideas and concepts as the absolute and sole truth.

The Bahá'í writings, however, tell us that when we become overly attached to an idea and a certain way of doing things, it can prevent us from searching for truth and veil us from deeper understanding:

In order to find truth . . . an open receptive mind is essential . . . The fact that we imagine ourselves to be right and everybody else wrong is the greatest of all obstacles in the path towards unity . . . we must be willing to clear away all that we have previously learned, all that would clog our steps on the way to truth; we must not shrink if necessary from beginning our education all over again. . . . When we are freed from all these bonds, seeking with liberated minds, then shall we be able to arrive at our goal.[1]

All my life I have heard Christians attest that the only way to God and salvation is through Christ. I have heard Jews avow that the only path to God and His knowledge is through the Torah. Muslims testify that the only ladder to Heaven is through complete submission to God and His teachings as revealed in the Koran. However, the teachings of the Bahá'í Faith explain that there is spiritual truth found in all of these religions.

As a Bahá'í, the God I believe in is the same God spoken of by Abraham, Moses, Krishna, Buddha, Zoroaster, Christ, Muḥammad, the Báb, and Bahá'u'lláh. I believe in the God of all humanity.

As a child, I was extremely happy with the religion that I had been born into, but I was also very curious to learn about other faiths, customs, and peoples. I was a young woman when I became a Bahá'í in 1979, after ten years of investigating the world's religions and traveling to more than fifteen countries. I was initially attracted to the Bahá'í Faith because of its scripture, particularly its teachings about the love of God, the message of the oneness of humanity and religion, and its emphasis on the education of children and the advancement of women. And I especially loved the prayers. The very first prayer from Bahá'í scripture that I recited aloud touched the core of my soul. It began, "From the sweet-scented streams of Thine eternity give me to drink, O my God, and of the fruits of the tree of Thy being enable me to taste, O my Hope!"[2]

I think it is relevant to note that although I am a member of the Bahá'í Faith, the prayers that I say daily remind me that what is far more important than the name of my religion is the purity of my relationship with God. I strive to show my love for God through daily prayer and through my deeds and action.

Inspired by the teachings of the Bahá'í Faith, I strive not to be judgmental of anyone, and I endeavor to treat each soul with respect and kindness. I have a strong marriage, three wonderful sons, one marvelous daughter-in-law, I sing with two choirs, have traveled to twenty-nine countries to date, and I am involved with local social and economic development projects that focus on promoting race unity and advocating for education and services for children with developmental disabilities. Oh—and I write, too.

I have also had my share of trials and difficulties. Two of my three beloved sons were born with a genetic condition that causes mental impairment. When my third son was diagnosed with the same condition as our middle son, I felt like a truck had run over me. My initial reaction was a mixture of shock, heartbreak, despair, denial, disappointment, fear, guilt, and perhaps some anger. The pain was so excruciating it was paralyzing. I asked myself, "Why did this happen to me? How could this happen? What did I do wrong?"

I turned to God with all my heart and prayed fervently. Two of my children had disabilities. And yet they were so beautiful and healthy looking. I cried and I begged God to give me fortitude and strength so that I could meet head-on the lifelong challenges and limitations my precious children would face as a result of their debilitations. I prayed for strength and fortitude so that I could effectively do whatever it took to help maximize their potential. I reflected on a verse from the Bahá'í writings that explains that trials and difficulties happen "in order that man's faith may be increased and strengthened. Therefore, although we feel sad and disheartened, we must supplicate God to turn our hearts to the Kingdom and pray . . . with faith in His infinite mercy."[3]

Facing the challenges of raising two children with disabilities did indeed cause me to turn to God and place my trust in Him, and this in turn increased and strengthened my faith. Quite frankly, I believe that without prayer and confidence in God at that time, I would have been unable to cope and would have plunged into hopeless depression. Through prayer and by directing my soul to the Holy Spirit, my eyes were opened, enabling me to recognize my children as blessings—as two angels on this earth who seemed to make everyone who is close to them a better person. Through prayer I was able to enjoy my children, take pride in them, and see the beauty and purity of their souls. There is a prayer from the Bahá'í writings that I say daily for my children and for all the children in the world:

O Thou kind Lord! These lovely children are the handiwork of
the fingers of Thy might and the wondrous signs of Thy greatness.
O God! Protect these children, graciously assist them to be educated

and enable them to render service to the world of humanity. O God! These children are pearls, cause them to be nurtured within the shell of Thy loving-kindness.[4]

Through prayer and basking in the love of God, I was able to see my children as precious pearls, and I was assisted to love my children with God's love—an unconditional love—which helped me to be a happier, more nurturing and effective parent. Through the power of prayer and giving up my pain to God, I was assisted in looking at the bigger picture and channeling that negative energy into something purposeful and productive. I have always found that turning a crisis into something positive and meaningful helps dissipate the pain.

What also particularly inspired and motivated me was a verse from Bahá'í scripture about the importance of educating children: "Every child is potentially the light of the world—and at the same time its darkness; wherefore must the question of education be accounted as of primary importance."[5]

And so, inspired by the Bahá'í teachings on the critical importance of the education of children, in 1987, I went through a training course at the Child Advocacy Commission in my hometown of Durham, North Carolina. Shortly after receiving certification as a Child Advocate, I was hired to work at Duke University Medical Center's Child Development Unit in Durham. There I served five years as editor of a periodical that provided the latest findings about education, medical treatments, and other services to help ameliorate the conditions and maximize the potential of children and adolescents with developmental disabilities.

At times it seemed very funny to me that I was working at Duke. My background was in music, theater, and writing. How on earth had I ended up working as a professional child advocate in one of the most prestigious medical centers in the nation? I believe it was the fruition of my prayers and turning to God. Through the years, I saw vast improvements made in my town regarding the education and services for young people with special needs, which was immensely gratifying.

On February 15, 2001, the Durham Human Relations Commission presented me with the Advocacy Award "In Recognition of Dedication and Commitment to Civil and Human Rights Advocacy, especially on behalf of People with Developmental Disabilities." In truth, I felt unworthy of the award because any good works I contributed, I believe, came as a result of guidance and assistance from heavenly forces.

Nearly every human being, at some point in his or her life, faces health challenges. I, too, have had to deal with health challenges. Last year, in an episode similar to a story in this book, I fought blindness due to an eye condition and had to undergo eye surgeries. I was declared legally blind and lost my driver's license. I never stopped praying, nor lost my faith in God—and it was a miracle to me the way my spirit was sustained with fortitude and a sense of radiant acquiescence.

Losing my eyesight and going through the surgeries was quite an ordeal for both me and my family, but the prayers kept us unified and enabled us to maintain a measure of calm, courage, and clarity of action. It is a heavenly blessing to feel, through prayer, the guidance and assistance of the Holy Spirit. I received material blessings as well because the surgeries were a success and my sight in both eyes was restored. Of course I am thrilled and profoundly grateful to have clear vision again, but I feel that during that time of personal crisis, prayer and trust in God helped my inner vision become clearer.

Of course, I am a frail, imperfect being, and I am as prone to mistakes as anyone. But I have such an internalized trust and faith in the mercy and forgiveness of God that my soul is happy and content in the knowledge that God loves me even with my shortcomings. There is no question in my mind that He loves me even during difficult trials and ordeals.

And as for making mistakes, I have found that through prayer and meditation combined, I am able to learn and benefit from my mistakes. When we use our mistakes to learn and grow, they are good. When we fail to learn from them, they create problems.

I also recognize that the infinite love and mercy of God is not a license for me to do whatever I want to do. On the contrary, knowing His love for me fuels me with inspiration to try my best to please Him by obeying His commandments as set forth in the holy writings of the Bahá'í Faith. The wonderful news is that the teachings of my faith assure me that when I strive in earnest to achieve something of merit—even when I fail to achieve it—I am nonetheless blessed if my motives and intent are pure.

I feel my life would be dead without the love of God and without daily prayer to sustain my soul. When I was a little girl, with the innocence and purity of a child's tender heart, I believed in God and loved Him profoundly with all my soul. I loved talking to God, and I especially loved the sensation of feeling immersed in His love when I prayed. I guess on some level I instinctively recognized that talking to God and praying to Him were the same thing—as long as my supplication came from my heart.

Perhaps prayer and trust in God come easily to young children when they are taught to do so because their hearts are pure and receptive. On the other hand, adults, and teenagers too, often require self-discipline to pray regularly and turn their hearts to God. My own personal experience is that daily prayer cleanses my heart, purifies my motives, and restores that childlike innocence and receptivity to God's infinite love.

The inner reality of prayer is the motive and nature of our supplication. It is personal communion with the Holy Spirit of God. More important than the outward techniques and physical gestures is the personal intent and endeavor of prayer. Do we worship God to grandstand our piety as pillars in the religious community? Do we worship in fear of superstitious beliefs? Do we go through all the motions of worship without any real feeling or meaning? Do we worship, convinced that our way is the only right way to practice faith?

Or do we worship, praise, and glorify God with humility and sincerity because we love Him? When we pray for the love of God, we learn to love each other for the sake of God because the very essence of faith is love. When we pray for the love of God, we ourselves are transformed into loving creatures—and we cannot help but want to show kindness and love to all. The very essence and inner reality of prayer is the love of God.

> By the fire of the Love of God the veil is burnt which separates us from the Heavenly Realities, and with clear vision we are enabled

to struggle onward and upward, ever progressing in the paths of virtue and holiness, and becoming the means of light to the world.

There is nothing greater or more blessed than the Love of God! It gives healing to the sick, balm to the wounded, joy and consolation to the whole world, and through it alone can man attain Life Everlasting. The essence of all religions is the Love of God, and it is the foundation of all the sacred teachings.[6]

CHAPTER 1

What Is Prayer?

From time immemorial, in humankind's quest to attain the nearness of the divine Creator, prayer—a universally accepted, essential element in the worship of God—has quickened the hearts of countless souls through its mystifying power. In our longing to know God and to commune with Him, sincere believers of all creeds and of all nations have offered prayer as a sweet call of faith to the eternal realm. With hearts uplifted in awe and ecstasy, myriads of souls through the ages have joyfully testified to the miracle of prayer and to its incalculable benefits.

The laws, customs, and traditions may differ greatly, but common threads linking all the world's major religions and their respective followers are the belief in God and the practice of prayer. Many independent seekers as well, who endeavor to investigate spiritual truths on their own while not adhering to an organized religion, believe in God and view prayer as an important aspect of their lives. In short, the belief in God and the practice of prayer are not only a unifying factor found in all major religions, but also signify a commonality in the spirit of humanity.

Prayer—supplication to God—is seen by believers as an expression of faith, a source of hope, and a key to spiritual fulfillment and happiness. It has been associated with invocation, sacrifice, devotion, atonement, salvation, redemption, benediction, submission, petition, healing, praise and gratitude, and more. Although it is one of the purest acts of worship, prayer has often been expressed with great elaboration and pomp through ceremonial ritual and congregational pageantry. Regardless of the mode of expression, though, whether it is through chanting, recitation, meditation, fasting, singing, or even dancing—what is most important is the purity of intent behind the prayer.

In its simplest definition, prayer is talking to God in a spirit of love. When one removes the exterior, often ornamental and ritualistic practices that have long been associated with prayer, its inner reality is revealed as a personal conversation and intimate connection of the heart with the Holy Spirit of God. While a person may appear pious because he or she is reciting the words and going through the motions of prayer, if there is no love for God and no sincerity in the words, the act is meaningless. In the Bible, St. Paul warns, "If I speak in the tongues of men and of angels, but have not love, I am a noisy gong or a clanging cymbal."[7]

Likewise, in the Bahá'í writings we find, "Words without love mean nothing," and "In the highest prayer, men pray only for the love of God, not because they fear Him or hell, or hope for bounty or heaven."[8] God created us because He loves us, but only when we love God can we know and reap the joy of His infinite love for us. Bahá'í scripture describes prayer as an expression of our love for God that originated in God's eternal love for us and in our creation:

O Son of Man! Veiled in My immemorial being and in the ancient eternity of My essence, I knew My love for thee; therefore I created thee, have engraved on thee Mine image and revealed to thee My beauty.

O Son of Man! I loved thy creation, hence I created thee. Wherefore, do thou love Me, that I may name thy name and fill thy soul with the spirit of life.

O Son of Being! Love Me, that I may love thee. If thou lovest Me not, My love can in no wise reach thee. Know this, O servant.[9]

If we think of prayer as our own personal hotline to God, then surely love is its signal. Love is the force that binds us to God. The scriptures found in all the world's major religions confirm this message, each exhorting us to love God. In the Hindu scripture we are told, "Worship Me well, with hearts of love and faith."[10] In Judaism we find, "If ye shall hearken diligently unto my commandments which I command you this day, to love the Lord your God, and to serve him with all your heart and with all your soul."[11] In Christianity, "You shall love the Lord your God with all your heart, and with all your soul, and with all your mind."[12] In Islam we read passages such as "Those of Faith are overflowing in their love for God."[13]

Of course, there may be times when we feel empty of love and down in spirit. If we think we have no love in our hearts should we even bother to pray? Absolutely yes! Those are the times when we need more than ever to pray. There is a special blessing that occurs when we pray for the love of God and turn to Him in moments of difficulty. During times of unhappiness, pain, confusion, and fear—even when we feel as if we are thoroughly void of love and spiritually bankrupt—a prayer from the heart, supplicating God is an act of love in itself. Whatever amount of love we deposit into our own personal "spiritual bank," we can be assured of multifold profits.

God's love is always there, but sometimes it requires an extra measure of faith to plug into it. The more we trust, revere, and seek the nearness of God, the stronger and purer our faith. The Bahá'í teachings tell us,

> When a man has faith, all the mountains of the world cannot turn him back. No, he will endure any trial, any disaster, and nothing will weaken him.[14]

> A man of faith bears every trial, every hardship, with self-control and patience. One without faith is always wailing, lamenting . . . he cannot endure hardship, he never thinks of better times coming that will take the place of present ills.[15]

Faith in and love for God, like all spiritual qualities, are sustained through prayer. The Bahá'í teachings say that "prayer is absolutely indispensable" to our "inner spiritual development"[16] and that "love and good faith" should "dominate the human heart."[17] The lyrics from an old African-American spiritual effectively convey that message through a sweet, simple metaphor: "Prayer is the key to the kingdom, faith unlocks the door." That door, when opened, leads us to the pathway of God's unconditional love. Through love and faith, sustained by the power of payer, we find that we can face even the harshest ordeals with a measure of courage, patience, and hope.

In describing the state and nature of prayer, the Bahá'í teachings attest, "There is nothing sweeter in the world of existence than prayer. . . . The most blessed condition is the condition of prayer and supplication. Prayer is a conversation with God. The greatest attainment or the sweetest state is none other than conversation with God. It creates spirituality, creates mindfulness and celestial feelings . . . and engenders the susceptibilities of the higher intelligence."[18]

Through daily, personal prayer we connect with our spiritual reality and develop virtues that enrich our lives, enable us to be happier and better people, and help us cope with everyday stresses, both large and small. Daily prayer is particularly important because it is a means to cleanse and purify our spiritual channel to God. We know that the cleanliness of our physical bodies is dependent upon daily washing. If we allow even one day to pass without bathing, we may feel unclean. Ironically, when people are in a situation in which they go long periods without bathing, they may tend to become less aware, and perhaps even oblivious, to their unhygienic condition. Through the daily practice of bathing, not only do we keep ourselves clean, but also we are more sensitive to the state of cleanliness, the fragrance and health of our bodies.

In the same manner, the longer we go without prayer, the more prone we are to be forgetful of our spiritual reality and purpose. Through the daily practice of prayer, as we bathe our souls in the depth of the ocean of God's love, awareness of our spirituality is enhanced and our faith is sustained. Daily prayer enables us to tap into the power of the Holy Spirit of God and to attune our hearts and minds with greater clarity, perception, and enlightenment. We are told in Bahá'í scripture that every day a person should "commune with God, and, with all his soul, persevere in the quest."[19]

It may require discipline to incorporate prayer into our daily routine, but the rewards are immeasurable. Discipline in striving to maintain a spiritual attitude when we pray is essential as well, since the effectiveness of our prayer is dependent upon the purity of our motive. Bahá'í scripture explains, "The most acceptable prayer is the one offered with the utmost spirituality and radiance . . . the purer the prayer, the more acceptable is it in the presence of God." [20]

Therefore, regardless of form and mode, whether we choose to pray while sitting, standing, bowing, kneeling, lighting candles, burning incense, reciting, chanting, singing, dancing, wearing a certain headdress, closing our eyes or opening our eyes, reaching our hands upward or keeping them at our side, the Bahá'í teachings stress that what is most important is the spirit and motive of our supplication. Bahá'í scripture asserts that a single prayer offered with radiance of spirit and genuine reflection is more acceptable in the eyes of God than the most lengthy and outwardly ceremonious display of pious worship.

Bahá'í scripture tells us that privately communing with God is the purest form of prayer and that prayers offered in this manner have a powerful effect on ourselves as well as others: "Whoso reciteth, in the privacy of his chamber, the verses revealed by God, the scattering angels of the Almighty shall scatter abroad the fragrance of the words uttered by his mouth, and shall cause the heart of every righteous man to throb." [21]

Furthermore, Bahá'í scripture explains, "The reason why privacy hath been enjoined in moments of devotion is this, that thou mayest give thy best attention to the remembrance of God, that thy heart may at all times be animated with His Spirit, and not be shut out as by a veil from thy Best Beloved. Let not thy tongue pay lip service in praise of God while thy heart be not attuned to the exalted Summit of Glory, and the Focal Point of communion." [22]

There is nothing in our lives that we can possibly achieve which is more important and beneficial to our spiritual growth and well-being than the personal, intimate relationship we form with God: "Throughout, it is the relationship of the individual soul to God and the fulfillment of its spiritual destiny that is the ultimate aim of the laws of religion." [23]

Through private communion with our Creator, and in yearning for His nearness, a sweet serenity calms our spirit like a soothing, gentle balm as we supplicate with words such as in the following prayer from Bahá'í scripture:

O my Lord! Make Thy beauty to be my food, and Thy presence my drink, and Thy pleasure my hope, and praise of Thee my action, and remembrance of Thee my companion, and the power of Thy sovereignty my succorer, and Thy habitation my home, and my dwelling-place the seat Thou hast sanctified from the limitations imposed upon them who are shut out as by a veil from Thee. [24]

Prayer is a means to lighten and cheer our hearts, not burden them. One of the loveliest things about prayer is that we are free to supplicate to God whenever or wherever our hearts so desire and feel the need. When we are in a place or situation in which it may be inappropriate to pray aloud, we can still offer prayer silently in our thoughts. At other times, sharing prayers aloud with others at devotional gatherings can be very spiritually uplifting and unifying. However, as wonderful as devotional gatherings are, Bahá'í scripture tells us that what is most crucial for the progress of the soul is to pray to God in private, as affirmed in the following prayer:

Intone, O My servant, the verses of God that have been received by thee, as intoned by them who have drawn nigh unto Him, that the sweetness of thy melody may kindle thine own soul, and attract the hearts of all men. Whoso reciteth, in the privacy of his chamber, the verses revealed by God, the scattering angels of the Almighty shall scatter abroad the fragrance of the words uttered by his mouth, and shall cause the heart of every righteous man to throb. Though he may, at first, remain unaware of its effect, yet the virtue of the grace vouchsafed unto him must needs sooner or later exercise its influence upon his soul. Thus have the mysteries of the Revelation of God been decreed by virtue of the Will of Him Who is the Source of power and wisdom. [25]

Prayer gives voice to the soul as an expression of divine reality, whether it is spoken out loud or offered in silent reflection. Prayer is more than uttering words and sounds. It is more than a mere petition. Prayer is speaking to God from the heart with sincerity and feeling. Prayer is about connecting with God, internalizing His love, and reflecting upon His divine attributes. Prayer extends to our actions. A fundamental teaching in all the world's religions is that our actions should reflect our prayers so that our deeds—our very lives—may be purposeful, virtuous, and beneficial to our fellow man. The Bahá'í writings indicate that such action is a form of worship in itself, as explained by Bahá'u'lláh's eldest son, 'Abdu'l-Bahá: "Briefly, all effort and exertion put forth by man from the fullness of his heart is worship, if it is prompted by the highest motives and the will to do service to humanity. This is worship: to serve mankind and to minister to the needs of the people. Service is prayer."[26]

When we pray and our thoughts are of God and aspiring towards heavenly subjects, it is of the essence that we strive to carry out those thoughts through action. It is through action that prayer is bestowed power and life. A passage from the Bahá'í writings explains,

> Thoughts may be divided into two classes:—Thought that belongs to the world of thought alone [and] thought that expresses itself in action. Some men and women glory in their exalted thoughts, but if these thoughts never reach the plane of action they remain useless: the power of thought is dependent on its manifestation in deeds.[27]

Prayer doesn't prevent us from facing trials and difficulties. However, when turning our hearts to God, offering supplication with love and faith, it is possible to endure even the harshest ordeals with fortitude and radiance.

Jean, a woman in her seventies who is a dear friend and one of the most spiritual people I have ever known, was in a dreadful car accident some years ago. She had several broken bones, and her lovely face was severely injured. A retired college professor and longtime champion of racial and gender equality, Jean was beloved and well known in her city. Many people from all around came to the hospital to see her. A reporter who was familiar with Jean's advocacy work wrote a beautiful tribute to her in the local newspaper after learning about her accident. Many of her friends held prayer vigils for her.

The hospital staff allowed only a few people to visit her at a time, and so on the day after the accident I arrived in the early morning to spend some time alone with her. I entered the intensive care unit and quietly tiptoed to her bed. I was immediately taken aback when I saw the extent of my friend's injuries. I gently took her hand and, knowing how much Jean enjoys music, I sang a healing prayer from Bahá'í scripture in a volume slightly above a whisper. The prayer began, "Thy name is my healing, O my God, and remembrance of Thee is my remedy."[28]

Jean was heavily medicated and groggy, but she clearly enjoyed the prayer. I will not elaborate on the severity of her wounds, but it was evident she would need to undergo a series of surgeries to repair her face. It was also clear that she was in pain. That is why I will never forget what Jean said when I asked her how she felt that morning—the morning after the awful crash. She responded with one word, "Blessed."

Standing there by her bedside, I paused to reflect on her single comment. I asked, "Why do you feel blessed, Jean?" Her eyes were half closed and her words came out slowly and slurred, but I sensed that her mind was crystal clear. "I'm blessed because of the prayers. I know that the friends are all praying for me. I can feel it." Jean, who has been a Bahá'í for more than forty years, then said, "I'm blessed because I have Bahá'u'lláh. I'm drowning in God's love."

Jean went back to sleep and I left. In all my life I had never seen anyone injured so badly, and yet when I asked her how she felt, she answered, "Blessed." And indeed she was. Many people continued to pray for her, and even her doctors were amazed that Jean made such a miraculous recovery. Today Jean walks with a cane, and her stamina is not quite what it used to be, but after a round of surgeries, her face is again lovely and her spirit is more radiant than ever. Throughout her ordeal her strength and courage remained a source of inspiration to all who know her. Never once did she complain, groan, or express unhappiness and fear. On the contrary, she laughed, joked, and brought cheer to the nurses, doctors, and to her friends.

Today, if anyone asks her, "Jean, how did you get through that terrible ordeal and still be such a glowing, exuberant soul?" She responds adamantly, "Prayers. I know that I would not be alive today if it had not been for the prayers." Yes, certainly, Jean is blessed.

Through prayer, we are able to draw power from the Holy Spirit, which fortifies our spiritual being and assists us in coping with whatever situations life hands us with a degree of strength, endurance, and calm. Through the power of prayer we are motivated to take affirmative steps to help remedy our difficulties. Through prayer we receive protection from behaving irrationally or recklessly, and from making decisions that can lead to harmful consequences. In essence, prayer helps us to take control of our lives. We may not always be in control of what happens in the world around us, but prayer enables us to take control of the way we respond to any given situation—and that is truly empowering. Yes, prayer is empowering. Prayer gives us direction and motivation to take a positive and productive course of action that benefits us as well as those around us.

Through the power of prayer it is possible for our hearts to transform from a state of sorrow and unrest to one of joy and contentment. Through the power of prayer it is possible to witness a crisis evolve into something wondrous and beneficial. That power is drawn from the all-merciful, all-loving God.

Prayer is rendering thanks and praise to God. Therefore, "Make a joyful noise unto God, all ye lands: Sing forth the honor of his name: make his praise glorious."[29]

CHAPTER 2

A Bahá'í Approach to Prayer

There is a short but compelling story about a youth who lived in nineteenth-century Persia (the country known today as Iran). While praying at a public holy place in the town of Kárbilá, this youth could be heard uttering with great frequency the following verse: "O God, my God, my Beloved, my heart's Desire."[30]

So wrapt was He in His devotions that He seemed utterly oblivious of those around Him. Tears rained from His eyes, and from His lips fell words of glorification and praise of such power and beauty as even the noblest passages of our Sacred Scriptures could not hope to surpass. The words "O God, my God, my Beloved, my heart's Desire" were uttered with a frequency and ardour that those of the visiting pilgrims who were near enough to hear Him instinctively interrupted the course of their devotions, and marvelled at the evidences of piety and veneration which that youthful countenance evinced. Like Him they were moved to tears, and from Him they learned the lesson of true adoration.[31]

This story is but one of many accounts about the founders and early believers of the Bahá'í Faith that are recorded in a fascinating book called *The Dawn-Breakers*. The book explains that some time later, in the year

1844, the same youth, Siyyid 'Alí-Muhammad, who had so profoundly touched the hearts of those pilgrims in Kárbilá, later became known as the Báb, the prophet-founder of the Bábí Faith, and one of the central figures of the Bahá'í Faith.

The eloquent writings of the Báb, which comprise a portion of the Bahá'í scripture, include the following counsel: "The most acceptable prayer is the one offered with the utmost spirituality and radiance; its prolongation hath not been and is not beloved by God. The more detached and the purer the prayer, the more acceptable is it in the presence of God."[32] The short but potent prayer offered by the Báb in the public square in Kárbilá, and the fervent, humble, and loving spirit in which he offered it exemplify perfectly and concisely the Bahá'í approach to prayer. There was not the slightest evidence of pomp, ritualistic clamor, sanctimonious fanfare, or proselytizing in the manner of his devotions. On the other hand, his prayer was not offered casually, nor was it lacking in reverence or spiritual intensity.

Who Is the Báb?

Born in Shiraz, Persia, on October 20, 1819, Siyyid 'Alí-Muhammad was orphaned as a young boy when his father died. He was raised by his maternal uncle, a merchant. As a young man, he followed his uncle's footsteps to become a merchant, gaining a high reputation for uncommon wisdom and fairness while also earning notice for his "godliness, devoutness, virtue, and piety."[33]

On May 23, 1844, he was only twenty-five when he assumed the title of "the Báb," (meaning literally "the Gate" in Arabic), and declared himself to be a prophet of a new revelation from God. He proclaimed himself to be the Promised One of the scriptures of the past and said that the mission of his dispensation was to alert the people to the imminent coming of another prophet, "Him Whom God shall make manifest," a claim that "marked the birth, and fixed the date, of the inception of the most glorious era in the spiritual life of mankind."[34]

In some respects, the Báb's role can be compared to that of John the Baptist, who prepared the way for the coming of Christ. The Báb was

Bahá'u'lláh's herald: his primary mission was to prepare the way for the coming of Bahá'u'lláh. Accordingly, the founding of the Bábí Faith is viewed as synonymous with the founding of the Bahá'í Faith—and its purpose was fulfilled when Bahá'u'lláh announced in 1863 that he was the Promised One who had been foretold by the Báb.

At the same time, the faith founded by the Báb is a distinct, independent religion. His major writings abrogated certain Muslim laws and replaced them with new ones, intended to assist in the spiritual progress of humankind and the advancement of civilization. His major work, the Bayán, stressed the importance of prayer and a high moral standard, with an emphasis on purity of heart and motive. His writings upheld the station of women as equal to men in the sight of God and promoted equality of all humanity, including the poor and downtrodden. His writings promoted education and useful sciences and called for the abandonment of superstition. Throughout, the central theme of the Bayán was the imminence of the coming of another messenger of God, one whose revelation would be far greater than the Báb's, and whose mission would be to usher in the age of peace and plenty that had been promised by all the holy scriptures of the past.

Following the Báb's proclamation, Persians of all classes were attracted to the Báb's message. The number of the Báb's followers grew rapidly and the new religious movement spread across the land. The Báb's teachings aided his followers in breaking free from the rigid mindset and trappings of their religious customs and traditions in preparation for the coming of Bahá'u'lláh.

As the new faith grew, intense fear and rage stirred within the religious and secular establishment. Determined to stamp out the new faith, authorities persecuted and eventually imprisoned him. Day by day, increasing numbers of his followers were apprehended, tortured, and executed. Despite these escalating persecutions, the new religion continued to spread.

One of the Báb's most remarkable disciples was a woman, Fátimah Umm-Salmá, the daughter of a prominent Muslim scholar. As a young woman, while independently seeking spiritual truth by studying the Koran and treatises of various religious scholars, she had discovered the writings of the Báb. Following a vigil of prayers and letter correspondence with the Báb, she embraced his cause and became a devout follower.

Though the women in Persia at that time were subjugated and treated as chattels, she was well versed in the Koran, an eloquent speaker, a brilliant poet, and a beautiful, courageous, audacious advocate for the emancipation and advancement of women. A passage in the Bahá'í writings describes her as "A woman chaste and holy . . . a burning brand of the love of God, a lamp of His bestowal."[35] Bahá'u'lláh, in concurrence with the Báb, gave her the title Ṭáhirih, meaning "the pure one."

Meanwhile, the Báb, though himself imprisoned, called for a gathering of eighty-one of his followers, "[T]he primary purpose [was] to implement the revelation of the Bayán by a sudden, a complete and dramatic break with the past—with its order, its ecclesiasticism, its traditions, and ceremonials."[36] Bahá'u'lláh, who stayed in close communication with the Báb and had not yet revealed his own station as "Him Whom God shall make manifest," hosted the gathering, which came to be known as the Conference of Badasht. He rented three gardens, one of which he assigned to Quddús (one of the Báb's appointed disciples) another to Ṭáhirih, and a third for himself.

During the twenty-two-day conference various arguments and differences of view and approach rose between Ṭáhirih and Quddús. Suddenly, Ṭáhirih made a symbolic gesture by appearing at a meeting without her veil. In doing so, she dared to break a law prohibiting a woman from publicly uncovering her face. She stood before the entire gathering with her face unveiled and made it clear to all that a new dispensation had begun. Bahá'u'lláh's eldest son, 'Abdu'l-Bahá, explains,

> Ṭáhirih, with her face unveiled, stepped from her garden, advancing to the pavilion of Bahá'u'lláh; and as she came, she shouted aloud. . . . "The Trumpet is sounding! The great Trump is blown! The universal Advent is now proclaimed!" The believers gathered in that tent were panic struck, and each one asked himself, "How can the Law be abrogated? How is it that this woman stands here without her veil?". . . [T]hus was the new Dispensation announced and the great Resurrection made manifest. At the start,

those who were present fled away, and some forsook their Faith, while some fell a prey to suspicion and doubt, and a number, after wavering, returned to the presence of Bahá'u'lláh. The Conference of Badasht broke up, but the universal Advent had been proclaimed.[37]

Considering that at that time women were generally regarded as inferior to men not only in that part of the world, but throughout the world, it is fascinating to ponder that a woman should proclaim the advent of a new revelation of God. From a Western point of view, the indignation and shock the conference participants suffered at the sight of Ṭáhirih's uncovered face may seem irrational: "Fear, anger, bewilderment, swept their inmost souls, and stunned their faculties."[38] One man at the conference was so upset that, "aghast and deranged at such a sight, cut his throat with his own hands. Spattered with blood, and frantic with excitement, he fled away from her face."[39]

Those in attendance had been conditioned to believe that it was a blasphemous act for a woman to uncover her face in public. When beliefs and patterns are deeply ingrained, it is difficult for people to change their mindset to accept change. However, despite the difficulty, change is not only unavoidable but essential for the spiritual and material progress of humanity. Thus the purpose of the conference was to implement "a complete and dramatic break with the past."[40] This could perhaps be perceived as the essence of the Bábí movement: preparing the way for the coming of a new prophet and revelation of God for all humanity.

The hearts and minds of the religious and secular authorities in Persia who lived in the time of the Báb were locked in a mindset that had changed little from centuries past, but true faith lies in attachment to God Himself, not to an ideology, nor to the material trappings of rituals and customs. One of the central principles of Bahá'u'lláh's teachings is the search for truth:

In order to find truth we must give up our prejudices, our own small trivial notions; an open receptive mind is essential. . . . Unless we make a distinction in our minds between dogma, superstition and prejudice on the one hand, and truth on the other, we cannot succeed. When we are in earnest in our search for anything we look for it everywhere. This principle we must carry out in our search for truth.[41]

Those who opposed the Báb argued that he was a heretic and a dangerous rebel and finally condemned him to death, a sentence that was carried out on July 9, 1850. The Báb and a young companion were suspended by two ropes against a wall in the courtyard of the army barracks of Tabríz. About ten thousand people crowded the rooftops of the barracks and houses that overlooked the yard. Standing before the Báb and the young man was a regiment of 750 Armenian soldiers, arranged in three files of 250 each. They opened fire in three successive volleys and the air clouded with a blanket of so much smoke and dust from the gunpowder that the sky darkened and the entire yard was obscured.

As recorded in an account filed with the British Foreign Office, the Báb was not to be seen when the smoke cleared. His companion stood in the yard alone, completely unscathed by the bullets. The ropes by which he and the Báb had been suspended were rent into pieces. The soldiers found the Báb back in his cell, giving instructions to one of his followers.

Earlier that day, the Báb had told the guards to not take him to be executed until he was finished speaking to the follower. The Báb had warned, "Not until I have said to him all those things that I wish to say can any earthly power silence Me."[42]

When the guards arrived for the second time, the Báb had finished giving his instructions to the follower and calmly announced, "Now you may proceed to fulfill your intention."[43] For the second time, the Báb and his young companion were brought out for execution. After what they had witnessed earlier that day, the Armenian troops refused to fire again. A Muslim firing squad was assembled and ordered to shoot. This time the bodies of the Báb and the young man were shattered by the spray of bullets. Yet, surprisingly, their faces were nearly untouched.

The Báb was only thirty-one years old at the time of his execution. Afterward, persecution of the Bábís greatly intensified. Even under severe torture, the Bábís refused to renounce their religion, and many were executed. Although his life and the lives of many of his followers had ended, the Báb's teachings prevailed and paved the way for Bahá'u'lláh.

Who Is Bahá'u'lláh?

Mírzá Ḥusayn 'Alí, whose title, Bahá'u'lláh, means the "Glory of God" in Arabic, was born November 12, 1817, in Tehran, Persia. He was the son of a wealthy government minister whose family could trace its ancestry to the great dynasties of Persia's imperial past. Bahá'u'lláh's childhood was one of privilege and comfort, and he was afforded every advantage to follow his father's path. However, he declined the ministerial career open to him in government and chose instead to devote his energies to a range of philanthropies to help the poor, the needy, and the desolate. These endeavors had, by the early 1840s, earned him widespread renown as "Father of the Poor." However, his life of privilege ended after 1844, when Bahá'u'lláh became one of the leading advocates of the Bábí movement.

After the execution of the Báb in 1850, Bahá'u'lláh was arrested and brought in chains and on foot to Tehran. Although the Muslim clergy demanded a death sentence, Bahá'u'lláh was protected by his personal reputation and his family's social station, as well as by protests from Western embassies. Instead of carrying out the death sentence, the government imprisoned him in the notorious Síyáh-Chál, known as the "Black Pit," a dungeon four levels below ground level. Bahá'u'lláh said of his imprisonment:

> We were all huddled together in one cell, our feet in stocks, and around our necks fastened the most galling of chains. The air we breathed was laden with the foulest impurities, while the floor on which we sat was covered with filth and infested with vermin. No ray of light was allowed to penetrate that pestilential dungeon or to warm its icy-coldness. We were placed in two rows, each facing the other.[44]

The conditions in the prison were so horrendous that the authorities were confident Bahá'u'lláh would not survive. In the four months Bahá'u'lláh spent there, not only did he survive poisoning and other attacks on his life from the authorities, but it was during that time, in that dark and dismal dungeon, when he realized his mission as a prophet of God. Referring to this revelation, he wrote,

> I was but a man like others, asleep upon My couch, when lo, the breezes of the All-Glorious were wafted over Me, and taught Me the knowledge of all that hath been. This thing is not from Me, but from One Who is Almighty and All-Knowing. And He bade Me lift up My voice between earth and heaven.[45]

Even while shackled in chains, to give comfort and solace to the other prisoners, Bahá'u'lláh taught them a prayer. Narrating that episode, *The Dawn-Breakers* reports Bahá'u'lláh to have said: "[E]very night, they chanted with extreme fervour. 'God is sufficient unto me; He verily is the All-sufficing!' One row would intone, while the other would reply: 'In Him let the trusting trust.' The chorus of these gladsome voices would continue to peal out until the early hours of the morning. Their reverberation would fill the dungeon" and pierce its massive walls.[46]

That such a spirit of gladness and succor was to be found among the prisoners in that wretched dungeon was wholly curious to the authorities in charge, who could hear the prisoner's joyous chanting, even in the palace of the Persian monarch a short distance away. Recognizing that Bahá'u'lláh's popularity among the people was growing, the government released Bahá'u'lláh and banished him and his family from their native homeland. They were to be exiled to Baghdad, Iraq.

With most of their material possessions confiscated by the government, Bahá'u'lláh and his family, along with other Bábís, embarked on their journey to Baghdad in 1853, which was the beginning of forty years of exile, imprisonment, and persecution.

After some years in Baghdad, Bahá'u'lláh gained tremendous popularity throughout the city as a spiritual leader. The Persian government, outraged that the people of Baghdad held Bahá'u'lláh in high esteem, urged the

Ottoman Empire, which ruled Iraq at that time, to order Bahá'u'lláh into deeper exile. In 1863, before leaving Baghdad, Bahá'u'lláh and several of his companions boated across the Tigris River and camped in a lovely garden on its banks. There, for twelve days, Bahá'u'lláh proclaimed that he was the Promised One foretold by the Báb and foretold in all the world's scriptures. Bahá'u'lláh revealed that he was the messenger of a new revelation of God for all humanity but attested, "I have never aspired after worldly leadership. My sole purpose hath been to hand down unto men that which I was bidden to deliver by God."[47]

For twelve days in that garden, which Bahá'u'lláh named the Garden of Riḍván (meaning "paradise" in Arabic), Bahá'u'lláh revealed his mission, and the Bahá'í Faith was established. He proclaimed the message that there was only one God, that God created all humanity as members of one human race, and that all are equal in the sight of God. He taught that all the world's religions have been stages in the progressive revelation of God's purpose for humankind. He taught that religion should be a source of unity and called for the eradication of all forms of prejudice, superstition, and fanaticism.

Although Bahá'u'lláh's initial proclamation occurred more than 150 years ago, he addressed issues that are profoundly relevant today, calling for the equality of women and men and advocating the advancement of education, the sciences, and the arts. His teachings confirmed the importance of the institution of marriage and family, and asserted the importance of good parenting, calling for both the spiritual and academic education of all children. His message promulgated the importance of independent investigation of truth, the essential harmony between science and religion, and the need for the elimination of extremes of wealth and poverty. Bahá'u'lláh called for unity and justice in the world of humanity so that global peace could be established, attesting, "So powerful is the light of unity that it can illuminate the whole earth."[48] He called for the spiritual development of humanity by enjoining all to acquire divine attributes, proclaiming:

> Be generous in prosperity, and thankful in adversity. Be worthy of the trust of thy neighbor, and look upon him with a bright and

friendly face. Be a treasure to the poor, an admonisher to the rich, an answerer to the cry of the needy, a preserver of the sanctity of thy pledge. Be fair in thy judgment, and guarded in thy speech. Be unjust to no man, and show all meekness to all men. Be as a lamp unto them that walk in darkness, a joy to the sorrowful, a sea for the thirsty, a haven for the distressed, an upholder and defender of the victim of oppression. Let integrity and uprightness distinguish all thine acts. Be a home for the stranger, a balm to the suffering, a tower of strength for the fugitive. Be eyes to the blind, and a guiding light unto the feet of the erring. Be an ornament to the countenance of truth, a crown to the brow of fidelity, a pillar of the temple of righteousness, a breath of life to the body of mankind, an ensign of the hosts of justice, a luminary above the horizon of virtue, a dew to the soil of the human heart, an ark on the ocean of knowledge, a sun in the heaven of bounty, a gem on the diadem of wisdom, a shining light in the firmament of thy generation, a fruit upon the tree of humility. We pray God to protect thee from the heat of jealousy and the cold of hatred.[49]

Soon the same authorities who had oppressed the Bábís began targeting followers of the new religion, who eventually came to be called Bahá'ís. Bahá'u'lláh's message spread, and the number of his followers increased throughout Persia and Iraq. The authorities did everything in their power to crush the religion by intensifying the persecutions and sending Bahá'u'lláh deeper in exile. Finally, in 1868, Bahá'u'lláh and his family and companions were exiled to the city of Acre in Ottoman-controlled Palestine (now Israel). In that city Bahá'u'lláh and his family spent nine years confined inside a filthy, dilapidated prison. In 1877, After being permitted to leave the prison doors, Bahá'u'lláh's eldest son, 'Abdu'l-Bahá, purchased a house in the countryside in the outskirts of Acre, and there Bahá'u'lláh and his family resided under house arrest until his passing on May 29, 1892, at the age of seventy-five.

Although technically still a prisoner of the Ottoman empire, Bahá'u'lláh resided in relative peace and freedom and spent his final years writing, teaching, and showing loving-kindness to all. Ironically, the two governments that tried everything in their power to crush the Bahá'í Faith were eventually overthrown, while the Bahá'í Faith evolved into a world religion that has spread to nearly every country on earth and continues to grow. Bahá'u'lláh's physical remains were laid to rest in a garden room adjoining the home in which he lived his last days, which is known as Bahjí (Arabic for "Place of Delight"). Bahá'ís worldwide consider this spot the holiest place on earth and travel there to visit, pray, meditate, and reflect on the life, teachings, and station of Bahá'u'lláh.

Prayer is the foundation and purpose of religion

Bahá'u'lláh's writings offer a treasure trove of prayers, laws, and spiritual and moral teachings that address virtually every aspect of life. These works, along with the writings of the Báb and of Bahá'u'lláh's son 'Abdu'l-Bahá, comprise Bahá'í scripture. These writings affirm that prayer is the very foundation and purpose of religion, and an essential element of the Bahá'í Faith. Bahá'í prayers celebrate the goodness of God and His wisdom, offer solace and opportunities for spiritual growth, and define a path for drawing closer to God. Bahá'í prayers are not exclusive—they are for the benefit and spiritual happiness of every soul on the planet, regardless of religion, culture, ethnicity, or nationality.

In daily life, prayer plays an extremely important role for Bahá'ís, who are enjoined to pray both in the morning and in the evening in addition to reciting daily one of three "obligatory prayers," which are to be said during one's private devotions. The primary purpose of such prayers is to draw us into a closer communion with God.

The shortest of the three obligatory prayers consists of a single verse, which is recited once between noon and sunset. This simple yet profound prayer not only explains the purpose of our creation but also reminds us of our human frailty and of our need to turn to our Creator: "I bear witness, O my God, that Thou hast created me to know Thee and to worship Thee. I testify, at this moment, to my powerlessness and to Thy might, to my poverty and to Thy wealth. There is none other God but Thee, the Help in Peril, the Self-Subsisting."[50]

The term "obligatory" as applied to these prayers implies for Bahá'ís an understanding that humans have certain spiritual duties before God. The Bahá'í teachings tell us that the purpose of life is to know and love God and to progress spiritually; these obligatory prayers reinforce that message. Some of the most deeply stirring and potent verses in Bahá'í scripture can be found in the longest of the three obligatory prayers: "O Thou Who art the Lord of all names and the Maker of the heavens! I beseech Thee by them Who are the Daysprings of Thine invisible Essence, the Most Exalted, the All-Glorious, to make of my prayer a fire that will burn away the veils which have shut me out from Thy beauty, and a light that will lead me unto the ocean of Thy Presence."[51]

The exhortation to pray daily is a duty unto God, and this law, like all divine ordinances, is not intended as an onerous task, and should be regarded as a precious gift bestowed upon humanity to benefit and exalt our souls. Another verse from one of the prayers states, "Whatever duty Thou hast prescribed unto Thy servants of extolling to the utmost Thy majesty and glory is but a token of Thy grace unto them, that they may be enabled to ascend unto the station conferred upon their own inmost being, the station of the knowledge of their own selves."[52]

To deny ourselves this heavenly gift of prayer is to deny our souls the spiritual sustenance they need to survive and grow, just as our bodies need nourishment to sustain our physical existence. Through prayer the soul awakens to divine realities and is enabled to inhale the fragrances of the Holy Spirit. "Spiritual progress," 'Abdu'l-Bahá says, "is through the breaths of the Holy Spirit and is the awakening of the conscious soul of man to perceive the reality of divinity. . . . Spiritual progress insures the happiness and eternal continuance of the soul."[53]

Beyond a few specific prayers that Bahá'ís are obliged to recite in particular instances or on particular occasions, such as the obligatory prayers, Bahá'ís are free to pray as they wish. They may use prayers that come from Bahá'í or other scripture and writings, or they may pray spontaneously in their own words. Even so, many Bahá'ís derive the utmost pleasure in turning to the beauty and potency of prayers found in Bahá'í scripture.

In addition to the daily prayers, the writings of the Bahá'í Faith also prescribe the practice of meditation. While our prayers may be recited, chanted, or sung aloud, meditation awakens our inner reality through silent reflection and contemplation. No particular technique of meditation is advocated in Bahá'í scripture; however, we should meditate on those things that will lead to spiritual illumination and remembrance of God.

Another common thread found throughout the world's religions is the use of fasting as a means of spiritual purification, and many religions teach that the purest prayers occur during times of fasting. The Jews offer prayers for atonement and cleansing of their souls during their fasting period on Yom Kippur, marking the beginning of the Jewish New Year. Muslims abstain from food and drink between sunrise and sunset for twenty-eight days in a row during their period of Ramadan, which is a sacred time for prayer, meditation, and purification of the soul.

Bahá'ís also fast, from sunrise to sunset for a period of nineteen days each year from March 2nd through March 20th. Bahá'u'lláh explains the purpose of this endeavor in the following words: "[T]his physical fast is a symbol of the spiritual fast. This Fast leadeth to the cleansing of the soul from all selfish desires, the acquisition of spiritual attributes, attraction to the breezes of the All-Merciful, and enkindlement with the fire of divine love."[54] The fasting period is a time for prayer, meditation, and personal reflection, spiritual cleansing and rejuvenation, and taking account of one's deeds.

Why pray for truth in our quest for the nearness of God?

Bahá'í scripture confers great importance on the independent investigation of truth for the spiritual progress of every soul: "Man must cut himself free from all prejudice and from the result of his own imagination, so that he may be able to search for truth unhindered. Truth is one in all religions, and by means of it the unity of the world can be realized."[55]

When we pray for an open mind in our independent search for truth, we embark on a spiritual journey. The search for truth unhindered is search for the knowledge of God. Therefore, the search for truth with an open mind, unclouded by superstition and prejudice, is an essential component of our spiritual life.

The spiritual life of an individual is the relationship between the soul and God. Again, there is no relationship that is more intimate or important than the one we have with our Creator. Because the ocean of God's knowledge is infinite and unfathomable, the journey to the nearness of God is eternal. The soul's ability to comprehend the knowledge of God is "the most precious gift bestowed upon man by the Divine Bounty."[56]

Striving to maintain a constant mindset of learning is an important tenet of the Bahá'í teachings and is a crucial step in personal spiritual growth. That is why every individual Bahá'í is enjoined to study and investigate Bahá'í scripture on his or her own. There is no clergy in the Bahá'í Faith, and every individual is accountable for his or her own spiritual development. Therefore, it is incumbent upon every Bahá'í to engage in daily prayer, offered privately. From the perspective of Bahá'ís and true believers of all faiths worldwide, the regimen of daily prayer is not an encumbrance but a means to uplift and radiate the soul.

The purpose of prayer is to refresh and gladden our spirits, not to burden them. While it behooves us to make prayer an integral part of our everyday lives, we also need to refrain from being obsessed with it. Bahá'í scripture exhorts the practice of moderation in all things, urging us to avoid all practices of excess such as asceticism, mendicancy, monasticism, esotericism, proselytizing, and fanaticism. Bahá'u'lláh wrote, "Whatsoever passeth beyond the limits of moderation will cease to exert a beneficial influence."[57]

Moderation is desirable even in the exercise of prayer. Moreover, the duration of time spent in prayer is less significant than the intent behind it: "The most acceptable prayer is the one offered with the utmost spirituality and radiance; its prolongation hath not been and is not beloved by God."[58] Furthermore, Bahá'u'lláh wrote, "Lay not upon your souls that which will weary them and weigh them down, but rather what will lighten and uplift them."[59]

What is the source of Bahá'í scripture?

Bahá'í scripture was inspired by the same source that inspired the sacred scriptures of all the world's major religions: the Holy Spirit of God. It is intriguing to note the similarities of the spiritual message that pervades the various sacred texts. The Bhagavad-Gita, the holy scripture of Hinduism, is a book of prayerful meditations, the title of which means "The Song of God." The Hebrew scripture, the Torah, is seen by both Jews and Christians as a revelation of the laws and principles of God and a meditation on biblical history turned into prayer. The Buddhist scripture is regarded as a meditation to the path of God and spiritual enlightenment. The Christian Gospels are embraced as a prayer book of God's love and spiritual redemption. Muslim followers adhere to scripture found in the Koran, which they revere as a revelation of God and a book of prayer, with submission to God being its principal message.

Each of these religions has been endowed with its own book of sacred scripture. The adherents of each religion regard their scripture as a revelation from God and a holy book of prayer. From the Bahá'í perspective, all of these scriptures comprise different chapters in the never-ending book of God's revelation to humanity. Bahá'í scripture is its latest chapter, and just as in all the sacred scriptures of the past, there is a special power invested in Bahá'í scripture.

Prayers written by Bahá'u'lláh, the Báb, and 'Abdu'l-Bahá have been translated into hundreds of languages. They are for anyone who yearns for the nearness of God, desires to explore spiritual mysteries, and longs for spiritual solace. Bahá'í scripture is written with an eloquence and poetic beauty that contrasts strongly with our usual manner of speech and thought. This dignified, elevated style may at first require more effort on the part of the reader, but ultimately it reinforces a sense of reverence toward God and helps to elevate our souls and enhance the transcendent quality of the prayers.

There is a particularly beautiful prayer from 'Abdu'l-Bahá imploring God "that the holy ecstasy of prayer may fill our souls—a prayer that shall rise above words and letters and transcend the murmur of syllables and sounds."[60] Oh, what a wonderful gift God has given us—this gift of prayer! Prayer gives us joy, and joy gives us wings! Through prayer our strength becomes more vital, our intellect keener, and our understanding less clouded. We seem better able to cope with the world and to find our sphere of usefulness. 'Abdu'l-Bahá, who was a prisoner with his father, talked about his years of incarceration and how turning to God enabled him to cope with a lifetime of hardship and persecution:

I myself was in prison forty years—one year alone would have been impossible to bear—nobody survived that imprisonment more than a year! But, thank God, during all those forty years I was supremely happy every day, on waking, it was like hearing good tidings, and every night infinite joy was mine. Spirituality was my comfort, and turning to God was my greatest joy. If this had not been so, do you think it possible that I could have lived through those forty years in prison?

Thus, spirituality is the greatest of God's gifts, and "Life Everlasting" means "Turning to God." May you, one and all, increase daily in spirituality, may you be strengthened in all goodness, may you be helped more and more by the Divine consolation, be made free by the Holy Spirit of God, and may the power of the Heavenly Kingdom live and work among you.[61]

How and when should we pray?

With the exception of a few specially revealed prayers in Bahá'í scripture, such as the obligatory prayers, there is no particular form or mode of prayer prescribed in Bahá'í scripture. Bahá'ís are enjoined to shun idolatry, the worship of icons, and all manner of rituals, and they are encouraged to use moderation and common sense in all endeavors, including prayer. They are thus free to express their devotions however they wish to do so—whether through reciting, chanting, singing, or other means.

Bahá'í teachings, however, do provide some guidance in creating an appropriate environment and attitude. The ideal atmosphere for prayer is a quiet, orderly, and clean place in which we can pray freely without disruption or distraction. A place that is dirty or disorderly is not conducive to creating a spiritual and serene atmosphere. And while Bahá'í scripture neither advocates nor shuns any particular attire, it does prescribe cleanliness of the body and clothing, as well as modesty in dress.

More important is the modesty of our behavior and attitude. Bahá'í teachings tell us that before we begin to pray, we should first take a moment or two to clear our minds, focus our thoughts in remembrance of God, and strive to achieve a reverent and sincere attitude and posture. Bahá'ís often memorize various prayers from Bahá'í scripture so that they may close their eyes when offering devotions. Closing our eyes may not only help us feel more relaxed and restful, but it may also assist in our efforts to direct our thoughts towards God and spiritual subjects.

Some people lower their heads when they pray because they feel it is a sign of humility and reverence to God. But from the Bahá'ís perspective, whether one prays with closed eyes, bowed head, or kneeling, sitting, or standing is an entirely personal decision.

Finally, when we offer our prayers, we should do so lovingly and humbly. The more radiant our spirit, the more receptive we are to God's blessings. What is of the essence when we offer prayers is the spirit that is behind the words.

> Praise be to God, thy heart is engaged in the commemoration of God, thy soul is gladdened by the glad tidings of God and thou art absorbed in prayer. The state of prayer is the best of conditions, for man is then associating with God. Prayer verily bestoweth life, particularly when offered in private and at times, such as midnight, when freed from daily cares.[62]

Again, by its simplest definition, prayer is talking to God in a loving spirit, and there should be no boundaries or limitations to prevent a true believer from turning his or her heart towards the Heavenly Kingdom. The only limitations that prevent one from turning to God are the veils of ego and vain imaginings. The more one strays from the path of God the deeper the spiritual consciousness sleeps—until the soul is in such a state that it is as if the soul is dead. Even so, the potential is always there for even the most deadened soul to be stirred and awakened to divine realities.

Bahá'í scripture offers the assurance "Pray to God day and night and beg forgiveness and pardon. The omnipotence of God shall solve every difficulty."[63] Every soul has been bestowed with the potential to draw on the power of the Holy Spirit and supplicate for the boundless mercy of God. Through prayer and the love of God, we awaken to the reality that every single human soul was created to be noble. In our love for God and in our prayer, we strive day and night so that our own potential nobility might radiate forth—and recognize the potential nobility of every soul we meet:

> I created thee rich, why dost thou bring thyself down to poverty? Noble I made thee, wherewith dost thou abase thyself? Out of the essence of knowledge I gave thee being, why seekest thou enlightenment from anyone beside Me? Out of the clay of love I molded thee, how dost thou busy thyself with another? Turn thy sight unto thyself, that thou mayest find Me standing within thee, mighty, powerful and self-subsisting.[64]

So where, when, and how best to pray? We can pray anywhere and anytime, of course. But for our hearts to be most receptive to the glorious power of prayer, it behooves us to supplicate with a loving spirit, yearning for the nearness of God, striving with the utmost humility to realize the nobility of our souls, and recognizing the nobility latent in every member of the human race.

CHAPTER 3

Was Blind but Now I See

Amazing Grace! (how sweet the sound)
That sav'd a wretch like me!
I once was lost, but now am found
Was blind, but now I see.

—JOHN NEWTON

Ray is no stranger to the heart-stirring message testified in that song, particularly in the verse, "I was blind, but now I see." During a period of extraordinary suffering and trials his heart was lifted out of darkness, and his soul was transformed through the power of prayer. During a time that could have led to bitterness and despair, he turned, body and soul, to the light of the Holy Spirit. While seeking new insights into the infinite knowledge of God, his vision cleared, paving the path onward to a new dawn of spiritual awakening and understanding.

In 1980, Ray was leading a good, upstanding life—one that many could take pride in and enjoy. He worked as a store designer, and his business was prospering. He dearly loved his wife and five children, resided in a lovely community in Coeur d'Alene, Idaho, and was greatly admired and respected by his friends and acquaintances.

Nevertheless, Ray was troubled. He was troubled about the decaying morals and conditions of society. He looked at the holy scriptures of Christianity, Judaism, Islam, the Bahá'í Faith, and other religions, and it troubled him that these sacred texts seemed to be unable to bring about positive change in American life. Was there something missing from them? Or, he wondered, was it that society lacked the knowledge and understanding of the scriptures to use them more effectively in tackling the ills of society?

Ray decided to take a month off from work to pray and meditate, calling upon God to guide him to a deeper understanding. During that time he received an unexpected phone call from Claire, the woman who had first introduced him to the Bahá'í Faith.

Although raised in a German Lutheran home, Ray had, at the age of nineteen, become a born-again Christian and joined a fundamentalist Church. By the age of twenty-three, although Ray considered himself devoted to Christ, he was excommunicated and declared a "heretic" because, based on his own intent Biblical studies, he believed that Jesus Christ was not the only messenger of God, and dared, quite audaciously, to inform the congregation of his conviction.

Four years later he met a young Presbyterian woman who, upon discovering Ray's belief that Christ was not the only divine messenger and that there were spiritual truths to be found in all major religions, accused him of being a Bahá'í. Appalled to be associated with an "Eastern cult," Ray immediately responded with denial and skepticism. Challenged by curiosity, though, and with an unquenchable thirst for knowledge, he later attended a meeting at the young woman's home, where Claire gave a talk about the Bahá'í Faith. Five days later, attracted to the Bahá'í spirit of oneness and unity, and after reading ninety-three pages of the book, *Gleanings from the Writings of Bahá'u'lláh*, Ray became a member of the Bahá'í Faith.

Ray and Claire enjoyed a close friendship until he left Eugene in 1971. Ten years passed with no contact, and so it was quite a surprise for Ray when the phone rang and he heard her voice on the other end. She explained that her call was the result of an intuition that she must bring him a book that she felt was relevant to his life. Because of her advanced age and her medical problems, Claire seldom left her home, and traveling to Idaho was a significant journey for her.

When she arrived several days later, Ray watched her get out of the car, driven by another woman. Claire held a white cane, which she used to find her way up the stairs from the driveway up to the porch where Ray was standing. After the two ladies were comfortably seated, Claire shared her experience of having detached retinas and the medical profession's inability to restore her eyesight. She told him how she refused to let blindness slow her down in the things that were most important, such as her relationships with her sons, her friends, and her spiritual life. Ray was amazed at her resilient attitude.

She gave him the book *The Aquarian Conspiracy*, by Marilyn Ferguson. The two women then returned to their car for the ten-hour drive back to Eugene. After so much effort on her part to bring the book, Ray felt compelled to read it and was in awe of Claire's insight. The book dealt with current scientific knowledge about how the two sides of the brain function. After reading the book, Ray came to the conclusion that although he had long been a spiritual seeker, he was a "left-brain learner," which meant that he comprehended information intellectually and analytically, based on fact and logic.

Additional findings reported in the book explained that the "right brain" learning style was based more on intuition and feelings connected with the heart, which led to a deeper, more internalized and somewhat more creative understanding. Ray was inspired by what he read. He began to realize that his heart's desire was to have greater receptiveness to divine guidance. He realized that intellect wasn't enough when it came to comprehending spiritual knowledge. He yearned to internalize the knowledge of God in his heart. He prayed for a spiritual awakening of his soul. He prayed for spiritual sight.

Two months later, Ray was flying to Atlanta, Georgia, on a business trip. While flying cross-country, he watched the movie *Somewhere in Time*, starring Christopher Reeves and Jane Seymour. In the final scene Christopher Reeves's character dies and ascends upward, viewing his body below while seeing his beloved running toward him in the afterlife.

Suddenly Ray fell into a trancelike state and saw a vision of a young woman coming towards him. As this heavenly image continued to approach him, Ray heard a clear voice utter the words, "This is the Truth, this is the truth, this is the living truth." Still approaching him, the lovely vision came into his arms, and he experienced an ecstasy beyond words. He sobbed uncontrollably at the wonder of the joy he felt holding her in his arms. Again the voice spoke to him and said, "This is how beautiful your soul can become if you are faithful to the end!"

"Wake up!" fellow passengers called to Ray as they jerked him out of his trance, concerned that he was convulsing. Ray, somewhat startled, stoically assured them that he was okay. But in truth, he realized that his tie, shirt, and jacket lapels were soaking wet. He quickly left his seat for the restroom and stood in shock when he saw blood-red eyes staring back at him in the mirror. He realized at that moment that all was not okay.

Back on the ground at the airport, a business associate who was there to greet Ray stared at him with stark worry, asking, "What happened to you?" Ray's response was a curt "I don't know and I don't want to talk about it!"

That evening Ray checked into his hotel and asked the clerk to give him a wake-up call at 7:00 a.m. Before going to sleep, he finished reading a book on the life of St. Francis of Assisi. He reflected on the final words in the last chapter: "Trust in God, trust in God, no matter what, trust in God." Ray was deeply touched by the man's faith. He prayed that God might grant him just a portion of the faith St. Francis had, and fell asleep.

Ray had cloudy vision in his left eye, which had a severe cataract, and had long been accustomed to using his right eye for good vision. When the wake-up call rang the following morning, the left side of his face was still deep in the pillow as he opened his right eye and reached for the phone. He was confused. He knew it could not possibly be 7:00 a.m. because all he saw was darkness. He challenged the clerk, but the woman insisted that it was 7:00 a.m. Ray sat up and realized that he saw daylight with his left eye, but saw only blackness with his right. He asked the operator to call an ambulance to take him to a hospital.

As soon as he hung up the phone, while waiting alone in his room for the ambulance, he thought about his prayers for greater faith and said aloud, "Boy, God, do you work fast!"

After returning home, Ray was besieged with a seemingly endless array of trials. He had a family to support, bills to pay, and a profession that relied on good eyesight. After undergoing a series of operations, he was informed by his doctors that the final verdict was a forty percent chance that he would regain his sight. Blood was on the macula of his right eye, and his diagnosis was indeterminate until it healed. So what could Ray do? He turned his heart and soul to God and prayed. He prayed fervently night and day. And the more he prayed, the more he felt that he was being guided. He says, "I felt I was being tested and prepared for a spiritual journey."

The surgeons were successful in restoring just enough eyesight in Ray's left eye to make it possible for him to read a few words at a time, providing that his face was close enough for his nose to touch the page. But as a recuperating patient, he had all the time in the world. He used that time to pray, meditate, and do a great deal of reading, particularly of the Bahá'í sacred writings, which he discovered, to his delight, offered a fathomless ocean of knowledge to explore. His reading proceeded at a snail's pace, but again to his pleasure, he discovered that there was much to be gained when one reads very slowly. He began to discern in the writings of Bahá'u'lláh very interesting subjects that he had never noticed before, and it began to change his understanding of the Bahá'í Faith.

Now that Ray had to rely on Social Security benefits, the life of material comfort that he and his family had previously enjoyed was transformed into one of hardship. And yet Ray, who came to view the sudden turn of events in his life as a fascinating and bountiful spiritual journey, had never known a greater sense of contentment. He was in ecstasy! He felt his soul was bathed in the ocean of God's mercy, and his heart luxuriated in God's love. In addition, he had never felt closer to his wife and five children. Through it all, Ray's family surrounded him with love and support. The family prayed together, and they, too, were benefiting by Ray's trials. The whole family deepened in their understanding that prayer and trust in God enabled them to face their difficulties with fortitude, radiance, hope, and unity.

Many wondrous and mysterious happenings took place in the next few years. It is probably accurate to say that Ray's life had catapulted into a series of crises and miracles, which often seemed to occur simultaneously.

On one such occasion, during a painful moment of self-doubt, Ray felt defeated and confused about what to do with the rest of his life. He turned to God and begged with all his heart for guidance. Suddenly an overwhelming sense of illumination seemed to shake his very soul. The feeling was so powerful that it frightened him.

Ray had prayed for guidance, and it was clear to him that his prayers were being answered. Ray loved Coeur d'Alene but believed that God had a plan for him on the East Coast. He felt guided to move his family to the New York City area. Logically, it was inexplicable. Ray turned to his prayer book, opened it, and read a Bahá'í prayer for protection. The words in the prayer seemed to speak to him directly—particularly one of its passages, which said, "I can utter no word, O my God, unless I be permitted by Thee, and can move in no direction until I obtain Thy sanction."[65]

After pondering the prayer, he was inspired to turn the pages to read another prayer—one that had been written specifically for the Northeastern States of America. Ray was unfamiliar with the prayer, so he was taken aback when he read the following passage:

> O Thou kind Lord! Praise be unto Thee that Thou hast shown us the highway of guidance, opened the doors of the kingdom and manifested Thyself through the Sun of Reality. To the blind Thou hast given sight; to the deaf Thou hast granted hearing; Thou hast resuscitated the dead; Thou hast enriched the poor; Thou hast shown the way to those who have gone astray; Thou hast led those with parched lips to the fountain of guidance. . . . Thou hast suffered the thirsty fish to reach the ocean of reality; and Thou hast invited the wandering birds to the rose garden of grace.[66]

This confirmed Ray's belief that he was being guided to relocate to the New York area, and he consulted about it with his wife, Joanne, who was remarkably supportive of the move. When discussing the decision with their three older children, he told them that they could stay in the west if it was their wish. His oldest son, Jonathan, who was nineteen, responded, "Dad! All my life I have heard of these stories about how God guides us when we trust Him, and now I want to see how you are going to get through this one!" His seventeen-year-old daughter, Robyne, who was about to start her senior year in high school, agreed, saying, "I wouldn't want to miss the adventure of it all!"

And so it happened. Ray and his family moved, lock, stock, and barrel, to Teaneck, New Jersey, just on the other side of the George Washington Bridge from New York City. Shortly after the family was settled in their new home, Ray, who was still severely visually impaired, was appointed to serve on a Bahá'í committee that was in charge of an annual commemoration of the Unity Feast, an event that had first been held in Teaneck on June 29, 1912. To Ray the most significant confirmation in relocating to New Jersey was learning about this event, which had been initiated by the eldest son of Bahá'u'lláh, 'Abdu'l-Bahá, during his visit to the United States in 1912.

The first Unity Feast was an outdoor gathering of 250 guests, hosted by 'Abdu'l-Bahá, who, in a loving address to the entire group, urged them to be united. Following his talk, even though it appeared as if the day would be ruined by thunder and rain, the inclement weather lasted only a few moments; the guests offered prayers, the dark clouds dispersed, the sun shown through, and everyone basked in the beautiful summer day, feasting on plenteous food and sharing in fellowship and a spirit of unity.

'Abdu'l-Bahá said in his talk,

This is a new Day, and this hour is a new Hour in which we have come together. Surely the Sun of Reality with its full effulgence will illumine us, and the darkness of disagreements will disappear. The utmost love and unity will result; the favors of God will encompass us; the pathway of the Kingdom will be made easy. Like candles these souls will become ignited and made radiant through the lights of supreme guidance. Such gatherings as this have no equal or likeness in the world of mankind, where people are drawn together by physical motives or in furtherance of material interests, for this meeting is a prototype of that inner and complete spiritual association in the eternal world of being.[67]

After dark, each of the guests was handed a candle, and they were lit one by one by passing the flame from person to person—just as each heart was enkindled, passing the spirit of unity amongst them. As they sat contentedly next to each other in the dark on the grass, holding the lit candles, and after enjoying such an extraordinary day, they shared inspiring stories that were marked by faith, heroism, sacrifice, and selflessness. They shared laughter and tender moments, and they shared a unity that could be described as divine.

After learning the history of that momentous event, Ray was so inspired by its spirit and format that he not only helped to coordinate the annual commemoration, but he also initiated the development of monthly home gatherings that he hoped would reflect the same unity. The gatherings, which were open to people of all ethnicities, religions, cultures, and social and economic backgrounds, were hugely successful. People came together from all walks of life to share in devotions, dialogue, stories, music, food, and fellowship.

Ray's eyesight returned two years later, and today Ray can see well enough to drive a car and act as co-owner of a successful store-designing business. He continues to lead a full and very happy life with his wife. Ray acknowledges that he has much for which to be grateful—most of all for an experience that he believes would have been devastating without prayers and faith. He came away with the understanding that what is most important—far more important than the trials themselves and the outward results of those trials—is how one personally deals with them and learns from them.

"Because I had lost my physical sight, my inner eye opened to a degree I never would have dreamed possible," Ray says. "I would not trade that experience for anything. That experience led to my profound awe and appreciation in the power of prayer and in trusting in God. I think my wife, Joanne, expressed it best when she said to me, 'We were never afraid because you made it seem that we were on an adventure and God was our tour guide into an exciting future.' And indeed it was—and still is!"

CHAPTER 4

Why Pray?

Several years ago a Jewish friend, Jake, shared with me a deeply moving story. He told me about his father: a loving, warm, and artistic man, with quick humor and easy laugh, who was extremely devoted to the Jewish faith and to God. He prayed every morning and every evening and taught his six children that a truly religious person is one who loves God, prays every day, and obeys the Ten Commandments. He had taught them to carry the Golden Rule in their hearts and to live by its message: "What is hateful to you, do not to your neighbour."[68]

Jake's father, who had escaped Russia as a young man during the pogroms of the early twentieth century, was a firm but doting patriarch of a religiously observant, affectionate, and close-knit family. Their home was typically filled with singing, dancing, laughter, and the heavenly aromas of Jewish European cooking, lovingly prepared by Jake's mother. Jake adored his family, and his early childhood was very happy.

But his home life took a drastic turn when tragedy struck. Jake's father, once a warm, wonderful, spiritual man, had turned bitter, hardened, and had become an atheist after losing his beloved wife to cancer. Jake was only ten years old when his mother died and it was a devastating time for him. Not only had he lost his mother—but in a way, he had also lost his father. It was as if his father had become an empty shell of the person he had once been.

Many years later, when Jake was in his early thirties, he went to the hospital to see his father, who was dying and had been in a deep coma for two days. As Jake sat by the bed, alone in the room with his father, he prayed. Suddenly, his father opened his eyes and looked at his son. He smiled warmly and tenderly, and then, as his eyes gazed upward, he spoke. The words that came out of his mouth were praise of and love for God. He was praying! And he was smiling and happy! Jake was speechless. He took his father in his arms and embraced him. And while he held him with the utmost love and affection, his father died—content and at peace.

As Jake told me the story, tears welled in his eyes: "My father was very happy and serene at the moment of his passing. He died in my arms, and I could feel his joy and his love for God. After what I had witnessed, for the rest of my life, no matter what happens, I will never doubt for a single second that there is a God in heaven and that He is good, loving, and merciful. After a lifetime of so much suffering, my father found God again. I will always believe that God is watching over us, protecting us, and ready to answer our prayers."

A few years ago, I saw Jake when he was terminally ill with the same disease—cancer—that had killed his mother, father, and two of his sisters. But Jake's faith in God never wavered. Although he suffered horribly for two years with the disease, never once did he show a lack of courage or dignity. His faith and his prayers sustained him and provided him with fortitude and inner strength, which he demonstrated nobly to the very end of his days in this world.

What could have possibly occurred in Jake's father to cause him to suddenly come out of his coma with a restored faith in God? After all, this was a man who for decades had claimed to be an atheist. Did an angel appear before his eyes? Did he see an apparition of his beloved wife? Did the shutting down of his physical body from the cancer awaken his soul to bear witness to the love and glory of God? Whatever happened, Jake believed that he had witnessed a powerful and miraculous testimonial to the truth of God's existence and mercy.

Jake's story, while deeply stirring, is not unique. There are a myriad of similar stories reported by relatives, friends, doctors, and others who have been present at the bedside of loved ones or patients approaching death. Those stories are about people of all walks of life and of all beliefs—as well as those who had claimed to have no faith at all. The stories are virtually the same: moments before death, they open their eyes and call out to God in remembrance and praise, often imploring for forgiveness and salvation. Following their heartfelt supplications, they die serenely and peacefully. Of course, not all people die in such a pleasant manner. For those souls who have no faith and no belief in the hereafter, death may be very frightening. It is curious that some souls turn to God as they are approaching death, and some turn away.

Bahá'í scripture reminds us that everything in the material world is transient, but it also testifies to the eternal life of the human soul. The purpose for our creation is to continually develop spiritually in our ongoing quest to be nearer to God. We sustain our love of God and attain spiritual growth through prayer and by turning to the light of the Holy Spirit. God has bestowed the gift of prayer on each and every one of us. But He has also given us free will. That free will allows us to choose to turn to God, or to stray from His path.

Be that as it may, Bahá'í scripture affirms that even those who have walked astray from His path will be immersed in the ocean of God's mercy if in their dying breath they turn to God and beseech His forgiveness: "How often hath a sinner, at the hour of death, attained to the essence of faith, and, quaffing the immortal draught, hath taken his flight unto the celestial Concourse."[69] Another passage from Bahá'í scripture attests,

> The sinner should, between himself and God, implore mercy from the Ocean of mercy, beg forgiveness from the Heaven of generosity and say:
> O God, my God. . . . I beseech Thee by the mysteries which lie enshrined in Thy knowledge and by the pearls that are treasured in the ocean of Thy bounty to grant forgiveness unto me and unto my father and my mother. . . . Thou art in truth the Most Merciful. No God is there but Thee, the Ever-Forgiving, the All-Bountiful.[70]

This idea of prayer as a means for salvation is one that is repeated throughout the sacred scriptures of the world's religions. Hindu scripture exhorts prayer and meditation as a means for the soul "to find and hold [God] in the hour of death."[71] In Islam, we have Muḥammad's reported words that "Prayer is a ladder by which everyone may ascend to Heaven."[72] Prayer is integral to the cycle of our being. Life in this world often begins with prayer and ends with prayer. We offer prayers at birth when we pray for the health of a newborn. We offer prayers at death when we pray for a departed loved one. We pray at weddings, we pray for our children, and we pray for our parents. We pray for healing and we pray for peace. Our prayers may be a tearful, bended-knee supplication, or impulsive but heartfelt thoughts, silently imploring God to shed His heavenly bounties upon us. We pray for all the major events in our lives, both the good and the bad. But why do we do it? What is the motivating force that compels us to pray?

I recently had the opportunity to ask a group of young people if they pray every day, and if so, why? A ten-year-old boy answered, "I pray every day because I love God and God loves me! And when I pray it makes me feel real good!" A thirteen-year-old girl replied, "I like to say prayers at night right before I go to bed to cleanse my mind of unpleasant thoughts so I can sleep peacefully. Another reason I like to pray is to feel closer to God and communicate with Him."

An eleven-year-old girl said that she likes to pray every day at school. She explained, "I think the prayers help me do a better job with my schoolwork. When I pray it makes me happy, and when I'm happy I do better at everything. But I can't pray aloud at school, so, I 'think' the prayers in my head."

A twelve-year-old commented, "I usually pray when I need help. It really makes me feel that I am being watched and protected." Another twelve-year-old added, "I pray every day because prayers make me feel joyful and delighted. I like to say prayers to help other people in their struggles and difficulties. I also say healing prayers for people when they don't feel good. But mainly, I pray everyday because I love God. And when I pray, I can feel that God loves me."

In their innocence and remarkable insight, those children affirm, by their own personal testimonials, that the impulse to pray is a natural one, inspired by the love of God. This is affirmed in Bahá'í scripture: "Love is the cause of God's revelation unto man, the vital bond inherent, in accordance with the divine creation, in the realities of things. . . . Love is the light that guideth in darkness, the living link that uniteth God with man, that assureth the progress of every illumined soul."[73]

'Abdu'l-Bahá explains, "If one friend loves another, is it not natural that he should wish to say so? Though he knows that that friend is aware of his love, does he still not wish to tell him of it? . . . It is true that God knows the wishes of all hearts; but the impulse to pray is a natural one, springing from man's love to God."[74]

God created us because He loves us, and although we humans do not always show it, it is our inherent nature to love. Certainly we see that quality in children. From the earliest stage of infancy children crave the love of their parents. Throughout their childhood they instinctually turn to their parents for every basic need—love, care, food, shelter, protection, education, and training. It is a natural impulse for children to love and trust their parents and to turn to them for assistance, guidance, and all other things that pertain to their welfare. The most blessed and happiest of all children are those who are not only loved by their parents with unconditional and selfless love, but also taught to love others for the sake of God, free of prejudice.

Unfortunately, when children have no knowledge of parental love, whether it is because they are homeless orphans or victims of parental abuse or neglect, their natural impulse to love may be thwarted, perverted, and misdirected. Likewise, when a person has no knowledge of the love of God, his or her natural impulse to pray and turn to a higher power may also be misdirected.

Prayer is the very foundation and purpose of religion. No matter how lofty our goals, prayer is essential for spiritualizing our hearts and our endeavors. Through prayer and turning to the light of God, we manifest the potential that is endowed and latent within each one of us: "All the virtues which have been deposited and potential in human hearts are being revealed . . . as flowers and blossoms from divine gardens."

Through prayer we draw closer to God and become able to both fully receive and to return His love. Through prayer the latent qualities of our spirit unfold. So why do we pray? What better testimony is there than in the heartfelt words of a thirteen-year-old boy who told me, "I pray every day to keep in touch with the Lord. The prayers make me feel like God loves me, and that makes me feel safe and very happy. It's awesome!"

A poignant testimony as to why we need prayer in our lives—as well as proof to the transforming power of prayer—is an extraordinary story of a man I know who plunged into such deep, aching despair that he believed himself to be spiritually dead. He testifies that it was through prayer, finding faith, and through divine intervention that he found complete redemption and spiritual resurrection.

Daryl grew up in a segregated, African-American neighborhood in northeast Washington, DC, in the 1960s. His parents insisted that he and his six brothers and sisters go to church every Sunday, though the parents themselves rarely attended because of the many jobs they held to make ends meet. While prayer did not overtly play a significant role in Daryl's childhood, he was raised to believe in God and to follow the Ten Commandments. Daryl says, "My parents were hard-working, responsible, and extremely loving. They instilled in us a moral foundation to know right from wrong. Our family was very close, and that closeness extended to our neighborhood. White people were afraid to go into our section of the city because of its negative connotations, but the folks on our block were very warm and loving, especially to the children. I always felt protected and safe there."

Beyond the safety of the four-block radius in Daryl's neighborhood existed a very different world. To venture out there, even just to go to school, Daryl had to learn to fight to protect himself. "Drugs, alcohol, gambling, and crime were everywhere," he recalls. "A lot of illegal stuff happened, but no one thought anything about it and no one did anything to stop it."

Despite the spiritual foundation in Daryl's home, he was exposed to corruptive influences on the streets that were impossible to elude. At twelve Daryl began smoking, and by the time he was in high school he was consuming alcohol, shooting pool, and cutting classes with his friends. Ironically, at six-foot-one and large-boned, he bullied one of his teachers into giving him a passing grade so that he could graduate from high school and join the police academy "to fight crime."

Determined to better his life, he entered the police academy after graduating from school in 1970. He married in 1973 and became an officer in the DC police force. It looked like Daryl was moving up in his life, but by 1975 his life was falling apart.

"My wife and I were separated, I was drinking heavily, smoking two packs a day, smoking marijuana, going to strip joints with my friends on the force, and I knew I was sinking to a spiritual low." Desperate to change his life and leave DC, he joined the Air Force.

In 1996, while stationed in San Antonio, Texas, Daryl, who grew more aware of racism while living outside the DC area, began reading books that described accounts of heinous mistreatments suffered by the African-American community, past and present. The more he read, the angrier he became. Daryl continued his heavy drinking and smoking and was so desperate to get a high that he would eat the marijuana to avoid getting caught with it on base.

He says, "I had reached the very bottom. I was lost, unhappy and spiritually bankrupt. I was desperately searching for a spiritual foundation, but I didn't know where to look." Never would he have imagined finding what he was searching for through the help of his base sergeant. Daryl said, "He was a little white guy. And I never hung out with white guys. All my friends were black guys. But when this guy learned that we both loved jazz, he invited me to his home to hear some of his collection. It turned out that he was a Bahá'í.

"I had never heard of the Bahá'í Faith, and I had no interest in learning about it. He gave me a pamphlet with some information, and I stuck it in my pocket without bothering to look at it. I didn't even pay attention to what he was saying.

"But, later, when I got home, I picked up the pamphlet and read it. I was surprised because some of it made sense to me. Later, my sergeant gave me more Bahá'í materials to read and I was attracted to the Bahá'í teachings about the progressive nature and oneness of the world religions. I concluded that if there is one God and oneness in the all the religions—that if you love God—how could you not love all people? That is when it dawned on me that we are all one people.

"But it was the power of prayer that did it for me. I felt God's mercy through prayer. For years I had been trying to get a high from whiskey and drugs—but when I read the Bahá'í prayers, I experienced an intoxication and joy that I realized could only come through a spiritual connection with God. There was one night when I was alone and reading Bahá'í prayers and I was consumed with a sense of grace and wholeness. I felt like God said, 'Son, I'm giving you one more chance.'"

Daryl became a Bahá'í three weeks after first learning about the religion in the home of the "little sergeant." "I immediately gave up the drugs, drinking and smoking," he says. "That was nearly thirty years ago. I have not touched that stuff since, nor have I any desire to do so."

Daryl remained in the military for three years before returning to DC. His friends and family were in disbelief when they learned he had given up alcohol. But Daryl was a changed man. He enrolled in college, went on to graduate school, and today has a doctorate and is a highly respected professor and department chair at a prominent university. He is actively involved with local and international agencies that advocate for human rights and race unity issues. He remarried, and he and his wife have one son.

Despite his success and achievements, Daryl remains humble and grateful and insists, "Daily prayer is what keeps me grounded and focused. God's love was there for me all the time, even when I felt spiritually dead. But I just didn't know it. Prayer keeps me spiritually connected and in tune with God's love and sustains my faith."

Looking back at that time of his life in the military when he first felt a spiritual connectedness with God, Daryl reflects, "There is a prayer revealed by Bahá'u'lláh that particularly reaches into my soul. I feel so blessed that by some miracle I turned to prayer and was spiritually awakened. The words in this prayer convey perfectly what is in my heart.

My God, my Adored One, my King, my desire! What tongue can voice my thanks to Thee? I was heedless, Thou didst awaken me. I had turned back from Thee, Thou didst graciously aid me to turn towards Thee. I was as one dead, Thou didst quicken me with the water of life. I was withered, Thou didst revive me with the heavenly stream of Thine utterance which hath flowed forth from the Pen of the All-Merciful.

O Divine Providence! All existence is begotten by Thy bounty; deprive it not of the waters of Thy generosity, neither do Thou withhold it from the ocean of Thy mercy. I beseech Thee to aid and assist me at all times and under all conditions, and seek from the heaven of Thy grace Thine ancient favor. Thou art, in truth, the Lord of bounty, and the Sovereign of the kingdom of eternity.[75]

Why do we pray? So that we may follow the natural impulse bestowed upon each and every human being to attain the knowledge and love of our Creator, endowing our souls with spiritual life and immeasurable blessings and happiness.

CHAPTER 5

Train to Chongqing

In late May of 1995, Jason and Mike, two twenty-year-old American college students, embarked on what promised to be a fascinating journey to the People's Republic of China. They hoped to teach English at a Chinese university for the summer and at the same time learn some Chinese.

In preparation for their two-and-a-half-month trip, they loaded large and cumbersome bags with enough books, clothes, cameras, and other paraphernalia to last them quite nicely for a few years, if not more. But they were determined that this was not going to be a touristy holiday.

Their attitude was to basically "go with the flow," and they were prepared to get their hands dirty. After all, they were two big guys: tall, healthy, and strong. They were young and college educated. What could go wrong?

Their limited plans did include some practical preparations. They received the appropriate inoculations and made room in their overstuffed bags for bottled water and antimalarial pills. Also, they had arranged to stay with an American friend in Macau, a small island off China's southern border. From there they would begin their journey to the city of Chongqing, Sichuan Province, directly east of Tibet. After arriving in

Chongqing, if all went well, they would find jobs as English teachers at a local university.

The first leg of their trip went smoothly. Their long flight to Macau arrived on schedule, and, as arranged, they stayed with their friend. After obtaining a guidebook and travel directions to Chongqing, Jason and Mike treated themselves to dinner at a local McDonald's. It was their last night in Macau, and as they enjoyed gobbling down their American cuisine of burgers and fries drenched in ketchup, neither of them had the slightest idea of the ordeals and mishaps that awaited them. The boys were about to get a lot more than their hands dirty.

The following morning Jason grabbed his enormous duffel bag that matched the length of his six-foot body, and slid his arms through the straps of one very heavy backpack. Mike, six feet four inches tall in bare feet, had three humongous backpacks, one of which he carried on his back, one in the front, and the other on his side. Wanting to get an early start, the boys skipped breakfast and crossed into the border town of Xuhei in the People's Republic of China. From Xuhei they would take a bus to the city of Guangzhou, where they would then board a train bound to Chongqing.

In Xuehei they encountered their first minor snag when they realized that no one at the bus terminal spoke English, and, of course, neither of them spoke Chinese. But the situation was easily remedied when Jason offered a friendly smile to the ticket agent, held up two fingers, and pronounced loudly and clearly "GWONG-JOE!" The agent understood him and sold him two tickets. The boys boarded the bus and were in high spirits for their journey.

Their spirits, however, plunged after reaching Guangzhou, their first real stop in mainland China. The boys were stupefied. In addition to feeling helpless and debilitated by their inability to communicate with anyone around them, they felt alienated and unprepared to deal with a host of unexpected challenges, one of which was their physical appearance. Jason and Mike felt like towering giants, and with their fair complexions and light eyes, the two were definitely an oddity.

"Everywhere we went, people stared at us," recalls Jason. "They didn't just stare—they gawked. Some stares seemed hostile, many were very amicable, but I think that most of the stares were just out of curiosity. It was 1995, and I think many Chinese had never seen a white foreigner in person. It was a very strange feeling to be the focus of everyone's attention everywhere we went."

An even more unpleasant aspect was the sweltering heat that was typical summer weather in southern China. The town was not only unbearably hot, but it was also bustling, crowded with hordes of people going and coming from every direction. People walked, ran, rode bicycles, and jumped in and out of noisy taxis that never seemed to stop honking. The town was the train hub of southern China, and people came to it from all regions of the nation.

In addition to the heat, the noise, the dense crowds, and the two American boys' inability to communicate with anyone but each other, they also became aware of an odious scent. That scent, which permeated the air, indicated an absence of certain amenities that are taken for granted in Western culture, such as modern plumbing and sanitation facilities, central air conditioning, and rodent control. The pollution from the fumes and other waste was overwhelming.

Although the people were genuinely warm and friendly, Jason and Mike lacked any means to communicate with them and felt lost. In fact, they *were* lost. They had no idea how to get to the train station, and no matter how many people they asked, no one could understand or help them.

They eventually managed to find the train station. It was supposed to be a short walk from the bus, but it took them almost two hours to locate it. Their clothes were completely drenched from perspiration, from the heat and humidity and lugging their heavy bags. Their last meal had been the celebration dinner at McDonald's the previous night, but, perhaps due to the excessive heat, the exhaustion, the odors, or just plain adrenalin, neither of them had an appetite at this point.

Their sole desire was to buy their tickets, get on the train, and sleep away the ten hours they had been assured by friends in Macau it would take to get to Chongqing. But after just one glance at the station, the boys knew that purchasing their tickets was going to be no easy feat.

Jason says, "I'll never forget my first image of the train station. It was this looming, monstrous, giant amalgamation of green-black metal. A huge clock stood in the middle of an enormous courtyard that was the size of a few football fields. And every square inch of the place was filled with masses of people running this way and that way. People were rushing about, shouting, fighting, eating, singing, and many were just lying down on the ground. It was mayhem. Inside the terminal it was dark, dank, and decayed. As far we could tell we were the only foreigners in the entire place. Many of the people were very friendly and it was obvious that they wanted to help us, but the language barrier made it impossible."

There were several very long lines in front of the ticket counter. Mike agreed to sit with the luggage while Jason ventured boldly through the massive crowds to stand at the end of one of the ticket lines. After what seemed like an eternity, he finally made it to the ticket counter and tried desperately to communicate with the agent, who spoke no English. Once again, showing his best smile, holding up two fingers, and attempting to articulate the clearest phonetic pronunciation possible, he shouted, "CHUNG-CHING." The agent looked at him as if he had two heads. Jason frantically waved two fingers in the form of a peace sign and repeated the name over and over again. She had had no idea of what Jason wanted. She motioned for him to get into another line.

Jason stood and waited at the end of every line in the terminal—all with unsuccessful results. None of the agents understood him. He anxiously attempted to find a foreign language desk, which he was sure existed somewhere in the train station, but his search was in vain. He tried to find anyone who could speak English, but that was also a futile effort. Finally, he returned wearily to Mike to inform him of his failure to purchase the tickets.

Poor Mike had been baking under the sun in front of the station for nearly two hours. When Jason updated him on their dilemma, Mike gravely hung his head down in despair. As if he were drowning in a cesspool, Jason struggled for air and swallowed the bitter taste of fear and rising panic. Feeling helpless, dirty, exhausted, hungry, and immobil-ized by their heavy bags, Jason began to wonder seriously whether they were going to be stuck there forever in front of the train station. Simply too hungry and tired to think clearly, they had landed in a crisis, and there seemed to be no apparent rescue at hand.

At that moment, as Jason felt his spirit sink to its lowest ebb, he turned his heart to God and began to pray under his breath. Over and over again he prayed, begging for divine intervention. As he prayed, he heard a man's screaming voice rise above the crowd's clamor, "Chongqing! Chongqing!" No sound had ever resonated so sweetly. Mike ran like the wind, weaving through the heavy mobs, following the voice. He came upon a small black market, and the ticket seller could actually speak a little English. Mike shouted excitedly, "How much for two tickets to Chongqing?"

"Five thousand yuan," the man responded. Mike was ready to give the man all his money, and probably his shoes as well. He opened up his wallet when Mike, in a somewhat more pragmatic frame of mind, thought that 5,000 yuan—the equivalent of 400 American dollars—sounded a bit pricey. After some negotiating the boys agreed to pay the man 2,000 yuan, which they later discovered was still a ridiculously high sum. But at the time they were too relieved to worry about the expense.

The man, obviously overjoyed at his financial killing, led the boys through the massive crowds to the entrance of the station. Once again on their own, the boys searched for their platform, trudging upstairs, downstairs, through one platform after another. Mike says, "I remember going inside the train station and showing our tickets to various people. One of them directed us to the wrong platform. We went all the way to the top of a long flight of stairs leading to the platform and were informed by an employee that our train was boarding on the other platform. We looked across the tracks and saw people running like lemmings for the train. Jason and I ran down the stairs with Jason's bag banging and bumping."

They sprinted up another set of stairs to reach the correct platform, towing their heavy, bulky bags and trying not to bang them into people or drag them over the many bodies that lay resting on the ground. Miraculously, they arrived at the correct platform just as their train was arriving. They were on their way to Chongqing!

Jason says, "When our train stopped, I stood there looking at it and all I could think of was that it reminded me of a punctured Styrofoam cup, but instead of water pouring out, it was people. Hordes of people poured out from the windows and doors of the train. People entered the train the same way. They climbed in through the windows; they jumped down on the tracks to grab onto the sides; they entered into every opening of the train they could find. Of course, Mike and I were bigger than everyone, and we used it to our advantage. We realized that if we wanted to get into one of the cars, we would have to literally push and claw our way in. We made it through and got ourselves seats. We were elated!"

It was late in the afternoon on Saturday when the boys finally boarded the train. They tried to get comfortable on a small wooden bench that seated three people. Jason sat by the window, and Mike sat in the middle, between Jason and another man. They faced another wooden bench about three feet away, where three young women sat.

Travelers continued to pour into the train. With no vacant seats available, they sat or reclined, crammed tightly next to each other on the floor. Some hunched their bodies to fit into the luggage racks above the seats. Others scrunched themselves under the benches. Everywhere there were people. They ate, drank, chattered loudly, and seemed perfectly at ease with their surroundings.

There was no air conditioning or electric fan, and just about everyone smoked cigarettes. Frequent spitting without taking aim in any particular direction was commonplace. The car was hot, humid, filthy, and the air was fetid. A mysterious yellow, acidic, gooey substance, which coated the ceiling and walls, dripped from a valve directly on top of Jason, canvassing his hair and clothes. The toilets of the two bathrooms overflowed and spilled into the car.

There were people on racks above Jason and Mike, and people were under their bench. The boys still hadn't eaten anything since the previous night, but as the train took off, heading north, they were feeling too happy to care about their discomforts. They were absolutely euphoric to finally be on their way. And they knew that they were only going to be on the train for ten hours. They could handle it. They had their bottles of water. They would be okay. After all, they had wanted a rough adventure, and they were getting just what they wanted. Or, at least, that's what they thought.

Jason explains, "We later found out that there are four kinds of seating on a train in China: 'hard seat,' 'soft seat,' 'hard sleeper,' and 'soft sleeper.'

Hard seat is the lowest rung on a Chinese train. In fact, the hard seat train is so impoverished and squalid, and its traveling conditions are so brutally arduous, that only those on a shoestring budget will travel on it. We found out later that it is considered completely intolerable for a foreigner. Mike and I found that out firsthand!"

Their spirits first began to decline after riding for about thirty minutes, when a beggar with no hands, who had been crawling on his knees while approaching passengers for money, spotted the "two rich foreigners." The beggar crawled over to the boys and rubbed his amputated limbs on Mike as he grunted and gestured for charity. Jason and Mike were warned in Macau not to give to beggars, as one small act of generosity could potentially attract others to clamor for gifts. Besides, the boys, who had limited funds themselves after being thoroughly scalped by their black market friend, had no change available.

Mike shook his head and motioned for the man to leave. The beggar was relentless. He stood rubbing his nubs against Mike's arm. Jason says, "It was really strange what happened. When this beggar approached us, every single person in our car stopped what they were doing, and for the first time since we had been on the train, there was complete silence. Every single face in that car focused on Mike. He tried to be polite, shaking his head 'no.' But the man kept rubbing his limbs on Mike's arms and grunting. Out of frustration Mike grabbed the beggar by his shoulders and pushed him away. The beggar started scrambling towards Mike again, but to our astonishment, the other people in the car began to yell at the beggar. It was pretty clear to us that they were telling him to leave us alone. The beggar moved on to another car."

Shortly afterwards, they experienced a considerably more pleasant encounter when they heard a female voice call out to them in English, "Are you Americans?" They looked up and saw a young woman approaching them. She was a student, and they were delighted to finally have an opportunity to engage in a conversation with an English-speaker.

Mike says, "She had been very kind to us and had asked the conductor, who came to check tickets, to upgrade us to 'hard sleeper.' The man laughed and told her that there were no hard sleeper vacancies." But the crushing blow was when she informed Mike and Jason that they had another twenty hours to go before reaching Chongqing! To add to their dismay, their one and only English speaking friend and translator stayed on the train for a mere five hours, leaving the boys, once again, feeling hopelessly alone, isolated, and unable to communicate with the people around them.

The journey, which, thus far, certainly could not be described as eventless, produced another unsettling incident. Mike recalls, "As I remember it, this event happened late at night, after about twelve hours of train travel. The girls who were sitting on the bench opposite us were sleeping, and a young man who wanted to sit down pushed one of the girls awake in order to take her seat."

"When the girl refused to budge, the man resorted to punching her in the face."

Jason and Mike, who were a lot bigger than the girl's attacker, were shocked and unsure of what to do. Their friends in Macau had warned them to not interfere in fights, because Americans who did so could easily attract danger from a hostile mob or be thrown into jail. Unfamiliar with the culture, they reasoned, albeit uneasily, that it was best to stay out of it. What seemed particularly odd to Jason and Mike was that with all the attention they had drawn when the beggar had approached them, none of the other passengers seemed to notice or care even remotely that the man had assaulted the girl.

Finally, the other two girls on her bench came to her defense, shouting and shooing away the aggressor. The man belligerently retreated and pushed his way through the crowd. But still, none of the other passengers appeared upset or surprised by the incident. Everyone carried on as if nothing out of the ordinary had occurred.

Jason and Mike, however, were deeply troubled. In the last few days they had observed ill-treatment towards women. In addition, hunger, fatigue, dehydration from the heat, and nausea from the stench were kicking in. They drank water from their bottles, but it hardly satisfied the emptiness in their stomachs.

The remaining hours through the night passed slowly. Mike was suffering from sleep deprivation as well as from extreme hunger. Although the putrid-smelling, acidic, sticky goo continued to drip on Jason, his body and brain seemed to shut down, which enabled him to fall into a fitful sleep as he crossed his arms and rested his head.

Twenty-eight hours passed. The boys were now deeply concerned that they had either missed their stop or had taken the wrong train. Jason dug into his bag and pulled out his guidebook. He noticed that there was a dictionary in the back of the book. Using the book, he managed to communicate with the three women who sat opposite him. The women giggled when they realized what Jason was asking them. Also using Jason's book, the women broke the news to the guys that Chongqing was still another twenty-four hours away.

Jason, who felt numb at hearing the news, fell into a complete stupor. Mike, on the other hand, was fully conscious and aware of the impact another day of travel would have on his psyche. He stood up, began pulling down his bags, and announced emphatically to Jason that he was getting off the train. He made the offer to Jason to get off with him. But, no matter what, he was getting off the train at the next stop.

Jason was horrified. Getting off the train? They had absolutely no knowledge of where they were. Jason wondered how they could possibly survive in some remote, backwoods area of China when it was impossible for them to manage in a large city like Guangzhou. He attempted to be rational about this, but his brain refused to function. He certainly didn't want to head off to Sichuan by himself, but he also didn't want to get off the train. He hated the fear and helplessness that assaulted his senses. He sat there, glued to his seat as if paralyzed. Drenched in the yellow, sticky goo, he was also stuck to his seat literally.

Once again, he felt as if he had sunk to the lowest ebb. He turned with all his heart to God. He pulled out a Bahá'í prayer book and quietly read one of his favorite prayers, which offered comforting words:

> [B]e thou so steadfast in My love that thy heart shall not waver, even if the swords of the enemies rain blows upon thee and all the heavens and the earth arise against thee. . . . Rely upon God, thy God and the Lord of thy fathers. . . . By God! Should one who is in affliction or grief read this Tablet with absolute sincerity, God will dispel his sadness, solve his difficulties and remove his afflictions. Verily, He is the Merciful, the Compassionate. Praise be to God, the Lord of all the worlds.[76]

Deeply immersed, Jason read the prayer over and over again and began to relax. His breathing slowed, and a sense of calm and strength renewed his spirit. While praying, he was also oblivious to the ruckus that was emerging around him. Apparently Mike's agitated state had caused quite a commotion among the other passengers. Everyone was shouting! Mike says, "The people were incredibly kind to us, and once they realized that we hadn't eaten for hours, they began to pass us their own food."

Jason, who was too nauseated to eat, continued to pray while everyone else on the train continued to shout. And then something very strange happened. The train stopped. It came to a complete halt! The train's conductor, this time a woman, entered their car and walked directly to Jason and Mike. She could speak some English and asked to see the boys' tickets. They told her how much they had paid for them, which caused her to raise her eyebrows in surprised indignation. She motioned for the boys to get their bags and to follow her. When she led them off the train, Jason was shocked. Was she throwing them off the train for causing a disturbance? Meanwhile, the other passengers on the train cheered and clapped them on the back as they were leaving the train.

The boys continued to follow her to the very last car of the train. When they entered the last car, they saw several bunk beds, two empty beds among them. She pointed to the empty beds, and Jason and Mike placed their bags on the racks and threw themselves on the beds. Stretching out on those hard, wooden beds felt like heaven to them. They were in ecstasy.

Mike says, "It does seem that the people in our car, who made such a commotion, told the conductor in Chinese that we didn't belong in the hard seat cabin. Apparently, the conductor told the other passengers that two hard sleeper spots had opened up, which is why the passengers were cheering—they were happy for us!"

But no one was happier and more grateful than Jason and Mike.

The pair had been given the name of a university in Chongqing that had become somewhat of a sanctuary in their minds all though the journey. However, when they arrived at the university's main office after traveling on the train for three days, now dirty, ragged, disheveled, and starving, they were told that there were no teaching positions available. No one would help them. It was Monday, and the dusk of early evening was falling upon them as a gloomy, gray curtain.

This time it was Jason who lost his composure. His hair was covered with the smelly, yellow goo from the train. It was on his clothes. His giant duffle bag was in shreds. He felt too weary to go on. He sat down on the ground, covered his face, and cried.

He felt himself plunging into deep despair. Mike, who recognized that there was nothing else for him to do but to put all of his trust in God, in a low, whispered, hoarse voice, prayed with all his heart and soul. While Mike prayed, Jason could think of only two things. He thought about his faith in God. And he thought about his love for his girlfriend, Julie, who was back home in the United States. It was the first time that he had realized that he wanted to marry her.

During their darkest hour, the two young men's thoughts had turned to prayer, faith, and what was most meaningful in their lives. A young Chinese man who spoke good English and had earlier directed them to the main office at the university suddenly appeared and came over to them. The man, whose English name was "Thomas," explained that he was a student at another university in town. He offered to help them but explained that he would first need to conduct some business in the school's administrative office, which would require an hour or two. Jason and Mike had absolutely nowhere to go anyway and were desperate for assistance. They agreed to wait.

Mike says, "Throughout the trip, as far as prayer goes, that was Jason's department. I was a bit too shocked to pray. I do remember, however, praying during Jason's collapse while waiting for Thomas to return. I was saying over and over the prayer: 'Is there any Remover of difficulties save God? Say: Praised be God! He is God! All are His servants and all abide by His bidding!'"[77]

When Thomas returned, he hailed a taxi and took Jason and Mike to a student's hotel near the campus of his university. The boys checked into a room, dumped their monstrous bags, washed up, and changed their clothes. Thomas then took them to a restaurant where he graciously treated them to dinner.

Jason and Mike devoured their food, which was their first meal in more than three days. That night, they went to their room and took showers for the first time in several days. Jason says, "I'll never forget that shower! Finally to wash all that goo off me was like being in paradise! Before we both passed out, I can remember us lying there in our real beds with clean sheets, with full stomachs, and feeling amazingly grateful to God. It was heaven!"

After spending a month in Chongqing, they departed for another city, Chengdu, where they finally taught English at a university. They made many close and wonderful friends that summer, among them Thomas, the young man who had rescued them in Chongqing. After getting a little more acclimated and learning to appreciate the culture, they also enjoyed traveling to different parts of China, where they encountered a number of fascinating and memorable experiences.

Jason traveled again to mainland China the following summer and returned a third time to stay for six months after he graduated from college. During those visits, he taught English at different universities, traveled, and enjoyed seeing again many of his Chinese friends.

The two young men now often laugh about their first journey through China. Jason says, "We realize that there were hundreds of things we could have done differently to have been better prepared. But we were young, inexperienced, and I guess we thought we knew everything. Amazingly, we got through it okay. We made a lot of great friends that summer and came to respect and admire the Chinese people and their culture."

Jason adds, "But Mike and I have talked about this a lot. And we agree that the most valuable aspect of that experience was realizing how essential it is to turn to God and to completely trust in Him. We realized that prayer is this amazing thing of power! I have never had any experience in my life in which I felt so deeply plunged into despair and pushed to the limits as I felt during that three-day journey through China. And yet every single time when our struggles became unbearable, there would be this visceral, almost brutal need to turn to God and to just give all our problems to Him.

"It was amazing! As soon as I began to pray, I immediately felt better, and I knew in my heart that God would take care of us and everything would be okay. When I look back at that experience, it astonishes me that each time we prayed, these miracles would happen. A poignant example is an entire train stopping just so that these two, completely worn out, grungy Americans could be given two beds! There is no question in my mind that God took care of us. It was as if all we had to do was turn to God and say, 'Please?' And bam! Everything was okay!"

Jason and Mike matured quite a bit that summer. Through prayer and trust in God, they learned humility, patience, and deepened in their level of compassion, respect, understanding, and appreciation for diverse populations. They have no regrets for their experience, because, without question, they learned firsthand the power of prayer and the benefits that come from complete reliance on God.

CHAPTER 6

What Is Our Spiritual Reality and Purpose?

Alex appeared to be a beautiful, healthy baby boy, but he was born with a genetic condition called fragile X syndrome, the leading known hereditary cause of developmental disabilities. When Alex was two years old, he was diagnosed positive through a cytogenetic blood test. He functioned in the moderate range of mental impairment and was significantly delayed in speech and language skills.

When he was three-and-a-half years old, a speech and language pathologist came to evaluate him. Through most of the session Alex spoke only a few words for the therapist. And then, out of the blue, Alex almost shocked the pathologist out of her chair by reciting from memory the following Bahá'í prayer: "Thy name is my healing, O my God, and remembrance of Thee is my remedy. Nearness to Thee is my hope, and love for Thee is my companion. Thy mercy to me is my healing and my succor in both this world and the world to come. Thou, verily, art the All-Bountiful, the All-Knowing, the All-Wise."[78]

I know this as a fact because I happen to be Alex's mother, and I was there. I will never forget how the therapist, in utter disbelief at what she witnessed, insisted that Alex had absolutely no understanding of what he was saying. She was adamant that Alex was merely parroting words that he had been exposed to in our home. While I freely admitted to teaching the prayer to Alex, I also told her that if what she said was true, then why was Alex unable to parrot other phrases and sentences?

From my perspective, it wasn't simply a matter of faith and recognition of Alex's spirituality. It also was a matter of logic. If he had no grasp of spiritual realities, then why was he more receptive to learning the prayer than other things that we tried to teach him? And why did he always choose to recite that particular prayer on his own initiative at the most appropriate times, such as when he or someone else around him appeared ill, sad, or troubled? It was, after all, a prayer that asks for healing and comfort.

Notwithstanding, the therapist refused to accept the possibility that Alex could understand that he was reciting a prayer to God. She was convinced that Alex could not possibly comprehend the concept of God and prayer because of his cognitive deficiencies. She seemed to be annoyed that I believed otherwise. I wonder what her reaction would have been to an interesting encounter I had with Alex a few years later.

Alex's language skills had improved considerably as he grew older, but, nonetheless, I was taken aback one day when he was about nine years old. I was passing his bedroom when I heard him engaged in what sounded like a serious conversation. I looked into his room and saw that he was alone. I asked, "Who are you talking to Alex?" He responded quite cheerfully, "I'm talking to God, Mommy!"

"Oh," I said. "What are you saying to God?"

"I told God that I love Him." He added, "God talked to me too!"

My curiosity aroused, I asked, "God talked to you too?

Alex smiled broadly and said, "Yes, He did!"

Now even more curious, I asked, "What did God say to you?"

"God told me he loves me too!"

My husband and I consider it a tremendous blessing to be the parents of three sons, who are all, praise God, very loving and spiritual people. My oldest son, Justin, was identified as academically gifted when he was in first grade, and today he is an attorney and married to a lovely young woman, Amy, a very talented artist. My youngest son, Ben, like Alex, was born with fragile X syndrome and is also mentally impaired.

Unless the scientists someday discover a cure for their condition, Alex and Ben will have very little independence or ability to choose their own course in this world. They will endure a multitude of challenges and will be dependent on others for their welfare for the rest of their lives. Their options for jobs and lifestyles will always be limited and dependent upon the support, care, and kindness of others. Even so, with appropriate special education and related services, proper vocational training, and good job and residential opportunities, Alex and Ben can be productive, happy, and contributing members of the community.

Can a youth with a limited mental capacity, who can barely read and write at a five-year-old level, comprehend the love of God and prayer? As a mother who has raised two children with developmental disabilities, I have no doubt that Alex and Ben are two precious souls with pure hearts who are amazingly in touch with their spirituality.

Not too long ago, after returning home from the Special Olympics state soccer games, Ben, a grinning fourteen-year-old who was bubbling over with happiness and excitement, announced, "God is good! Our team won the gold medal! God is good! Thank you, God!"

What made that announcement so special was that Ben, who has never quite developed the verbal skills of his brother Alex, still had difficulty in formulating a sentence of more than a few words. In his enthusiasm, not only did he express joy in winning the games, but also to the best of his ability and in his own innocent way, he gave praise and gratitude to God. Those few words, "God is good" and "Thank you, God," were declared with such heartfelt sincerity that it was as if he had recited a long, beautiful prayer. In his earnest innocence, Ben praised God and gave Him thanks.

My children's spiritual growth is not debilitated by their physical impairments. Alex and Ben are mentally impaired, but they are not spiritually impaired. They love God and pray with all of their hearts. They are both quick to offer prayers for others as well as for themselves. They refuse to go to bed at night until we have said prayers together. What is particularly inspiring is the calming and joyful effect prayers have on their behavior and disposition. Their words may be few, but the absolute sincerity of their expressions of love for God affirm their inner spiritual reality.

What is the nature of our spiritual reality?

Bahá'í scripture explains, "The purpose of God in creating man hath been, and will ever be, to enable him to know his Creator and to attain His Presence."[79] To this most excellent aim, the soul was created to progress in this world and, after its separation from the physical body, to continue to progress in the spiritual worlds of God. This eternal quest of the soul to attain nearness to God is the purpose for which we were created, and that truth cannot be altered. However, what can be altered is the level of progress that our souls achieve in this world. As our understanding of the true nature of our spiritual reality deepens, we become more ardent in striving to fulfill our spiritual purpose, which is to know and worship God and to prepare for our spiritual destiny in the eternal realm.

The Bahá'í writings explain that humankind is endowed with five physical powers and five spiritual powers. The five physical powers enable us to perceive all things in the material world.

These are sight, which perceives visible forms; hearing, which perceives audible sounds; smell, which perceives odors; taste, which perceives foods; and feeling, which is in all parts of the body, and perceives tangible things. These five powers perceive outward existences.[80]

We also have five spiritual powers, which all pertain to the intellect: "imagination, which conceives things; thought, which reflects upon realities; comprehension, which comprehends realities; memory, which retains whatever we imagine, think, and comprehend;"[81] and the intermediary power, which acts between the physical and spiritual powers. That is to say that the intermediary power conveys to the spiritual powers whatever the physical powers discern. The intermediary power is also known as the "common faculty" because it communicates between the outward and inward powers.

For example, we use our sight, which is an outer power, to look at a flower. Our visual perception of the flower is conveyed to the intermediary power, which then transmits this perception to our inner powers: imagination, thought, comprehension, and memory. We then may derive pleasure in simply gazing at the flower. Perhaps we feel inspired to draw a picture of the flower or write a poem about it.

We may possibly feel inclined to touch the flower and inhale its fragrance, using more of our outer powers. Again, our intermediary power transmits the physical perception to our inner powers. Artists, jewelers, clothing designers, perfume makers, and architects are inspired by the shapes, colors, and fragrances of the flower. Our spiritual powers provide us with endless abilities to comprehend, appreciate, reflect, remember, and be creatively inspired by the flower's aesthetic beauty as well as by its practical uses.

While a bee drinks its nectar and pollinates a flower, and a bird may eat the flower's seeds, any interest a flower may elicit from another earthly creature serves in alignment with the dictates of nature. It is true that some animals are affectionate, loyal, playful, and can be trained by humans, but all creation, with the exception of humankind, is bound by the stern law of nature. "The sun, the stars, the oceans, the mountains, the rivers, the trees, and all animals, great or small—none are able to evade obedience to nature's law."[82]

Humans alone have the freedom and ability to control and adapt some of the laws of nature to meet our needs. Our intellect is

in truth, the most precious gift bestowed upon man by the divine bounty. Man alone, among created beings, has this wonderful power. . . . God gave this power to man that it might be used for the advancement of civilization, for the good of humanity, to increase love and concord and peace.

But man prefers to use this gift to destroy instead of to build, for injustice and oppression, for hatred and discord and devastation, for the destruction of his fellow-creatures, whom Christ has commanded that he should love as himself.[83]

God gave us this spiritual power of intellect for the purpose of contributing to the advancement of civilization, but He also gave us the free will to use it as we choose. "Study the sciences, acquire more and more knowledge," says 'Abdu'l-Bahá. "Use your knowledge always for the benefit of others; so may war cease on the face of this beautiful earth, and a glorious edifice of peace and concord be raised. Strive that your high ideals may be realized in the Kingdom of God on earth, as they will be in Heaven."[84]

When we use knowledge for our own self-interest to satisfy obsessive cravings for power and riches, we go against the very purpose for which God created us and bestowed upon us these heavenly gifts. The thought force and the animal force are partners in this world. Although the physical component of man is part of the animal creation, we possess a power of thought superior to all other created beings. Our everlasting reality is this power of thought and not the material body. This power of thought is our rational soul. All material things, including the physical body, are temporary, while the soul and the powers of the spirit are eternal.

Bahá'í scripture explains that in the world of humanity there are three degrees of reality: the body, the individual soul, and the spirit of humankind. Like an animal, man possesses the faculties of the senses, as described earlier, and is subject to heat, cold, hunger, thirst, etc. However, unlike the animal, man has a rational soul—the human intelligence. This intelligence is the intermediary between the body and the spirit. This spirit is a radiance drawn from the eternal light of the Holy Spirit of God, which sheds illumination upon the soul.

When we open our hearts and minds and turn to the blessings of the spirit, our souls become luminous, enlightened with understanding, and bear goodly fruits. When our souls turn to our material side, towards the bodily part of our nature, we become more brutal, vile, cruel, misguided, unhappy, and, in 'Abdu'l-Bahá's words, "inferior to the inhabitants of the lower animal kingdom."[85] By turning to our spiritual nature, our souls radiate the Mercy of God and stimulate spiritual progress.

Why is progress of the soul important?

According to Bahá'í scripture, the soul has its origins in the spiritual worlds of God. The soul is exalted above matter and the physical world. The individual has his beginning when the soul, coming from these spiritual worlds, associates itself with the embryo at the time of conception. But this association is not material; the soul does not enter or leave the body and does not occupy physical space. The soul does not belong to the material world, and its association with the body is similar to that of a light with a mirror that reflects it. The light that appears in the mirror is not inside it; it comes from an external source. Similarly, the soul is not inside the body; there is a special relationship between it and the body.

Spiritual progress—developing our spiritual qualities and strengthening our relationship with God—prepares the soul for life after its separation from the physical body, which occurs at death. The physical body dies, but the soul continues to progress onward through the spiritual worlds of God. The state and condition of the soul upon entering the next world is largely contingent upon how well the soul developed in this world. Bahá'í scripture compares the development of the soul to the development of the human embryo. At the beginning of life, we receive capacity and endowment for the reality of human existence. While still in the womb the fetus obtains eyes, ears, arms, legs, hands, feet, internal organs, and so on, in preparation for his or her new existence. 'Abdu'l-Bahá explains,

> The powers requisite in this world were conferred upon him in the world of the matrix [womb] so that when he entered this realm of real existence he not only possessed all necessary functions and powers but found provision for his material sustenance awaiting him. . . . Therefore, in this world he must prepare himself for the life beyond. That which he needs in the world of the Kingdom must be obtained here. Just as he prepared himself in the world of the matrix by acquiring forces necessary in this sphere of existence, so, likewise, the indispensable forces of the divine existence must be potentially attained in this world.[86]

The soul progresses in this world for the purpose of preparing for life in heaven just as the fetus develops and prepares in the womb for existence in this world. When the fetus does not progress normally, the infant may be born with a physical impairment such as a hearing impairment, visual impairment, or as in the case of two of my children, a mental impairment.

Fortunately, these physical impairments do not impair the spiritual progress of a soul. On the contrary, we are assured in Bahá'í scripture that those innocent souls who are born with disease or impairments, although they may have to endure tremendous challenges and hardships throughout their mortal lives, receive a special protection and blessing. God is the All-Merciful. Bahá'í scripture attests that all suffering in this world is compensated in the eternal realm—the Heavenly Kingdom of God: "I know of a certainty, by virtue of my love for Thee, that Thou wilt never cause tribulations to befall any soul unless Thou desirest to exalt his station in Thy celestial Paradise."[87]

A dear friend of mine wrote a letter to me a few years ago to share her thoughts about Alex and Ben and offered this comment: "I think your two boys are lovely children. Considering that ninety percent of the troubles of the world come from people who are brilliant intellectually but who certainly will not be rewarded on high, as far as we know, and all the trouble they cause, one can appreciate the virtues of children such as yours, however simple they may seem intellectually, whose hearts and souls are pure."

The message in my friend's letter was a soothing balm to my heart and was not only comforting, but also afforded me a new outlook. Focusing on the spirituality of my children helped me to better appreciate Alex and Ben, who truly are two very sweet, wonderful young people. Alex, who graduated from high school in June 2002, is extremely happy working full time at a candle factory—a commercialized component of his vocational center. He works diligently, receives a regular paycheck, derives tremendous pride from his work, and has many friends there. Ben, my youngest, is also a hardworking student in a special education class at a public high school. He loves school, his teachers and classmates all seem to be exceedingly fond of him, and he enthusiastically enjoys his participation in the year-round local Special Olympics activities.

One of my favorite passages from Bahá'í scripture affirms the essential, crucial need of spiritual education for our children:

Training in morals and good conduct is far more important than book learning. A child that is cleanly, agreeable, of good character, well-behaved—even though he be ignorant—is preferable to a child that is rude, unwashed, ill-natured, and yet becoming deeply versed in all the sciences and arts. The reason for this is that the child who conducts himself well, even though he be ignorant, is of benefit to others, while an ill-natured, ill-behaved child is corrupted and harmful to others, even though he be learned. If, however, the child be trained to be both learned and good, the result is light upon light.[88]

Alex and Ben are limited in what they can comprehend intellectually, but to me, they are two shining, brilliant stars. They are not out to hurt, cheat, steal, manipulate, or take advantage of others in any way for their own gratification. Alex's speech and language pathologist failed to acknowledge his spirituality and believed it to be impossible for him to grasp the concept of God. But, in fact, both Alex and Ben love God.

Very recently my mother passed away, and, once again, my children amazed me by bearing witness to their spiritual reality. They loved their grandmother very much and, naturally, they were sad when they heard the news of her passing. Our family attended the funeral, and my husband and I were curious as to how the boys would react to being at the service. Coming from out of town to attend the funeral, we were given no warning in advance that the grandchildren who were present would be invited to stand up and say a few words about their grandmother at the gravesite. I almost stopped breathing when Ben's name was called, because, even today, as a teenager, Ben is extremely quiet and shy around groups of people, particularly those who are unfamiliar to him. Generally, Ben speaks only a few words at a time.

But when his name was called he shocked us all. Ben stood up, looking handsome in his black suit, crisp white shirt, and teal silk tie, cleared his throat, lowered his head, and said very reverently, in the manner of a prayer, "Grandmother, you were a wonderful woman. I love you and I miss you. You are happy in heaven with my grandfather. Amen."

Ben then quietly took his seat, and many at the funeral, so deeply touched by Ben's sweet, heartfelt little prayer, smiled warmly. There was such genuineness in the words and spirit of Ben's prayer that it was impossible not to recognize that this young person, although debilitated by mental deficiencies, had an understanding of the spiritual kingdom and the eternal soul. He understood that his grandmother still watched over him and that she was happy to be with her husband, his grandfather, who had passed away a few years earlier. Ben's comprehension of the afterlife certainly had little to do with his ability for intellectual reasoning. Ben could sense this spiritual truth in his heart.

Ben and Alex are able to grasp spiritual concepts because they are endowed, like all human beings, with spiritual cognition. Their spiritual reality is unscathed by their physical disabilities. My husband and I have come to believe that the reason their hearts are so pure and receptive to the knowledge and love of God is because of their impairments. They are protected from the veils of ego, prejudice, and vain imaginings that the rest of us so-called "normal people" struggle with throughout our lives.

Again, there are no words to adequately describe how blessed I feel to be their mother. They are an affirmation to me every day of my life that our spiritual reality is a power that is, "conferred upon man through the breath of the Holy Spirit. It is an eternal reality, an indestructible reality, a reality belonging to the divine, supernatural kingdom; a reality whereby the world is illumined, a reality which grants unto man eternal life."[89]

CHAPTER 7

What Should We Pray For?

A few years ago, my friend Cindy was in need of money. She was ecstatic because she had been invited to sing with her choir on a two-week European concert tour. Cindy wanted very much to go. In fact, it was something she desired with all her heart, but there was a problem: each of the choir members was expected to pay his or her own expenses. Cindy was low on funds at the time, and for her to find enough money for the trip seemed highly improbable.

But Cindy had faith. She prayed fervently to God, and she was so certain that the money would come from somewhere that she was among the first of the choir members to sign up for the tour.

When Cindy's relatives, who were scattered in different parts of the country, heard that she wanted to go on the tour, her uncles, aunts, and other relatives, some of whom she hadn't heard from in ages, sporadically mailed money to her not only enough to go on tour, but she even had a little extra left over to buy some new clothes.

Cindy was elated, grateful, and extremely humble about receiving the financial assistance from her family, but she was not surprised. She had put all of her trust and confidence in God, and never for one second had she lost faith. Cindy went on the tour with the choir and it was one of the most wonderful experiences of her life!

Cindy's faith and trust in God were not a guarantee that she would acquire the money needed for the tour, however she did take the appropriate steps to achieve the means. Her prayer was affirmatively answered, and she rendered heartfelt gratitude and thanks to God. Although Cindy undoubtedly would have been saddened if she had been unable to tour with the choir, her prayers afforded her a sense of detachment that would have enabled her to cope with disappointment. She had put all her trust in God and, whatever the outcome, Cindy believes that she would have been assisted and protected through prayer.

We offer prayers for all aspects of our lives: assistance, protection, healing, comfort, solace, relief of stress, and for all things that pertain to our spiritual and physical well-being. Personally, I pray for everything and everyone in my life. Not only do I pray for my family and friends, but also whenever I have a dispute or unpleasant exchange with an individual, I immediately pray for that person, regardless of whose fault it was and how he or she may have treated me.

Prayer not only increases our capacity to enjoy and appreciate our blessings both materially and spiritually, but when we offer prayers of gratitude, the Bahá'í writings assure us that it also increases our blessings: "God never forsakes His children who strive and work and pray! . . . So will success crown your efforts, and with the universal brotherhood will come the Kingdom of God in peace and goodwill."[90]

But what is of the utmost importance when considering the object of our prayers is the purity of our motive. Regardless of what we pray for, whether of a spiritual or material nature, it should ultimately serve a spiritual purpose. Taking the time to meditate and reflect upon the spiritual purpose of our activities and desires helps to spiritualize the various aspects of our lives. It fosters within us a higher aim and purpose in our goals, motives, decisions, and behaviors.

Our prayers are affirmatively answered only when they are in accordance with God's will. It is impossible for an individual to foretell the exact future and predict what God ordains, but we are more inclined to offer a prayer that is in harmony with the will of God if we combine our knowledge of spiritual principles with common sense. For example, certainly we see a distinction between praying for nutritious food and

[handwritten marginalia at top: "or sex involved with really purely of love & respect clean in mood" "disciplicone no drifting hygienic, contradictions cleanser 73 or not at all" "pure productive work"]

drink on the table to keep our family fit and healthy, and praying for an opulent table of rich, fat- or sugar-laden food and drink merely for the sake of pleasure and inebriation.

The request of the former prayer enables us to be healthy, happy, and productive, whereas the latter, although briefly pleasurable, is not only a mark of indulgence, but can also lead to hardening of the arteries and other potentially fatal diseases. It is illogical to think that a prayer offered for something that is harmful to the health of our body or soul would be in accordance with the will of God. The Bahá'í writings suggest that "The true worshipper, while praying, should endeavor not so much to ask God to fulfill his wishes and desires, but rather to adjust them and make them conform to the Divine Will. Only through such an attitude can one derive that feeling of inner peace and contentment which the power of prayer alone can confer."[91]

If we pray for a new washing machine, we may ask ourselves, "How can this washing machine help me draw nearer to God?" Well, we are told in many holy scriptures that cleanliness is next to godliness. This is affirmed in the Bahá'í verse "God hath enjoined upon you to observe the utmost cleanliness."[92] So, even when we pray for material things, we can think about how these material things may benefit our spiritual growth.

The prayers in Bahá'í scripture remind us that when we ask God for material blessings it is to lighten our physical burdens so that we may be freer to commune with our Creator: "Give us our daily bread, and grant Thine increase in the necessities of life, that we may be dependent on none other but Thee, may commune wholly with Thee, may walk in Thy ways and declare Thy mysteries."[93]

God gave us water to quench our thirst and a land rich in food to nourish our bodies. Why should we not enjoy earthly bounties when it is all part of God's creation? He endowed us with the natural impulse to pray, which is a means to nourish the soul. The soul, although it is a spiritual entity, operates through the physical body, and therefore the body and soul both demand sustenance, exercise, and activity to have a healthy, effective working partnership.

To ignore the needs of the soul is to deny our spiritual reality and stunt our spiritual growth. We sustain the soul through prayer and exercise

[handwritten at bottom: "~ Kola M."]

[handwritten marginalia: then sexuality is distorted that led them to act of]

it through spiritual activity. Likewise, to ignore, abuse, or renounce the needs of the body serves no fruitful purpose and, in fact, may cause both physical and spiritual harm: *[handwritten: deprivation.]*

> Prayer is like the spirit and material means are like the human hand. The spirit operateth through the instrumentality of the hand. . . . When man refuseth to use material means, he is like a thirsty one who seeketh to quench his thirst through means other than water or other liquids. The Almighty Lord is the provider of water, and its maker, and hath decreed that it be used to quench man's thirst, but its use is dependent upon His Will. If it should not be in conformity with His Will, man is afflicted with a thirst which the oceans cannot quench.[94]

We should strive to offer our prayers with humility, moderation, and detachment. From a Bahá'í perspective, detachment from the material world does not imply asceticism or apathy. On the contrary, when we love things of the material world for the sake of God and humbly praise and thank God for our daily blessings, our ability to enjoy and genuinely appreciate those things is enhanced. When we love things of this world to such a degree that they take possession of our heart, we lose perspective of who we are and what is most important in life and fall prone to unhappiness and disappointment.

Seeking God's forgiveness

We confess our sins to God and pray for His forgiveness, mercy, and compassion, and only God may grant pardon and offer salvation. Our relationship with God is entirely personal and sacred. According to Bahá'í scripture, no individual may judge the measure or sincerity of another individual's devotion to God, nor may any individual grant absolution on behalf of God for the sins of another: "When the sinner findeth himself wholly detached and freed from all save God, he should beg forgiveness and pardon from Him. Confession of sins and transgressions before human beings is not permissible, as it hath never been nor will ever be conducive to divine forgiveness."[95]

Bahá'í scripture provides many prayers for forgiveness and assures us that God will forgive us when we supplicate with sincerity and humility: "God would forgive him his iniquities were he only to repent."[96]

We are also enjoined to atone and ask for forgiveness for our transgressions in our everyday lives by turning to God in daily prayer and striving to exemplify spiritual qualities. In asking God to wash away our sins and help us to transform ourselves spiritually, prayer alone is not enough: "We must endeavor through the assistance and grace of God and by the exercise of our ideal power of intellect to attain all lofty virtues."[97]   *dignify   virtues*

How we choose to live our lives plays a crucial role in showing our repentance and seeking God's forgiveness. Bahá'í scripture tells us, "Bring thyself to account each day ere thou art summoned to a reckoning; for death, unheralded, shall come upon thee and thou shalt be called to give account for thy deeds."[98] When we live in a state of conscious atonement with the eternal world, our souls are awakened and quickened with the love of God.

While Bahá'í scripture enjoins us to confess our sins only to God, it is also appropriate to offer an apology to those whom we may have hurt or offended. When we feel that our actions have hurt another soul, even inadvertently, it behooves us to offer that person a sincere apology. Not only can a simple, heartfelt apology ease the tension and usually make the other person feel better, but it also frees us from a sense of guilt and lifts a burden that can weigh heavily on the heart. It is fascinating to consider that we may be the ones who benefit most from our own selfless deeds.

It is also important to be able to forgive others who may have offended us. How many marriages might have been saved if spouses had only been willing to forgive each other after simple disagreements which erupted into long-term, bitter resentments that were impossible to resolve? Countless relationships among families, friends, neighbors, business associates, political leaders, and so forth, have been destroyed over simple misunderstandings and the refusal on both ends to extend a sincere apology and a willingness to forgive.

A few years ago, someone I thought was a very good friend became furious with me and harbored a grudge against me for almost a year. I had absolutely no idea of what I could have possibly done to provoke her. The worst part about it was that she refused to speak to me, which made it impossible to resolve the conflict. And so I prayed for her, and I prayed for our unity. I prayed for her every day.

One day I was startled to receive a phone call from her. She asked if she could visit with me. With some initial trepidation, I welcomed her to my home and we sat in the parlor and talked. She explained that for a very long time she had been outraged because of a cruel act that she believed I had committed towards her. When she told me what it was, I was aghast.

Not only was I innocent of the deed, but I was also taken aback by my friend's assumption that I would have done something so vicious and petty. She explained that the reason she had finally decided to speak to me was because after all those months she realized that I was innocent and she had misjudged me. At that moment, I thought about all the prayers I had said for her. And now here she was in my home, offering an apology and asking to rekindle our friendship.

I forgave her and we became friends again, but I truly believe that if I had not turned to God and prayed about it for all those months, I would have not been able to forgive her so easily. I believe that the prayers greatly benefited both of us. Through the prayers my friend and I were once again united, but also, they afforded me a protection, enabling me to cope with an unpleasant situation with a degree of calm, clarity, and detachment. Deeply moved by my readiness to forgive her, she has proven to be a good, loyal friend ever since.

We should never underestimate the power of apologizing and forgiving in relationships. Because it is often extremely difficult for us to quickly forgive someone we think has offended us, there is great wisdom and merit in praying to God for help to do so. While it may sound martyr-like to pray for forgiveness towards those who have offended us, in truth, harboring hostile feelings towards another is unhealthy and creates a climate of dissension, distrust, and unhappiness. 'Abdu'l-Bahá states,

> Let not your heart be offended with anyone. If some one commits an error and wrong toward you, you must instantly forgive him.

Do not complain of others. Refrain from reprimanding them, and if you wish to give admonition or advice, let it be offered in such a way that it will not burden the bearer. Turn all your thoughts toward bringing joy to hearts. Beware! Beware! lest ye offend any heart. Assist the world of humanity as much as possible. Be the source of consolation to every sad one, assist every weak one, be helpful to every indigent one, care for every sick one, be the cause of glorification to every lowly one, and shelter those who are overshadowed by fear.[99]

Praying to God, whether for ourselves or for others, or for our beloved departed in the next world, reaps benefits for both the individual who prays and for the recipient for whom the prayer is offered. We pray for our families, our friends, and other people in our lives, and by so doing we connect their hearts through the love of God. Through the power of prayer, our anxieties can be relieved, dissensions resolved, misunderstandings reconciled, and troubles averted. It is particularly powerful when we pray for our departed loved ones and ask them to intercede for us:

> As we have power to pray for these souls here, so likewise we shall possess the same power in the other world, which is the Kingdom of God. Are not all the people in that world the creatures of God? Therefore, in that world also they can make progress. As here they can receive light by their supplications, there also they can plead for forgiveness and receive light through entreaties and supplications.[100]

What is the highest prayer?

Regardless of what we pray for, what is most important is having a pure motive when we pray. The purest motive of all is to pray for the love of God: "In the highest prayer, men pray only for the love of God, not because they fear Him or hell, or hope for bounty or heaven."[101] The most important relationship we will ever have in all our existence is the one we form with God, our Creator. He brought us into being and will judge our fate in the eternal realm. It is impossible to conceal from God what is truly in our hearts. God knows all our secrets, our hidden desires and thoughts. He knows what is in our thoughts better than we do ourselves.

One may ask, if God already knows what is in our hearts, then why bother to speak to Him? The answer to this is that in the process of speaking to God, we turn our hearts to Him in faith and trust, and through this personal, independent initiative, which we call "prayer," we spiritualize our lives, know His love, and reap countless benefits. We speak to God not for His benefit, but for our own.

Through the combined effort of prayer and goodly action souls arise and are blessed by the grace of God to be made "as standards of salvation and banners of redemption."[102] Countless faithful ones who have turned heart and soul to God, imploring His forgiveness and striving to walk a virtuous path, have experienced extraordinary transformations of the soul, mystical blessings of the merciful God:

> It is evident that nothing short of this mystic transformation could cause such spirit and behavior, so utterly unlike their previous habits and manners, to be made manifest in the world of being. For their agitation was turned into peace, their doubt into certitude, their timidity into courage. Such is the potency of the Divine Elixir, which, swift as the twinkling of an eye, transmuteth the souls of men![103]

Connecting the hearts through God's love

Rachael, an American singer, was touring with a chorale in Europe. Although Rachael had been a Bahá'í for several years, she was of Jewish background and had relatives who had been killed in the Holocaust. In 1996, her troupe was scheduled to perform a concert in Frankfurt, Germany, and Rachael felt conflicted. As a child, Rachael grew up hearing heart-wrenching accounts about the slaughter of six million innocent Jews. She had heard stories of unspeakable horrors inflicted upon the prisoners in concentration camps. Sometimes she heard those stories told firsthand by Jewish survivors from the camps, such as Rachael's best friend's parents. It greatly disturbed Rachael whenever her eyes fell upon the prison camp numbers branded on the arms of her friend's mother and father.

There was a part of Rachael that perceived the German people as monsters. Yet, as a Bahá'í, Rachael knew that it was imperative to rid herself of all hate and prejudice and to regard all people as members of one human family. She knew that such negative emotions were not only an obstacle to unity, but a harmful deterrent to the progress of her own soul. Rachael recognized that her hatred was so deeply ingrained that she would be unable to enter Germany and look upon the people there in a spirit of loving fellowship without God's assistance. So she prayed. She prayed for unity, she prayed for forgiveness, and she prayed for healing. She focused on a passage from a book written by Bahá'u'lláh called the Hidden Words: "O Son of Being! Love Me, that I may love thee. If thou lovest Me not, My love can in no wise reach thee. Know this, O servant."[104]

Rachael recited this verse repeatedly. She prayed to God, imploring Him to help her internalize its message so she could love the German people for His sake and asking that all traces of hatred, anger, and prejudice would vanish from her soul. She reflected on another verse from the Bahá'í writings: "Love the creatures for the sake of God and not for themselves. You will never become angry or impatient if you love them for the sake of God."[105]

As her troupe's bus crossed the border into Germany, Rachael held onto her Bahá'í prayer book as a talisman and read one prayer after another. A few days later, she experienced an extraordinary encounter that would affect her for the rest of her life.

Rachael explains, "Shortly after entering Germany, I found the people so warm and friendly that I had completely forgotten about all my worries and fears. Our chorale had been invited to sing at an outdoor picnic sponsored by the Bahá'í House of Worship in Frankfurt. And so there I was, sitting on a bench outside the vast, lush grounds of the Bahá'í Temple, laughing and joking with a few of the other chorale members as I gobbled down some really delicious, messy barbecue.

"It was summertime, the weather was gorgeous, and there were birds singing and flowers, trees, and grassy lawn all about. It was perfect! I was relaxed and feeling very happy. Thousands of people from the area were there, and a small party of Germans was sitting at our table. They were all speaking German, but I was in such a friendly mood and my heart felt so light that I turned around to speak to a woman who was sitting next to me. I asked her if she spoke English, and she smiled warmly and said that she did. I told her my name, and she said her name was Ingrid. I told her, 'I have fallen in love with the German people. Everyone is so nice here. I am having a wonderful visit.'

"This pleased Ingrid immensely, and she quickly translated what I said into German to share with her friends. This seemed to make them very happy, and they all turned to me, very politely, with large grins, laughing and nodding their heads in approval. Further into the conversation, I explained to Ingrid that this was an especially meaningful experience for me because I had Jewish relatives who had died in the Holocaust. I instantly regretted my words because seconds after I spoke, Ingrid burst into a storm of tears. Her friends turned around, and Ingrid passed on this news to her friends. Some of the others also began to cry. One of my fellow chorale members said jokingly, in an attempt to lighten the moment, 'Oh gosh, Rachael! What have you done? I think you have just singlehandedly created an international incident!'

"The look on Ingrid's face was one of such heartbreak that I found it difficult to find humor in the situation. I tried to tell her that it was not my intent to point blame, but she was inconsolable. Some of the other chorale members found us to inform us it was time to give our concert. I hated to leave Ingrid and the others at that moment, and the entire time I was on stage I thought about Ingrid and prayed to God with all my heart that I would find her after the concert.

"As soon as the concert was over, I rushed back to the table, but she and her friends were gone. I searched everywhere for her, and just as I was about to give up, Ingrid and I bumped into each other on my way to the ladies room. She was on her way out and not watching where she was going because she was too busy wiping her face with tissues. The poor woman was still crying! I stopped her and said, 'Ingrid, thank God! I have been looking for you everywhere.'

"Although Ingrid had a thick accent, her knowledge of the English language was impressive. She spoke slowly, 'Please. You must allow me to explain. When I was a little girl during the war, I would see the soldiers march the Jewish prisoners through our small town on the way to the camps. The soldiers pointed guns at them and beat them and even laughed at them. Such cruelty was sickening to watch. But the townspeople watched. I watched in horror and saw that many of the prisoners were children. All through my childhood I had nightmares about this, and the nightmares still come.'

"I gently took Ingrid's hands in mine and said, 'You were a little child when all that happened. You were completely innocent. You committed no crime. You did nothing wrong, and I only feel love and friendship towards you. My religion teaches that every human being on earth is a member of one human family. Dearest Ingrid, I hope you can feel my sincerity. I pray that God removes all the pain from your heart. Perhaps what you need in order to heal is just to hear someone of Jewish background give you some love. So, I am giving it to you now with all my heart. Ingrid, you are my sister.'

"Ingrid looked at me and seemed deeply moved. And then she said something that I had not expected. 'Yes, I do need to heal. But you need to heal too. Perhaps it was God's purpose for you to come to my country and meet the German people. You need to see that many of us here are heartsick over the atrocities that were inflicted on innocent people. You need to see that we are human and compassionate.'

"At that moment, I realized that Ingrid was right and it struck me to the core. I was so focused on easing her pain that I hadn't even thought about my own deeply rooted feelings. Now it was I who burst into tears. We hugged and smiled and laughed through our tears. The sisterly love I felt for this woman was very genuine. Our hearts were connected through the love of God. We couldn't stop smiling. We were jubilant. Before we said our final good-byes, we called each other 'sister.'

"Afterwards I walked to the Bahá'í House of Worship, sat down, and privately offered several prayers of praise and gratitude to the 'prayer-hearing, prayer-answering God.'[106] Something very powerful happened to both Ingrid and me that day. A process of healing had taken place in our souls, thanks to the miraculous, transforming power of prayer connecting our hearts through God's love."

CHAPTER 8

Using Prayer in Service to Humanity

Ramine, a young man with noble goals and a warm, jovial nature, entered medical school out of a desire to serve humanity as a physician, to care for the sick and the wounded. However, shortly after beginning his first year of medical school, it occurred to him that there was a spiritual component missing from his training.

As he endeavored to study and memorize the vocabulary of medicine, on his own initiative he also studied and memorized a prayer from Bahá'í scripture called the Long Healing Prayer. And while he acquired knowledge about the different illnesses and basic treatments, from the prayer he gleaned a deeper understanding about the spiritual attributes required of a physician—such as compassion, patience, and kindness. It was quite a challenge to memorize the 1,358-word prayer, but to Ramine it had become integral to his medical training.

As he studied the prayer, it dawned on him that each of the verses identified different attributes of God. The prayer's opening passage attests, "He is the Healer, the Sufficer, the Helper, the All-Forgiving, the All-Merciful. I call on Thee O Exalted One, O Faithful One, O Glorious One! Thou the Sufficing, Thou the Healing, Thou the Abiding, O Thou Abiding One!"[107]

Ramine also saw those attributes as qualities to which all physicians should aspire, such as the ones mentioned in a later verse: "I call on Thee O Thou Kind to all, O Thou Compassionate with all, O Most Benevolent One!"

"The prayer added another dimension to my training," says Ramine. "As with my other studies, learning the prayer required commitment, focus, steadfastness, and discipline. I made it a goal to memorize the Long Healing Prayer by the end of my first year of medical school. I would alternate between studying for finals and memorizing another page of the prayer. In the end, I felt that memorizing the prayer was my most meaningful accomplishment of medical school and the one of which I am most proud. It made me feel extremely good to have vested a significant amount of time in learning this prayer because I felt that it permeated my growth as a physician in both conscious and unconscious ways."

He adds, "To me, the ideal physician is one who combines excellent knowledge in the material aspect of medicine and provides service with a spirit of humility and love for one's patients. This prayer helped me focus on those latter qualities. Through communion with God and by asking for His help to be that kind of physician, I felt assisted and guided."

Ramine experienced an even deeper level of appreciation for the prayer after he began his residency.

"Residency is a time to take all that we learn in medical school and put that knowledge into practice. I felt that it was important to develop a daily relationship with prayer and apply that to my practice as well. So I made a commitment to say the prayer once a day before every shift for my patients, for my development as a physician, and for the people in my life."

He discovered early on, however, that keeping to that commitment required added discipline: "I became fairly strict and regimental about it. After working twelve-hour shifts, often nonstop, naturally, my tendency was to want to sleep as late as possible. Also, there were times when I was in a foul mood, perhaps after working the night before with a very ill patient who didn't get better. Those were the times when I had to really push myself to say the prayer."

Ramine established the habit of setting his alarm clock thirty minutes earlier to allow sufficient time to recite the prayer. He says, "I realized that rushing through the words with no feeling would serve little purpose. Giving myself time to relax, reflect, and say the prayer with the right spirit was worth sacrificing an extra half-hour of sleep."

During his term of residency, Ramine treated patients from all walks of life, with ailments ranging from minor head colds to heart attacks. His job was demanding, necessitating long and irregular hours of service, but he loved the work and was confident that he had found his niche.

To this day, Ramine, an emergency room physician, credits daily prayer with enabling him to meet the various challenges of his job with an ardent, conscientious, and positive spirit. He believes that his medical practice continues to reap incalculable benefits from daily prayer: "Incorporating the element of prayer into my career has elevated my sense of purpose as a physician. It helps to focus and orient me as well as guide me in some degree to make decisions. And I believe that prayer affords a protection to my patients."

He adds, "I don't think that the spiritual guidance and assistance that I feel are specific to the Long Healing Prayer—it has more to do with the daily connection with God and asking for His guidance and help in my development and efforts to be of service. I'll often say spontaneous prayers during my shift, especially when I am treating a very ill patient. On the other hand, I can't discount the power of the Long Healing Prayer. It is a particularly special and potent prayer, which is why I remain committed to reciting it once a day before every shift."

While Ramine continues to draw inspiration and assistance from the prayer and feels that it exalts his sense of esteem as a physician, it also has had a profoundly humbling effect on his attitude. It has helped him recognize that one of the most important qualities for a physician to attain is humility. The prayer is a daily reminder to him that all healing comes from God, a concept that is clearly expressed in the writings of the Bahá'í Faith: "All true healing comes from God! If the heavenly benediction be upon us while we are being healed then only can we be made whole, for medicine is but the outward and visible means through which we obtain the heavenly healing . . . All is in the hands of God, and without Him there can be no health in us!"[108]

Ramine says, "Bahá'í scripture tells us that if healing is right for the patient, God will grant it. And if healing is not right for the patient, He won't. Well, I absolutely believe this is true because I've seen many strange mysteries through the years."

He has seen his share of successes and tragedies and has witnessed numerous unexplained mysteries. He has seen patients in critical, life-threatening conditions miraculously defy death and fully recover, and he has seen other patients with less severe afflictions fail to pull through even after receiving the best possible medical treatment. "All physicians have seen this," he says. "Any truly smart physician should be humble, because no one knows everything and no one is infallible."

The prayer has made an impact on Ramine's practice in ways that he would have never imagined. He explains, "When I first started working in the emergency room and patients were pouring in with heart attacks and fatal wounds, it would annoy me when a patient with, say, a sprained wrist would ask me for a drink of water. But in reciting the prayer, it struck me that one of the verses says, 'I call on Thee O Quencher of thirsts.'"

"It occurred to me that if an attribute of God as the Divine Healer is the 'Quencher of thirsts,' then who am I to deny a patient a drink of water or juice? My entire attitude changed at that point. I no longer saw it as an annoyance when my patients asked me for a drink. In fact, to this day, whenever my patients request it, I fetch the water or juice and bring it to them myself, which always seems to mean a lot to them. They're usually pretty surprised that a doctor would take the time to do this. But it means a lot to me too. If quenching one's thirst is an attribute of God, than I see it as a privilege to serve my patients in this way."

Ramine believes that such small acts of kindness are extremely meaningful. He is aware that the needs of his patients often go beyond medical treatment. They also need assurance, respect, and kindness. Ramine recognizes that prayer increases his level of compassion and sensitivity to meeting a broader scope of the healing needs of his patients.

Ramine, who is also a talented guitarist, singer, and composer, offers this analogy for the benefits of daily prayer, "We learn motor memorization when we are playing a musical instrument through constant practice and repetition. Again, in the same way, when we pray on a regular basis, eventually the words of the prayer become ingrained in our memory and are internalized, making a fuller impact on our behavior and actions.

"To me, as a physician, this is very significant. Bahá'í scripture explains that work is a form of worship and is a means 'to serve mankind and to minister to the needs of the people.' It further explains that, 'Service is prayer.' In fact, one of my favorite passages from Bahá'í scripture says, 'A physician ministering to the sick, gently, tenderly, free from prejudice and believing in the solidarity of the human race, he is giving praise.'"[109]

"What this means to me is that when we strive to carry out the message of prayer through action, which is to serve others and contribute to the betterment of the community, we are in essence serving God. Daily prayer inspires and spiritualizes my work and enables me to better serve the needs of my patients. To me, this is a form of worship."

After completing his residency, Ramine relocated to Portland, Oregon, to accept a position as a staff physician in one of the city's major trauma centers. His life has become busier and fuller than ever, but Ramine continues to make time to recite the Long Healing Prayer every day before each shift.

It makes one wonder: What would society be like if everyone were to follow Ramine's example and take the time to pray each day before they left for work? What if parents prayed for their children every day? What if children prayed for their parents every day? What if husbands and wives prayed for the unity and well-being of their marriage everyday?

What would happen if the leaders of the world were to meet and pray together before beginning their deliberations? What if everyone in the world prayed every day for peace, justice, unity, and the elimination of poverty and inequity? Sounds unlikely? Actually, it sounds like we'd be working together to build a Kingdom of God right here on this planet.

Ramine realized that it all begins with one person. Through prayer and action he became more than an idealist who merely thinks and espouses the importance of goodly virtues but does not practice them. Through prayer and action he is manifesting his spiritual conceptions and ideals and contributing to the benefit of society. On his own initiative he prays everyday for his patients, his friends, and his family. He is making a difference.

That's all it takes to change the world. It begins with one person. That's where it has to begin. Bahá'í scripture tells us that all work done in a spirit of service is worship. It also tells us that service is prayer. Ramine has chosen to live a life of service. He has chosen to live as in a state of prayer. We all have the choice to spiritualize our lives. We all have the potential to make a difference. We all have the capacity to pray. It begins with each one of us.

CHAPTER 9

How Do We Know When Our Prayers Are Answered?

Several years ago I was visiting my older sister, who was residing at that time in a Mediterranean coastal city. One afternoon while my sister was out, I decided to spend an hour or so at the beach, which was a few blocks from her flat.

It was in mid-October, and as I stood barefoot on the vacant beach, gazing out meditatively at the turquoise sea, the beauty and magnitude of God's creation took my breath away. Although it was already autumn and late in the day, the weather was mild and the ocean appeared surprisingly tranquil. The sun, a glorious, fiery red ball, shone brightly against the azure sky as its iridescent rays streaked across the blue-green water.

The sea, a vision of grandeur, was too inviting to resist. Wearing a bathing suit underneath my jeans and T-shirt, I quickly removed my outer clothes and jumped into the water. I was petite and not a very good swimmer, but the water was so calm and refreshing that without realizing it I swam a considerable distance from the shore.

I suddenly found myself being pulled farther out to sea by an undercurrent. Before I could make sense out of what was happening, I was pulled downward and my right leg was trapped between jagged rocks undersea. As the waves swooshed over my head a sense of panic began to overtake me. I realized I could drown and I feared for my life.

I tried with every ounce of strength that I could muster to pull my leg out from between the rocks but with no success. In desperation, I threw a hand up in the air, hoping that someone might notice and rescue me. And then I remembered that there was no one on the beach.

My thoughts raced to my parents, who, back in the United States, would never know what had become of their youngest daughter. I thought to myself, "I'm going to die and no one will know where I am or what happened to me!"

I was gasping for air, my trapped leg refused to budge, the water was rising over my head, and the possibility of surviving seemed more remote as each second passed. I was frantic. In my moment of darkest despair and urgency, I turned with all my heart and soul to God. I prayed and prayed, begging God to help me, to save me—to keep me alive! I prayed for my parents and sister. I prayed that they would not have to suffer as the result of my death.

And then it all happened very quickly. A huge wave of ferocious power crashed into my body with such magnitude and stunning impact that my leg was literally ripped out from the entrapment, pushing me back towards shore. I had never been a strong swimmer, but I used every muscle in my aching body to swim against the undertow. Miraculously, I made it to the beach.

I panted with exhaustion as I crawled onto the sand. My leg, which was covered in blood, was cut and scraped, but I cared little about the injury. I was alive and safe! I cried with relief and thanked God with all my heart. My faith was sustained and I believed, without a trace of doubt, that I had witnessed the awesome, omnipotent power of God and the miracle of prayer.

Some naysayers may deny this was a miracle. They may insist that the huge wave crashing into my body and forcing my leg out of the rocks was no more than a fluke of nature. But God moves in mysterious ways. Why should the elements of nature not be utilized in the mystical workings of God? After all, God created all of nature.

Often when I recall the incident, the memory enkindles in my soul a profound stirring of love and gratitude. I can remember that, as frightened as I was when I thought I was drowning, my body relaxed as soon as I began to pray. My need to turn to God and pray for help was under dire duress and impulse, but even so, some part of me instinctively knew that my last dying thoughts should be of God. The thought of God comforted me.

There is no question in my mind that my prayer was answered affirmatively that day on the Mediterranean beach. After crawling to safety, I lay there on the sand, basking in the love, mercy, and benevolence of the almighty God and was grateful to the very depths of my soul.

Bahá'í scripture proclaims that our Lord, the Heavenly Creator of the universe, "is the prayer-hearing, prayer-answering God."[110] God's love for us has no bounds. There is a healthy logic in trusting that He loves us more than we love ourselves and that in His infinite wisdom, He knows better than we do what is best for us. God hears and answers all prayers of the faithful: "Thou art, verily, the Almighty, the Most Powerful, Who art wont to answer the prayers of all men. No God is there but Thee, Who hearest and art ready to answer."[111]

While God does not always grant our requests in the way that we may wish Him to do so, Bahá'í scripture assures us that all prayers are answered. Sometimes it is very clear to us when a prayer has been answered, but often it is not so clear, which is why it behooves us to be patient and trust in God. "Blessed are the steadfastly enduring, they that are patient. . . . God will add unto the recompense. . . . He, verily, shall increase the reward of them that endure with patience."[112]

In addition to enduring with patience, sometimes it requires independent initiative in taking a certain course of action for our prayers to be affirmatively answered. Often before we can change life externally, we first need to reflect on how we may change our life internally. When we make a sincere effort to change the patterns of our thoughts and behavior, focused on achieving spiritual attributes, our souls become more receptive to heavenly favor. Bahá'í scripture attests, "Say: Await ye till God will have changed His favor unto you. Nothing whatsoever escapeth Him. He knoweth the secrets both of the heavens and of the earth. His knowledge embraceth all things."[113]

God knows all that is in our hearts, and He knows our deeds. Nothing escapes Him. If our prayer is not affirmatively answered, we may consider praying for and meditating on changes we need to make within ourselves so that "God will have changed His favor." Striving to initiate positive changes within one's own life creates an avenue for spiritual growth and draws forth affirmations of the Holy Spirit. God's love and blessings are there for us all the time. But the greatest blessing and token of His love for humanity is endowing each and every human soul with spiritual potentiality. Each of us is individually accountable for realizing our own spiritual potential.

Affirming prayer through action

Marlene had just turned forty years old. She was sad because she greatly desired in life to be married and have a family, but it seemed as if she would never find her special person. Marlene was an extremely loving, sweet, and kind person and my heart ached to see her so forlorn. I asked her if she had been praying. She replied, "Oh yes! I pray every day to find a husband." I thought about that and said, "Please don't take this personally, because I think you are quite marvelous, but perhaps you should be praying for and reflecting upon the spiritual characteristics you think might be beneficial in preparation for marriage."

Having been married a long time myself, I added, "Marriage is a huge commitment and responsibility. People fall in love and marry all the time, but look how many people end up miserable and in divorce. I doubt that most people spend nearly enough time and effort in preparation for marriage. The Bahá'í writings tell us that the best marriages are built on a spiritual foundation, which is why before getting married we must 'exercise the utmost care to become thoroughly acquainted with the character of the other.'"[114]

I suggested to Marlene that she might consider saying every day a special prayer that begins, "O God, my God! This Thy handmaid is calling upon Thee, trusting in Thee, turning her face unto Thee, imploring Thee to shed Thy heavenly bounties upon her, and to disclose unto her Thy spiritual mysteries. . . . O my Lord! Make the eyes of my husband to see. Rejoice Thou his heart with the light of the knowledge of Thee."[115]

I remarked, "When you offer that prayer you are not simply praying to find a husband, but you are praying for your future husband's spiritual character—and for yours as well." Marlene loved the prayer, and she committed to saying it everyday. She also immersed herself in studying passages from the Bahá'í writings about marriage, and slowly, her life began to change. She began eating a healthier diet, joined a gym, and went swimming a few days a week. She spent more of her free time reading and less time watching television, and overall her life took on a more orderly pattern. She was slimmer, healthier, happier, more confident, and looked radiant.

She eventually met someone whom she believed she wanted to marry—a sweet, gentle man named George. There were problems, though, such as George's refusal to marry her until he found a job, and the fact that they lived a great distance apart, which was painful for both of them. Marlene was offering daily prayers for George to find a job so that they might marry, but two years later they seemed no closer to being answered. Finally, I said to her, "I wonder if you are praying for the right thing." "What do you mean?" she asked.

"What if it's the will of God for you to be married regardless of whether or not George has a job?" I asked her. "Maybe your marriage shouldn't depend on whether he gets a job. Maybe your marriage should depend on whether it is the will of God. Personally, I think that's what you should be praying about."

Marlene was grateful for the suggestion and shared it with George. After several consultations on the phone, Marlene came to grips with George's vacillation about getting married. She realized that she needed to reassess their relationship and her priorities. Through her prayers she began to feel empowered with a sense of independence and a healthy detachment that alleviated her feelings of desperation, loneliness, and despair. She realized that she already had a wonderful, full, rich life. She liked her job, her apartment, and her many devoted friends.

Marlene and George still discuss the possibility of marriage, and she is grateful for the friendship they share. But she is in an independent frame of mind, ready to accept whatever is meant to be and to forge on. Although her prayers to marry have not yet been answered affirmatively, she believes that she has found the answer she needs in her realization that she has control over her life and that she can lead a happy, spiritual, useful, and joyful life as a single woman.

Making our prayers conform to God's will

My friend Catherine believes that God's blessings are always there for us, but without prayer and trust in God we are spiritually blind to them. One of her favorite verses from Christian scripture is from the Book of Luke: "Give, and it shall be given unto you; good measure, pressed down, and shaken together, and running over, shall men give into your bosom. For with the same measure that ye mete withal it shall be measured to you again."[116]

Catherine explains, "What that means to me is that the more we love and give of ourselves in service to God, the more we receive His blessings. In other words, what goes around comes around. Whatever measure we give to God we not only receive in measure, but we receive in multifold. So when we pray, we need to make an effort to pray from our hearts and show God we love Him through our actions and deeds.

"I always told my children when they were little, 'Stay in tune with God! Pray and rely on the Holy Spirit. That is where we receive our guidance and direction. We don't always get what we want, but we always get what we need. Without prayer and faith we are blind to God's blessings. We need to trust that whatever God gives us is in accord with His will.

"Not too long ago, my family was having some money problems and I was trying to figure out what to do about it. And then I remembered that my cousin owed me a big sum of money. I prayed and prayed— 'Oh, please, God, if he gets the money, would you please help him remember that I gave him a loan?' Just as I was praying, the phone rang. It was my cousin! He told me that he had the money and was bringing it over right away! Boy, when it's God's will, He sure can move swiftly!"

As Catherine points out, the blessings are always there for us. God may not always fulfill our requests or meet all our desires, but He will assuredly respond to our prayers by granting us what is in accordance with His will. Passages from the Bahá'í writings also affirm that prayers that are answered affirmatively and more perceptibly are those that are in accordance with His will:

> We ask for things which the divine wisdom does not desire for us, and there is no answer to our prayer. . . . We pray, "O God! Make me wealthy!" If this prayer were universally answered . . . affairs of the world would be interfered with, energies crippled and progress hindered. But whatever we ask for which is in accord with divine wisdom, God will answer. Assuredly![117]

Another passage tells us that whatever we ask for, it behooves us to supplicate with a sense of urgency: "Spirit has influence; prayer has spiritual effect. . . . God will answer the prayer of every servant if that prayer is urgent. His mercy is vast, illimitable. He answers the prayers of all His servants."[118]

Even so, no matter how urgent our prayer, how pure our motive, or how loving and sincere our spirit, our prayers are answered affirmatively only if they are in accord with God's will, as illustrated in the following example:

> A very feeble patient may ask the doctor to give him food which would be positively dangerous to his life and condition. He may beg for roast meat. The doctor is kind and wise. He knows it would be dangerous to his patient so he refuses to allow it. The doctor is merciful; the patient, ignorant. Through the doctor's kindness the patient recovers; his life is saved. Yet the patient may cry out that the doctor is unkind, not good, because he refuses to answer his pleading. . . . God is merciful. In His mercy He answers the prayers of all His servants when according to His supreme wisdom it is necessary.[119]

Though God always assuredly answers our prayers, we often fail to recognize His answers and His wisdom. About fifteen years ago I engaged in a conversation with a friend, Emma, who was grieving inconsolably over the loss of her husband. When I tried to offer comfort by assuring her that the soul of her husband was waiting for her in the heavenly realm, my counsel, while sincere in its intent, caused Emma additional agitation. Although she insisted that she believed in God, she refuted quite scornfully the idea of the eternal soul and heaven. She adamantly proclaimed, "Dead is dead! There is nothing beyond!" She was far too upset to discuss the matter further, so I let it drop.

Very recently I was having a conversation with Emma, who is now in her eighties. She informed me of her plans to be cremated after death. I was surprised to hear of her decision because cremation is against the law of her religion. When I asked her if she was concerned about defying the principles of her religion, she responded, "Dead is dead! Once the body dies, that is it—the end! There is no such thing as heaven. There is no such thing as the soul. Trust me on this—I know what I'm talking about. I am a practical person. I believe only what I can see."

Baffled, I responded, "But I thought that you believe in God."

Quickly she answered, "Yes, I believe in God. I talk to Him all the time!"

I said, "Well, then, I am confused. You say you believe in God. Does that mean you can see Him? Can you physically touch Him? Hear His voice?"

She replied, "Of course not!"

I asked, "Then why do you believe in God and pray to Him every day when you can't see Him?" I waited for an answer, but Emma remained silent, apparently still thinking about it. I asked, "If you believe in God even though you can't physically see Him or touch Him or hear His voice—then why is it so inconceivable that God would give us eternal souls and a hereafter? Why is it that you are able to believe in the Creator but not in His ability or will to create eternal life for us?"

This is a woman who normally has quite a lot to say on most any topic, but this time she was unusually quiet. I added, "Can a rock see us or comprehend our existence? If the rock lacks the ability to perceive us, does that mean we must not exist?"

After a long, silent pause, she answered, "I'll think about this."

I also thought about it and prayed for her. About a week later, Emma called me on the phone to tell me that she decided not to be cremated. Her voice sounded lighter, younger, and more exuberant. She said, "I talked to God and told Him that I want to do whatever He wants me to do. I still don't know if there is such thing as heaven, but I realized that what you said made sense. Maybe there is a heaven. Maybe I'll see my husband again. Since cremation is not allowed in the Bible, and not in your religion either, then I figure I better not take any chances of doing something that might not please God."

Emma may not have been aware of it, but her prayer was answered affirmatively. Within a week she had changed her viewpoint dramatically so that she now considers the possibility of the eternal soul and heaven when only a short time ago she was adamant that neither existed. Although she may not be thoroughly convinced, her heart has awakened to a new awareness. For more than a decade and a half she had been convinced that she would never again see her beloved husband. As a result, she had become a bitter, unhappy person. New possibilities had now opened up to her, soothing away years of bitterness, filling her with a sense of hope, comfort, and even joyful anticipation.

Praying for Spiritual and Physical Health

Even people who rarely pray may turn impulsively to God when they find themselves or loved ones afflicted with poor health. Sometimes their prayers are affirmatively answered and good health is restored. Other times we see loved ones and friends who fail to recover from illness—including those who pray with the utmost love and confidence in God and receive treatment from highly skilled physicians.

Bahá'í scripture offers prayers for both physical and spiritual healing. Regardless of the condition of the body, the potential is always there for the soul to reap spiritual rewards. God may not always grant our requests to meet our physical needs, but He will assuredly grant our requests to meet our spiritual needs:

> The prayers which were revealed to ask for healing apply both to physical and spiritual healing. Recite them, then, to heal both the soul and the body. If healing is right for the patient, it will certainly be granted; but for some ailing persons, healing would only be the

cause of other ills, and therefore wisdom doth not permit an affirmative answer to the prayer. . . . The power of the Holy Spirit healeth both physical and spiritual ailments.[120]

Nina, a Bahá'í friend of mine, has consistently exemplified extraordinary fortitude in the face of personal tribulation and suffering in her battle with cancer. She has undergone countless surgeries and treatments of radiation, chemotherapy, and physical therapy. Living in excruciating pain has become commonplace for her. For most people the stress of enduring such physical hardship and uncertainty would surely be insufferable, yet amazingly she has managed to remain upbeat, optimistic, and spiritually radiant. A constant source of inspiration to her friends, she astonishes all who know and love her in the fact that she has not lost her delightful wit and her marvelous ability to laugh and joke at the absurd.

Nina attributes her positive attitude to the sustenance she receives from her faith. She says, "I would have never survived without prayers and faith in God. I don't know what people do without faith when they go through these kinds of trials. I don't believe that I would have lived without the prayers. They provide me with tremendous comfort and strength, especially the healing prayers from Bahá'í scripture."

Nina recognizes that her trials serve as an impetus to grow spiritually in striving for the nearness of God—a thought that gives her immeasurable solace. She believes that much of her ability and confidence in seeing the spiritual good in the face of physical suffering is due to the influence of her beloved, departed father, a Holocaust survivor who escaped from a concentration camp in Czechoslovakia in 1939.

"Knowing about all of the difficulties that my father faced in his life," Nina says, "and seeing his strength and joy for living was an inspiration. Despite all of the tests and trials he endured—especially his struggles in getting out of Europe—as long as I can remember, my father was always convinced that everything would turn out all right. He never had any interest in the trappings of religious customs, but he had this internal, spiritual belief and faith in God that helped me feel secure that no matter what happened, everything was going to be okay."

As illustrated in Nina's story, offering prayer with trust in God provides comfort and solace to the sufferer and emboldens one to face trials with courage and a radiant spirit. God is the Divine Healer for all afflictions, both spiritual and physical; turning our hearts in prayer and giving up our suffering to Him help to protect and fortify us against the onslaught of every possible test and trial.

It behooves us to trust that God's answers to our prayers are intended to benefit our spiritual growth, regardless of the physical outcome. Those answers are not always perceptible in this world, but the Bahá'í teachings attest to the spiritual rewards bestowed upon our souls when we submit wholly our trust in God: "The rewards of this life are the real luminous perfections which are realized in this world, and which are the cause of eternal life, for they are the very progress of existence."[121] Also, trials provide us opportunities to benefit spiritually:

> While a man is happy he may forget his God; but when grief comes and sorrows overwhelm him, then will he remember his Father who is in Heaven, and who is able to deliver him from his humiliations. Men who suffer not attain no perfection. The plant most pruned by the gardeners is that one which, when the summer comes, will have the most beautiful blossoms and the most abundant fruit.[122]

Even so, extreme tragedy, illness, and tribulation may cause us to fall into such a state of depression, panic, and anxiety that we feel emotionally paralyzed, mentally incapacitated, and spiritually dead. During such times, prayer and trust in God may require tremendous effort. There may be times when prayer alone is not sufficient. Certain actions may be required, which could include seeking help from a qualified psychiatrist or psychologist or other competent physicians. Bahá'u'lláh urges us to seek such help when it is needed: "Whenever ye fall ill, refer to competent physicians. Verily, We have not abolished recourse to material means, rather have We affirmed it."[123]

It is crucial that we turn to both prayer and to competent physicians when we are afflicted with poor health. "There are two ways of healing sickness," 'Abdu'l-Bahá writes, "material means and spiritual means. The first is by the treatment of physicians; the second consisteth in prayers offered by the spiritual ones to God and in turning to Him. Both means should be used and practiced. . . . they are not contradictory."[124]

A few years ago, my friend Tangela discovered the truth of that message during the course of an extraordinarily harrowing, yet wondrous and life-transforming episode. Having been blessed with a gorgeous soprano voice, Tangela was always singing. She came from a family of singers and had been raised in a warm and loving home filled with music and laughter. Tangela loved music and regarded it as an integral part of what made her who she was. Through high school, college, and as a married woman with two children, she continually sang in choirs, quartets, musicals, and ensembles. So when she fell gravely ill and was no longer able to sing, she sank into a deep depression.

It all began with what seemed like a simple cold. When her health continued to decline, she went to see a doctor, who told Tangela that it was nothing more than a virus. However, Tangela was not getting better. She was having extreme difficulty breathing and felt as if her lungs were about to burst. She was only in her mid-thirties, but her constant state of fatigue, discomfort, and shortage of breath was making her feel much older. Also, she was rapidly gaining weight. Her health deteriorated, and she persistently sought the help of doctors, who could find nothing wrong with her aside from her obesity, which, naturally they blamed as the cause of her weakened condition. And, of course, they blamed *her* for the obesity.

She was advised to seek psychological counseling, which she did. She saw many other physicians as well, who prescribed painkillers, anti-depressants, and a vast assortment of drugs, but nothing improved her health. More than a year passed, and she gained over one hundred pounds. It became difficult for her to breathe or move, and what was most painful to her was that she could no longer sing. Her voice was raspy and tired, and it was a drain for her even to talk.

When Tangela went to see various physicians, desperately seeking help, she sensed that they disregarded her as an obese African-American woman who required minimum medical attention. She wondered, "Where were the medical tests? Where were the physical examinations?" She says, "None of the doctors ever touched me. They took one look at me and blamed all my problems on my weight and depression."

She fell into such a deep depression that death was beginning to seem preferable. She had an adoring husband and two wonderful children, but she felt useless to them. In the past, she had been an active and vibrant member of the community, but now she rarely left the house. Every day had become more of a challenge for her to move and breathe, and she was so embarrassed about her weight that she hid in her home so that none of her friends could see her. She was in a constant state of nausea and pain, and she could no longer carry out her normal activities— work, cleaning the house, and taking care of the family. Worst of all, she could not do the one thing that had always unfailingly uplifted, refreshed, and gladdened her spirit—to sing.

One night in late spring of 1998, feeling completely debilitated and helpless, in her greatest moment of despair and desperation, she turned to God and prayed. This prayer was different from her normal devotions. This time, she gave all of her suffering up to God. She released every ounce of her anguish, frustration, and misery and gave it up to Him. She prayed with fervor and tearful urgency, imploring God for His love and assistance.

The next day, she was certain that she was dying. She felt half dazed, she could barely breathe; surely she was close to death. But she felt no fear—only relief that the end was soon approaching. The doorbell rang, and she struggled to the door to open it. Standing there were three very dear Bahá'í friends who had come to her home out of concern after not seeing or hearing from her in quite awhile. They had been especially worried when no one had answered the telephone at her house that day. It was unlike Tangela, who was normally an extremely outgoing and effervescent person, to suddenly be a recluse. Her friends sensed that something was terribly wrong. They took one look at her, and they rushed to her side. All three happened to be professional nurses, and before Tangela knew what was happening, they had her on the floor examining her. Tangela studied the faces of her three sisters who had come to her aid, and she thought silently, "Three angels."

One of the "angels," shouted out, "There's no pulse! I don't feel a pulse!" They quickly got her into their car and rushed her to a hospital in a nearby town. Tangela remembers lying on the gurney, hooked up to tubes and wires, when the doctor, examined her and wondered aloud, "Why is she still alive?"

Her vital statistics were dangerously off the charts, but what helped to save her life was putting her on catheterization. A few days later, after the physician performed a surgical procedure called cardiac catheterization, she was diagnosed with congestive heart failure due to post cardiomyopathy. By her ninth day in the hospital Tangela had lost 125 pounds, which had all been from water retention. She was now well enough to go home, which the doctors must have regarded as a miracle. Based on what was written on Tangela's medical chart, the physicians had not expected Tangela to live.

Tangela says, "All the time I was in the hospital my friends were visiting me and praying for me. It was the prayers that saved my life. I have no question about that. And I know that the prayer I had said the night before I went into the hospital was answered. I gave it all up to God. Before, when I prayed, I just kept asking God to make me feel better so that I could get on with my normal life. But this time, my prayer was different. I just gave it all up to Him. And then the next day, those 'three angels' came and saved my life! It was a miracle that they came the way they did—I have absolutely no doubt about that."

The doctors, who later gave her a heart implant for monitoring, were truly shocked at her speedy recovery. In the following years, Tangela's health continued to improve vastly. At the present time, feeling fully recuperated, she has a career in the field of education, thoroughly enjoys her time spent with her husband and two children, and her singing voice is more beautiful than ever.

Tangela believes that she is alive and well today because of the prayers and the intervention of God. She says, "I don't regret this experience because it helped me feel closer to God, and there is no question in my mind that I grew spiritually." She is exuberant and extremely grateful that her prayers were answered because she can now better serve her family and community—and she can sing again, which brings the utmost joy to her heart.

My friend Nina, who continues to struggle with cancer, also believes that her prayers were answered in that she has the strength and fortitude to cope with her suffering. Both women are truly blessed because of their trust in God, their recognition of His intervention, and their gratitude for His assistance in their lives.

The teachings of the Bahá'í Faith affirm that it is possible to attain happiness, optimism, and inner strength during times of stress, pain, and suffering. 'Abdu'l-Bahá, addressed the topic of joy and pain:

> In this world we are influenced by two sentiments, *Joy* and *Pain*.
>
> Joy gives us wings! In times of joy our strength is more vital, our intellect keener, and our understanding less clouded. We seem better able to cope with the world and to find our sphere of usefulness. But when sadness visits us we become weak, our strength leaves us, our comprehension is dim and our intelligence veiled. The actualities of life seem to elude our grasp, the eyes of our spirits fail to discover the sacred mysteries, and we become even as dead beings.
>
> There is no human being untouched by these two influences; but all the sorrow and the grief that exist come from the world of matter—the spiritual world bestows only the joy!
>
> If we suffer it is the outcome of material things, and all the trials and troubles come from this world of illusion.
>
> For instance, a merchant may lose his trade and depression ensues. A workman is dismissed and starvation stares him in the face. A farmer has a bad harvest, anxiety fills his mind. A man builds a house which is burnt to the ground and he is straightway homeless, ruined, and in despair.
>
> All these examples are to show you that the trials which beset our every step, all our sorrow, pain, shame and grief, are born in the world of matter; whereas the spiritual Kingdom never causes sadness. A man living with his thoughts in this Kingdom knows perpetual joy. The ills all flesh is heir to do not pass him by, but they only touch the surface of his life, the depths are calm and serene.

Today, humanity is bowed down with trouble, sorrow and grief, no one escapes; the world is wet with tears; but, thank God, the remedy is at our doors.... If we are hemmed in by difficulties we have only to call upon God, and by His great Mercy we shall be helped.[125]

God answers our prayers in different ways, but assuredly they are always answered. The degree to which we benefit from His answers is dependent upon our faith and trust in Him.

CHAPTER 10

Blessed Is the Spot

Saliha was born in the barren mountain town of Erzurum in Eastern Turkey, near the border of Iran. There she and her siblings were raised to be devoted followers of the Sunni Muslim religion. Steadfast in her belief in Muḥammad as a divine prophet, and firm in her obedience to the teachings of the Koran, Saliha learned in her earliest years to submit her heart wholly to God through prayer and worship.

Saliha's maternal great-uncle also lived with the family and was quite knowledgeable about the Koran. Saliha's mother and grandmother also knew how to read the Koran, which was an unusual achievement considering that many Islamic cultures did not permit women to study the holy scripture. Moreover, only ten percent of the entire Turkish population at that time was literate. Saliha was proud that her family was educated in the Koran and appreciated that she was encouraged to study the scripture as well. One of the great pleasures of her childhood was listening to her elders discuss the stories and teachings in the Islamic tradition in the parlor of her home. Her spiritual life was tremendously important to her.

Turkey, under the sultan-ruled Ottoman empire, had been the governing center of the Arab Muslim world for six centuries. At its height, the empire had encompassed southeastern Europe and the Middle East.

Combining the influence of Islam and the Christian Byzantine Era, the Ottomans made tremendous contributions to the civilized world with advances in the arts, sciences, and architecture. However, by the early nineteenth century the empire showed signs of decay and downfall. Horrific persecution of religious and ethnic minorities, tyrannical rulers, and widespread poverty and illiteracy created dissension and dissolution within the empire. Turkey, a nation that at one time had gloried in its progress, had taken a backward turn and fallen into an age of darkness.

The Ottoman empire and its decline also played a key role in the history of the Bahá'í Faith. Bahá'u'lláh and his family were prisoners of the Ottoman empire and suffered a series of banishments. In captivity, at the hands of this oppressive government, their exile led them to Baghdad, Constantinople (now Istanbul), Adrianople (now Edirne), and finally in 1868 to the city of Acre, Palestine, where they were incarcerated within the prison walls of the city until 1877. At that time, Acre was as a prison city, a destination for the worst of murderers, thieves, and political dissidents. The city had no source of fresh water, and the air was notoriously foul. Into this environment Bahá'u'lláh and his family arrived, and it was where he was destined to spend the remaining twenty-four years of his life. During all that period the Ottoman empire did everything in its power to vanquish the Bahá'í Faith. Nevertheless, despite Bahá'u'lláh's exile and imprisonment and the severe persecution of his followers, the Faith emerged as a world religion.

Following World War I, the Ottoman empire was almost completely destroyed, losing control of its territories. By 1922 it was completely crushed and replaced by a new government. Although the constitution at that time retained Islam as the state religion, in 1928 this religious clause was removed and Turkey officially became a secular republic. Although most of the population was Muslim, with Sunni Muslims forming the majority, the ideology of secular nationalism not only influenced all aspects of society but was infused into everyday life. The new reforms included the abolition of religious courts, religious schools, religious practices, and the wearing of religious garments in public places. This infringement was a tremendous blow to the nation's many devout followers of Islam.

Saliha and her family, who loved the traditions of Islam, were among those who were greatly saddened by these restrictive laws. The family considered it very important to recite their prayers five times a day, beginning at dawn, accompanied by the required ablutions (washing of hands, feet, and face in preparation for prayers) and genuflections (kneeling, bowing, and other physical positions associated with prayer). The family also believed that wearing religious garments traditional to their Islamic culture, such as the long robes and veils for women, and robes and certain headdress for men, were essential to prayer and worshipping God.

Along with many other Muslim families in Turkey, Saliha's family continued to follow the customs in their home and place of worship. However, the family was concerned that they would lose favor with God because the government forbade the people from practicing religious customs in all public places, and this meant the family could no longer carry out these practices in their places of work or at school.

While the government's restrictions remained a source of sadness and oppression for the family, they were grateful that at least within the privacy of their home they were free to observe their cherished traditions. They particularly enjoyed their nightly discourses with Saliha's elderly great-uncle, who was pious in his prayers and daily reading of the Koran. He firmly believed that the coming of the mehdi (messenger of God), as promised in the Holy Scripture, was imminent.

Tragedy fell upon the family, however, when Saliha's father passed away. His business building wood framework brought in the family's sole income, for the children were too young to work and the great-uncle was too old. To bring an income they rented out rooms on the first floor of their large house to boarders. Careful with their expenses, the family lived modestly and managed to make ends meet.

One day an elderly gentleman named Ibrahim, a stranger to Erzurum, came to their door to ask about renting a room. The family was delighted to discover that their new boarder was a scholarly man, extremely well versed not only in the Koran, but also in many other religions. They were so deeply attracted to his knowledge and wisdom and to the gentle, thoughtful manner in which he spoke that it gradually became a daily routine for the family to ask him questions concerning spiritual matters. Ibrahim's answers were impressively intelligent and insightful, yet he always spoke with great humility. The entire family grew to trust him and care for him very deeply.

Saliha was now a twenty-year-old college graduate and was working as an elementary school teacher. She grew close to Ibrahim, and he never failed to impress and enlighten her with his astute insights on spiritual topics. She and her family regarded him as a great religious scholar, perhaps the wisest and most knowledgeable person they had ever met. And so they shared with him their heartache about not being permitted to adhere to the sacred traditions in accord with Muslim law in public places.

Quoting verses from the Koran and from other religious scripture, he gently explained that what is most important about prayer is the purity of the motive behind it and the spirit in which it is offered to God. He said that the head coverings and genuflections were outer symbols of faith that served little purpose without an ardent, loving spirit. He pointed out that praying with sincerity and feeling was more meaningful than reciting prayers all day long without feeling, that the purity of one's heart is the greatest adornment in showing one's love to God. The family was extremely relieved to hear these words from Ibrahim. They accepted them as truth, for they saw in Ibrahim's message great wisdom and logic.

Because of Ibrahim's teachings, Saliha began to view prayer as a personal communion with God. It was a supreme joy to her to awaken to the spiritual realization that inner prayer and a pure heart were far more important to the nourishment of her soul than the exterior practices of ritual and the wearing of special garments.

Ibrahim had been living in the house for about one year when Saliha decided to talk to him about her great-uncle's prediction that the mehdi would come in their lifetime. The elderly man smiled and, as always, paused thoughtfully before he responded. Very gently, he explained that he was a Bahá'í and told her about Bahá'u'lláh, whom Bahá'ís recognize as the messenger of God for this age. He explained to her that all the knowledge that he had shared with her and the family, such as the nature of prayer as an intimate conversation with God, all came from the teachings of Bahá'u'lláh, which are found in the Bahá'í writings.

Then Ibrahim showed Saliha photographs of Bahá'u'lláh's eldest son, 'Abdu'l-Bahá, and Bahá'u'lláh's great-grandson, Shoghi Effendi. Her heart began to pound when she saw the photo of 'Abdu'l-Bahá's face. She was so excited that she bolted upstairs to tell her family about Bahá'u'lláh and to show them the photographs.

Saliha breathlessly rushed into her mother's bedroom and told her about the conversation she had had with Ibrahim. As soon as her mother saw the picture of Shoghi Effendi, she said, "I see in his face the beauty of Joseph." She was referring to the story of Jacob's son told in both the Bible and the Koran. It was nighttime and the family was already asleep, but Saliha and her mother quickly awakened the others in the house. Upon hearing the news about Bahá'u'lláh, nine people in all—Saliha, her mother, her six siblings and cousin—all became Bahá'ís that very night.

Unfortunately, their Muslim relatives, who were not nearly so receptive, were outraged when they discovered that all nine members of Saliha's family had become Bahá'ís. Although they knew absolutely nothing about the Bahá'í Faith and had no interest in learning about this new religion, they were convinced that Saliha and her family were misled and had strayed from the path of God. For a period of time she and her family were the targets of verbal assaults and hostile attitudes from the relatives. Eventually the relatives distanced themselves from Saliha and her family.

Saliha had married a Muslim man, Fikri. She relocated with him to Istanbul, where Fikri could advance in his career as a civil engineer, and Saliha immediately fell in love with the beautiful coastal city. The couple had two children, Ufuk and Isik. Saliha was very grateful for the good life she shared with her family even though she was denied the freedom of living openly as a Bahá'í. Her husband was not a religious man, but he considered himself a Muslim, and from his perspective it was unthinkable for his wife to practice her beliefs openly. He knew nothing about the Bahá'í Faith and had no desire to learn about it. Out of consideration and respect for her husband's wishes, and for the sake of harmony in their marriage, she remained a Bahá'í in her heart but rarely mentioned the Faith in her home. This was a great sacrifice for her, but she found solace in her daily prayers from Bahá'í scripture, which she offered silently and privately.

Although Saliha did not attend Bahá'í meetings or talk to her children about the Bahá'í Faith, she took comfort in the belief that her home and her heart were blessed, a bounty assured in the message of this prayer: "Blessed is the spot, and the house, and the place, and the city, and the heart, and the mountain, and the refuge, and the cave, and the valley, and the land, and the sea, and the island, and the meadow where mention of God hath been made, and His praise glorified."[126]

Saliha realized that what was most important of all was her personal relationship with God. Although she could not practice her religion outwardly, in her heart she was a Bahá'í, and to her that meant loving God through daily prayers and striving to live her life as a prayer, adorned, not by physical garments and customs, but with virtuous character, deeds, and action. Saliha trusted in God and knew that what mattered most was the sincerity of her prayer—the purity of her motive and spirit.

Without mentioning the Bahá'í Faith, she taught her children its fundamental teachings: that there is one God, that all the world's religions represent one changeless and eternal faith, and that all humanity is one race, destined eventually to live in peace and harmony. She taught them about the principles of unity and justice, the equality of women and men, the importance of education, and the harmony of science and religion. She taught her children to be truthful, trustworthy, kind, and courteous to all. But her children grew up never realizing that all those principles came from the teachings of the Bahá'í Faith.

In 1980, Saliha's husband died. And while she grieved for her departed husband, for the first time in twenty years she was free to openly worship God exactly as her heart desired. Saliha joyously recited prayers from Bahá'í scripture aloud in her home, she immersed herself in the study of the Bahá'í teachings, and she became actively involved in the Bahá'í community.

Saliha retired from teaching in 1990 and still leads a busy life as a volunteer for a nongovernmental organization that focuses on social and economic development. She says she can think of no better way to show her love for God than by serving humanity and helping to contribute to the betterment of the community.

Once able to openly practice her religion, Saliha became quite vocal in sharing with her children the teachings of Bahá'u'lláh. While she had already taught them many of the religion's fundamental principles, neither of her children had had much exposure to the prayers from Bahá'í scripture. Saliha's daughter, Isik, along with her brother, Ufuk, both embraced the Bahá'í Faith.

For Isik, it took time to understand the power of prayer as a means to personally commune with God. Her transformation occurred when she was in her twenties and attended a Bahá'í youth conference in Italy. Her exposure to the devotional gatherings there deeply affected her. The sense of tranquility, unity, love, and exhilaration she experienced in the devotions sparked within her such a profound sense of nearness to God that it left her breathless. At that conference prayer took on a new meaning for her. She not only viewed prayer as vital to her personal relationship with God, but she had also witnessed the unifying impact it had on people when they prayed together. She left the conference spiritually charged and knew that her life would never be the same.

In 1996, Isik bid her relatives a teary farewell to begin a new and exciting adventure working as a secretary at the beautiful Bahá'í World Center on Mount Carmel in Haifa, Israel. During the five years she spent there she met and married Glen, an American Bahá'í coworker.

In 2002 Isik and her husband, an educator, moved to the United States. Isik dearly misses Saliha and her other relatives in Turkey, but she takes comfort in sustaining a close bond with them through the daily prayers they say for each other. She says, "My mother taught me by the example of her life that prayer is a sacred gift from God to commune with Him and to fortify the soul. Prayer is extremely important in my life."

Isik also never forgot the transforming impact the devotional gatherings had made on her. She said, "After my husband, Glen, and I moved to the United States, we prayed and consulted about what types of service we could provide to benefit the community. The Universal House of Justice, which is the governing body of the Bahá'í world community, located at the Bahá'í World Center in Haifa, had sent out a letter explaining the benefits of devotional gatherings hosted in people's homes. Glen and I discussed this. We realized that we both love eating, we both enjoy having friends in our home, and we love to pray. So it was only natural that we decided to host devotional gatherings that would somehow be combined with sharing food. We decided to hold our devotional gatherings on Saturday mornings and serve brunch.

"We began hosting devotional gatherings a few months after our move to the States, and we have continued to do so every other Saturday since. The first few gatherings attracted only a few people. We extended our invitations to our friends, neighbors, and coworkers. We had hoped that many people would just flow to our apartment, and we were disappointed at first.

"So we started making individual phone calls to our friends and invited them personally. It worked. Attendance started improving. We also developed the habit of inviting the people we meet for the first time to our devotional gatherings. I was delighted when one of my coworkers easily and gratefully accepted my invitation after I had agonized for a long time over whether to invite him, how to invite him, and when to invite him. He not only accepted my invitation but has attended our devotional gatherings frequently.

"We continue to experiment with the format. For example, we realized that starting with breakfast works best. People arrive at our door between 10:00 and 11:00 a.m., help themselves to food, tea, or coffee, socialize, and settle by 11:00 a.m., when we move on to the devotional portion.

"We now have an average attendance of fifteen people at every gathering. At the beginning, we usually make a very brief introduction to the purpose of these gatherings, particularly for the sake of first time visitors. We simply say that the purpose 'is to remember God and His love for all of us and to reflect on our true purpose in life.'

"We usually select some readings from scripture and prayers around one particular theme, such as tests and difficulties, spiritual growth, race unity, the oneness of religions, the mystery of sacrifice, and so forth. Sometimes our themes reflect a topical issue. After Hurricane Katrina, our theme was 'The Mystery of Suffering and Spiritual Growth,' and we used the gathering as an opportunity to offer a round of prayers for the departed and the survivors of that disaster.

"We always make available the sacred writings of the world religions—scriptures from Christianity, Islam, Buddhism, Judaism, Hinduism, Zoroastrianism, and the Bahá'í Faith. We also always start with music played and sung by either Glen or our other musician friends. After we pass around the selected passages and they are read aloud, we tell our guests that any form of prayer, poem, or song is welcome.

"We sometimes include a group activity after the devotional portion. There have been times when we invite our guests to choose one of the verses from the scripture read that morning that inspired them most and to express their heart's response to it in the form of a collage, drawing, text, or words. We have an activity box available just for that purpose, with various photographs cut from magazines, colored paper, pens, glue, scissors. This is an optional activity that we sometimes offer, but people seem to enjoy participating in it and have a lot of fun. Mostly, we have a group discussion either on the verses read or on a variety of spiritual themes. We don't have a specific ending time, and friends stay as long as they want to, so our gatherings sometimes last until late afternoon!

"People who come to our devotional gatherings for the first time usually comment on how very relaxed and comfortable they feel in our home. I have to agree with them, because that's how I feel too. I believe that our home is continuously blessed and 'its air is purified' through these devotional gatherings. After all, that was our hope when we began these gatherings: to make our home a 'spot . . . where mention of God hath been made, and his praise glorified'—and everyone feels at home."

CHAPTER 11

Coming Together in Prayer: The Power of Devotional Gatherings

Bahá'u'lláh's eldest son, 'Abdu'l-Bahá, while traveling through the United States, addressed a public gathering in Washington, DC, on April 23, 1912. The meeting took place shortly after the tragic sinking of the *Titanic*, and 'Abdu'l-Bahá spoke about its impact:

> Within the last few days a terrible event has happened in the world, an event saddening to every heart and grieving every spirit. I refer to the Titanic disaster, in which many of our fellow human beings were drowned, a number of beautiful souls passed beyond this earthly life. Although such an event is indeed regrettable, we must realize that everything which happens is due to some wisdom and that nothing happens without a reason. Therein is a mystery; but whatever the reason and mystery, it was a very sad occurrence, one which brought tears to many eyes and distress to many souls. . . .
>
> But when I consider this calamity in another aspect, I am consoled by the realization that the worlds of God are infinite; that though they were deprived of this existence, they have other

opportunities in the life beyond, even as Christ has said, "In my Father's house are many mansions." They were called away from the temporary and transferred to the eternal; they abandoned this material existence and entered the portals of the spiritual world. . . . they now partake of a joy and happiness far more abiding and real, for they have hastened to the Kingdom of God. The mercy of God is infinite, and it is our duty to remember these departed souls in our prayers and supplications that they may draw nearer and nearer to the Source itself.[127]

In the aftermath of such tragedies, since the dawn of civilization, quite often the natural inclination of people is to gather together in prayer. They pray for the departed souls, they pray for the survivors and for their healing, and they pray to rebuild for whatever has been lost. Those who gather in devotion to God for the sake of praying for others and the world around them discover that it not only strengthens the community, fostering unity and healing, but it brings a sense of comfort and peace to their own hearts. "The practice of collective worship is one important ingredient in the flourishing of community life. It also reinforces individual spiritual development."[128]

Considering the condition of the world today, surely there has never been a more critical time for the peoples of the earth to join together in devotional gatherings in communities everywhere. No sermons, no proselytizing, no politics, no ancestral rituals, or rigidity should get in the way of people simply getting together to speak to God from the depths of their souls. Whether the prayers are from sacred scriptures, which carry a certain potency because they come from the divine source, or they are composed in one's own words spoken from the heart, what matters most is the spirit and intent with which they are offered.

When the ultimate aim of the gathering is to achieve nearness to God and unity with our fellow man and woman, the Holy Spirit will shed illumination upon the hearts and unify the souls through His love. Bahá'u'lláh attests, "So powerful is the light of unity that it can illuminate the whole earth."[129] Try to imagine what could happen if people were to gather together in spiritual meetings all over the world just to pray for unity. While such a vision may seem unrealistic right now, it can start with each of us taking initiative in our own little corners of the world.

My friend Kathy, who is a Bahá'í, did precisely that. She explained, "Whenever disaster strikes at a colossal magnitude, the human heart is touched profoundly. This is a truth I discovered immediately following the tsunami that swept away more than 220,000 lives in Southeast Asia and East Africa. As I prayed, read the teachings of Bahá'u'lláh, and pondered the significances and human toll of this disaster, it occurred to me to try to reach out to my neighbors, to connect with them and acknowledge this human tragedy in some way.

"I only knew the neighbors to my immediate right and left. My first thought was to bring as many neighbors as possible together to pray for the victims and survivors of this disaster. So with the help of God, I dug deep down to find some courage to hand deliver an invitation to each of my other neighbors to attend a devotional gathering at my home about a week after the tsunami struck.

"I made the invitations as beautiful and reverent as possible, stating the purpose of this devotional meeting and asking each neighbor to bring any inspirational reading, poem, or anything that moved them. As I knocked on the first door, a young man opened it and looked at me as if I were trying to sell him something. I explained I was a neighbor, that I didn't know many of my neighbors, and that I'd like to meet as many as possible. I also told him that the tsunami disaster is an occurrence that can help all of us as members of the human family to reach out to each other and, at the very least, send the victims and survivors our best thoughts, wishes, and prayers.

"His face immediately changed from suspicion to a dropped jaw. He said, 'Awesome! I wish I had thought of that! How good of you to think of such a thing!' After that, the remaining fourteen doors were easy to approach. I felt confirmations from above helping my small efforts and making every step easier for me to take. Each new neighbor made similar comments, much to my amazement.

"In preparation for the devotional gathering, I had conducted research and created two compilations on guidance from the world's sacred texts: one from all the major religions, including the Bahá'í Faith. All these sacred texts spoke about taking care of those in need, the orphan, the widow, the ill, the wounded, the distressed, the purpose of suffering in this life, how to respond to tragedy and to 'be generous in prosperity and thankful in adversity.'"

> Be generous in prosperity, and thankful in adversity. Be worthy of the trust of thy neighbor. . . . Be a treasure to the poor, an admonisher to the rich, an answerer to the cry of the needy, a preserver of the sanctity of thy pledge. Be fair in thy judgment, and guarded in thy speech. Be unjust to no man, and show all meekness to all men. Be as a lamp unto them that walk in darkness, a joy to the sorrowful, a sea for the thirsty, a haven for the distressed, an upholder and defender of the victim of oppression. Let integrity and uprightness distinguish all thine acts. Be a home for the stranger, a balm to the suffering, a tower of strength for the fugitive.[130]

Kathy continued, "When the evening for the devotional meeting arrived, I placed candles up the stairwell, on the fireplace mantel, and on the coffee table. Three neighbors showed up. As none of them had brought any inspirational readings, I passed both sets of readings around to each person. I had soft music playing in the background and invited anyone to read from any of the selections they wished; I also gave them the option of not reading anything if they didn't feel comfortable.

"When there were quiet intervals, I played some inspirational music from various backgrounds: Native American flute, African-American spirituals, classical music, and so on. Then someone else would read another sacred verse. This went on for an hour and a half until everyone present had read every verse from both compilations. The readings were followed by refreshments and deeply engaging conversation on related spiritual topics. We discussed issues such as the purpose of trials, tribulations, and suffering, life after death, and the purpose of life. It was heading towards midnight when we all realized that the time had flown by.

"I was delighted when my neighbors asked if we could do this again. So we scheduled one for the following month. This time two new neighbors joined our gathering. And once again, the friends stayed for hours reading the sacred guidance from the world's religions with astonishment at the consistency of the spiritual message. It had never before occurred to them that there was complete agreement in the spiritual message of all the religions of God.

"By the grace of God, the tsunami disaster created the opening of hearts of strangers to gather together and pray for victims. One of the best things that came out of this is that I've met some wonderful people, and now these 'strangers' are friends."

Harmony between material and spiritual progress

Tragic disasters resulting in the loss of lives and in chaos and suffering, whether they are caused by nature or by the hand of man, are not a recent development in the history of humankind. To many, the devastation left in the wake of the 2005 Gulf Coast hurricanes seemed shockingly unprecedented and even somewhat surreal. But as history has repeatedly proven, no nation is impregnable to such forces. We can read in textbooks about mighty empires that seemed completely invincible in their time, yet later fell to complete ruination. In truth, only God is invincible, and everything in the material world is fleeting and is under His domain.

Only when the material progress of a nation is in harmony with its spiritual development will it bring forth the favor and blessings of the heavenly kingdom, as affirmed in a verse from a Bahá'í prayer that specifically addresses the American people:

O God! Let this American democracy become glorious in spiritual degrees even as it has aspired to material degrees, and render this just government victorious. Confirm this revered nation to upraise the standard of the oneness of humanity, to promulgate the Most Great Peace, to become thereby most glorious and praiseworthy among all the nations of the world. O God! This American nation is worthy of Thy favors and is deserving of Thy mercy. Make it precious and near to Thee through Thy bounty and bestowal.[131]

We have seen evidence of the potential greatness of our nation at times when we are drawn together in devotional gatherings, offering up prayers for our fellow man and for the conditions of the world in which we live. Following the tragic attack on the United States, September 11, 2001, civic and religious leaders alike called on the American people to gather together in prayer. From large cities to small, rural towns nationwide, peoples of diverse religions, creeds, ethnicities, ideologies, political orientations, and classes all came together to pray as one people in massive multicultural devotional gatherings.

People met in churches, schools, parks, and other public facilities. They carried candles, sang together, cried together, and complete strangers often embraced each other. Suddenly, there was an exhilarating unity and solidarity among the American people. It sparked a new consciousness—a sense of strength, courage, and rejuvenation in the spirit of the nation. Perhaps the glimmerings of spiritual unity lasted for only a brief period, but the goodness, compassion, courage, and decency of the American people as a whole shone forth and it was glorious.

The following year, in commemoration of the one-year anniversary of the September 11th tragedy and in memory of the thousands of souls who lost their lives, devotional gatherings were again held throughout the nation. I had the privilege to participate in such a gathering, which turned into a momentous event for the community and a testimonial to the unifying and healing power of devotional gatherings.

The event was held at a Christian Presbyterian Church in Durham, North Carolina. Nearly 1,000 people came, and the attendees reflected the diverse population of the city. People of various ethnicities and religions gathered together at this event, which at first began solemnly, in remembrance of the horrors of the previous year. However, once the program commenced, the spirit of the gathering gradually turned from sadness and grief to awe and exhilaration.

The program began, surprisingly, with a cantor blowing the ancient instrument known as the shofar. A cantor is a Jewish official who presides over the musical portion of a religious service, and the shofar, a ram's horn, is traditionally blown to trumpet in the Jewish New Year during the holy days of Rosh Hashanah and Yom Kippur. Most of the people who were in attendance at the multifaith observance had never before heard a shofar blown. All seemed entranced by the reverberating, haunting sound of the ancient Hebrew instrument. The blowing of the shofar at that gathering seemed to signify the trumpeting in of a new day of hope, peace, and unity.

Several local religious leaders took turns at the pulpit offering prayers in the traditions and languages associated with their faith. Buddhist, Hindu, and Native American Indian prayers were offered. A Catholic priest and male and female pastors from churches of different Christian denominations stood up to read passages from the Bible and offer prayers for peace and unity.

An especially inspiring highlight of the program was when a rabbi chanted a prayer in Hebrew, immediately followed by an African-American imam (a Muslim official who leads prayer) chanting a prayer in Arabic. Listening to the two men pray one after the other in their respective languages was deeply stirring, but seeing them afterwards embrace each other like two brothers was a memorable sight indeed.

About midway through the program, a young Bahá'í woman stood up to recite a Bahá'í prayer. She was the only religious representative to come to the pulpit who was neither a member of the clergy nor an official prayer leader. Because there is no clergy in the Bahá'í Faith, any Bahá'í may serve as a representative of the Bahá'í Faith. Choirs and various musicians representing various local churches and faiths were also invited to present, including my own local choir. Although I am a classically trained soprano, and I had no background in singing gospel-style music, I joined a multifaith, multiethnic gospel choir in 1997 and have had the time of my life singing and touring with the choir in concerts, churches, devotional gatherings, festivals and at a variety of venues in cities throughout the South and Midwest.

On that particular evening, only seven members of our choir were available to attend, all of whom happened to be Bahá'í women. Even so, we were a diverse group in ethnicity and color, and we sang our hearts out. The spirit was splendidly unifying that evening, and our souls quickened with all the love and joy we sensed in the room. When our little choir stood up to sing, all seven of us experienced a somewhat mystifying sensation. We all felt as if a band of singing angels was circling around us. We were further astounded when several people in the audience, even in the back of the large sanctuary, later told us how "amazed" they were because we sounded as if we were a full-sized choir.

The program closed with a Baptist minister delivering a benediction, followed by the cantor, who again blew the shofar, signifying the end of the program. People stood up from their seats and hugged each other or shook hands, smiled, wept, and conversed in fellowship. It was apparent that everyone was greatly moved—no one seemed to want to leave the building.

Those who gathered there that night bore witness to the power of prayer and to the unifying power of multicultural devotional gatherings. The collective unity and joy experienced at the gathering was a testimonial that when humanity as a whole recognizes that there is one God and one human race, the reality that "world peace is not only possible, but inevitable" will shine forth.[132] The people who were there that evening embraced that message, and the atmosphere was ablaze with the love of God.

All sacred scriptures promise that the day will come when all humanity will dwell together in peace and harmony, building God's Kingdom on earth. The Hebrew scriptures foretold, "Behold, how good and how pleasant it is for brethren to dwell together in unity!"[133] The gathering's attendees saw a glimpse of such a possibility at that evening's event. The program succeeded in honoring the departed through a spiritual celebration of the diversity of the human race, which afforded the meeting a sense of hope and new vision for a better day. Through the expression of prayer, the memory of those departed souls was granted a sense of higher purpose and meaning.

Praying for unity

Bahá'í scripture affirms that devotional gatherings, which bring people together in unity, warrant special blessings of the Holy Spirit: "[A]ll should gather together, and, harmoniously attuned one to another, engage in prayer with the result that out of this coming together, unity and affection shall grow and flourish in the human heart."[134]

The reality of people of diverse populations living, working, and worshipping God together in unity is not merely an idealistic concept or wishful dreaming. Dialogue and action are unquestionably crucial in addressing social ills, but through prayer we draw assistance from the Holy Spirit, which lends us a power that is impossible to attain when left solely to our own devices and imaginings.

Bahá'u'lláh wrote, "The well-being of mankind, its peace and security, are unattainable unless and until its unity is firmly established."[135] In striving to carry out this message, American Bahá'ís have been fervent in their efforts towards building a foundation for models of unity at the community level, and many of their endeavors in this area have been hugely successful. Those efforts first began at the prompting of 'Abdu'l-Bahá, who, during his travels through the United States and Canada in 1912, initiated an outdoor Unity Feast picnic in Englewood, New Jersey.

Addressing the gathering, 'Abdu'l-Bahá said,

This is a delightful gathering; you have come here with sincere intentions, and the purpose of all present is the attainment of the virtues of God. The motive is attraction to the divine Kingdom. Since the desire of all is unity and agreement, it is certain that this meeting will be productive of great results. It will be the cause of attracting a new bounty, for we are turning to the Kingdom ... seeking the infinite bestowals of the Lord. ... Rejoice, for the angels of heaven are your assistants and helpers.[136]

The prayers at that gathering uplifted and united the hearts of the participants, establishing a precedent for future Bahá'í gatherings. Although there are no prescribed rituals and customs in the Bahá'í Faith, praying for the love of God and promoting unity are among the essentials of every Bahá'í meeting.

During his tour through America 'Abdu'l-Bahá was invited to speak at many different venues, including churches, synagogues, schools, libraries, and other public facilities, as well as at gatherings in private homes and at outdoor events. At each meeting, 'Abdu'l-Bahá expounded on Bahá'u'lláh's teachings, offering words such as "God is one, the effulgence of God is one, and humanity constitutes the servants of that one God . . . God has created mankind from the same progeny in order that they may associate in good fellowship, exercise love toward each other and live together in unity and brotherhood."[137]

He also stressed Bahá'u'lláh's teachings on the essentiality of prayer: "[O]nly in the remembrance of God can the heart find rest."[138] He encouraged devotional gatherings among peoples of diversity, extolling the benefits of such meetings, "Whensoever a company of people shall gather in a meeting place, shall engage in glorifying God, and shall speak with one another of the mysteries of God, beyond any doubt the breathings of the Holy Spirit will blow gently over them, and each shall receive a share thereof."[139]

Encouraged by 'Abdu'l-Bahá, who returned to his home in Haifa, Palestine, the American Bahá'í community sponsored a series of "Race Amity" conferences in the 1920s. The largest of those meetings was held in 1921 in Springfield, Massachusetts, and was attended by some twelve hundred people. Amazingly, the attendance was completely integrated— blacks and whites sat next to each other—in the year 1921. The conference was a tremendous success, but, again, while talks were presented and dialogues were exchanged, the nature of the meeting was spiritual. A devotional component played a significant role at the meeting. Through the collective prayers and heavenly spirit of the conference, the hearts of the participants were connected through God's love—which opened new possibilities for learning, understanding, and healing.

In striving to follow 'Abdu'l-Bahá's example for nearly a century, Bahá'ís in the United States have been actively engaged in a number of race unity efforts. However, in the last few years, a growing number of Bahá'ís are discovering that one of the simplest, most effective and enjoyable methods to promote unity and spiritual healing is by hosting multifaith devotional gatherings in homes, at local Bahá'í centers, or at neighborhood churches and other public venues.

What are the elements of a Bahá'í devotional gathering?

Devotional gatherings hosted by Bahá'ís are open to everyone. All are welcomed and embraced in fellowship at such gatherings, regardless of religious background, creed, or ethnicity. Proselytizing is forbidden in the teachings of the Bahá'í Faith, and the idea of conversion is not the purpose of devotional gatherings. Their purpose is best explained in the following passage from Bahá'í scripture: "[A]ll should gather together, and, harmoniously attuned one to another, engage in prayer; with the result that out of this coming together, unity and affection shall grow and flourish in the human heart."[140]

Many people who come to these devotional gatherings for the first time may feel surprised at the lack of rigidity in custom and stirred by the reverence of spirit. The gatherings are animated by the guidance that "Prayer is essentially a communion between man and God, and as such transcends all ritualistic forms and formulae."[141]

From the Bahá'í perspective, it is especially important to avoid ritualistic patterns in gatherings: "When one is praying in private, one may do what one's heart prompts in such matters. However when prayers are read at meetings, care should be taken not to develop rigid practices and rituals."[142]

The Bahá'í teachings shun rigidity in devotional practice so that the focus of the gathering may be on the pure motive of prayer rather than on the ritual of prayer. Bahá'í scripture states, "These spiritual gatherings must be held with the utmost purity and consecration, so that from the site itself, and its earth and the air about it, one will inhale the fragrant breathings of the Holy Spirit."[143]

While there are no clergy in the Bahá'í Faith and no Bahá'í officials to lead congregational prayer, and Bahá'ís are thus left to follow their own inclinations, they are urged to "take the utmost care that any manner they practice should not acquire too rigid a character, and thus develop into an institution."[144]

Regarding which prayers are offered, Bahá'ís themselves are encouraged to use the revealed prayers of Bahá'u'lláh and the Báb as well as those of 'Abdu'l-Bahá, but all participants are free to recite prayers and readings from the sacred scriptures of other religions because the Bahá'í teachings recognize that they all come from the same source. Spontaneous prayers are also permitted, however, the Bahá'í writings explain, "Bahá'ís are generally encouraged to use the Creative Word, including those prayers and Tablets revealed by Bahá'u'lláh, the Báb and 'Abdu'l-Bahá . . . [and] while spontaneous prayer is permitted, the revealed verses are preferred because 'the revealed Word is endowed with a power of its own.'"[145]

Music often plays a prominent role in these devotional gatherings. Bahá'í scripture explains: "[I]n this new age the Manifest Light hath, in His holy Tablets, specifically proclaimed that music, sung or played, is spiritual food for soul and heart."[146] There is room for great creativity in such devotional expressions. Some Bahá'ís may sing or chant prayers and verses from Bahá'í scripture set to lovely melodies, and some Bahá'í teenagers may even rap prayers to a "hip-hop" beat, which is acceptable as long as the tone and manner are reverent. While the encouragement of creative and artistic freedom in expressing our love for God makes the devotional gatherings more fun, participatory, and enjoyable, reverence is the one essential characteristic governing all of these devotional activities.

Extending the spirit of unity

In the summer of 2005 I attended a devotional gathering at my local Bahá'í center that focused on the theme of race unity. The room was packed, with standing room only, and it was filled with people of marvelously rich diversity in religion, ethnicity, and color. Many of the people there were Bahá'ís, but a large portion of the group included their neighbors, friends, family, and coworkers. There was one very lovely family, a couple with five children, who had been attending the devotional gatherings for a few months. At this particular gathering, about midway through the program, the husband suddenly stood up and announced that he had something to say. He was a large man with a gentle voice and demeanor, and everyone quieted down to listen.

He looked at the different faces in front of him and said, "I am not a Bahá'í, but my wife and I have been bringing our family here for the last three months. The genuine level of unity I have seen and felt here among people of so much diversity is something that I thought I would never live to see. But it's not just unity I'm talking about. I'm talking about love. I need to try to share with you the feeling of love I feel in this room. I don't even know most of you, and yet I can honestly say that I feel love for every single person in this room. I know it is God's spirit I'm feeling."

The man's eyes began to well with tears, and he paused. He said, "This unity we are feeling here today is the real thing, and I'll tell you why I know. There are white people here who have invited my family and me to their homes. In fact, we are going to have lunch with a white family in their home this afternoon. As an African-American man, this is very meaningful. In all my life, even though I went to school with white people and work with white people and have white neighbors, not one single white person has ever invited me or my wife into their home.

"It's not enough to just see each other at our jobs or for our children to go to the same schools—we have to pray together, get to know each other, and invite each other into our homes. But it's got to start with us praying together because we need to feel that spiritual connection before we can learn to talk to each other. I feel so much love for every person here—and I feel love from of all you too. Well, I guess that's all I have to say." As soon as he sat down there was an explosion of applause. People were wiping their eyes, and all were deeply touched. After the gathering, several people ran over to embrace him. It was a wonderful gathering of souls.

Testimonials such as those affirm that achieving unity in diversity is not a fantasy but a very real and tangible possibility. In a worship service where all members are of the same ethnicity and from the same economic and social stratum, there may be a strong feeling of solidarity, but that sense of commonality may often be more the result of physical and cultural similarities than spiritual realities. It is only natural to gravitate towards people of similar backgrounds and lifestyles, for it does appear to provide a comfort zone. However, when we cling and restrict ourselves to one particular group of people, we are unable to gain perspective and understanding of other people's cultures, and this potentially creates distrust, misconceptions, misunderstandings, prejudice, animosity, dissension, and strife.

We can achieve unity and promote peace in our community by expanding our associations with peoples of different backgrounds beyond the workplace and school. We need to associate with each other more intimately in a spirit of fellowship. The Bahá'í teachings assert that when people strive to develop an intimate, spontaneous, and informal association with people of diverse ethnic and cultural groups and genuinely seek their friendship with sincere intentions, respect, and kindness— racial barriers will break down, mutual understanding will emerge, grievous and deeply rooted wounds will heal, and distrust will transform into trust, loyalty, and goodwill.

What better method to help achieve such a lofty goal than by praying together at multicultural devotional gatherings? Bahá'í scripture affirms, "All should gather together, and, harmoniously attuned one to another, engage in prayer; with the result that out of this coming together, unity and affection shall grow and flourish in the human heart."[147] Chilled hearts of strangers, even of those who are enemies, can be thawed and connected through the love of God. But that love must be so sincere that they love God more than they hate each other, and all must be willing to give up their hate and prejudices for the love of God.

It is also extremely beneficial for families and friends to pray together as well as for each other. Bahá'í scripture offers several beautiful prayers for marriage, children, and parents, and for the unity and well-being of the family. The family unit is, after all, the pillar and foundation of society. Peace and unity must be first established within the immediate family before it can be extended to the community, the nation, and beyond:

> If love and agreement are manifest in a single family, that family will advance, become illumined and spiritual; but if enmity and hatred exist within it destruction and dispersion are inevitable. This is likewise true of a city. If those who dwell within it manifest a spirit of accord and fellowship it will progress steadily and human conditions become brighter whereas through enmity and strife it will be degraded and its inhabitants scattered. In the same way the people of a nation develop and advance toward civilization and enlightenment through love and accord, and are disintegrated by

war and strife. finally, this is true of humanity itself in the aggregate. When love is realized and the ideal spiritual bonds unite the hearts of men, the whole human race will be uplifted, the world will continually grow more spiritual and radiant and the happiness and tranquility of mankind be immeasurably increased. Warfare and strife will be uprooted, disagreement and dissension pass away and universal peace unite the nations and peoples of the world. All mankind will dwell together as one family, blend as the waves of one sea, shine as stars of one firmament and appear as fruits of the same tree. This is the happiness and felicity of humankind. This is the illumination of man, the glory eternal and life everlasting; this is the divine bestowal. I desire this station for you and I pray God that the people of America may achieve this great end in order that the virtue of this democracy may be insured and their names be glorified eternally.[148]

CHAPTER 12

Coping with Crisis

The aftermath of Hurricane Katrina, which rained catastrophic destruction upon the Gulf Coast of the United States in August 2005, created a crisis in our nation. Many people died, and scores were displaced. They lost their homes, belongings, livelihood, and loved ones. Entire families suddenly found themselves homeless and destitute.

In the weeks following Katrina, more hurricanes, flooding, and tornados pummeled the coast, resulting in death and destruction on a scale unprecedented in contemporary America. The nation mourned the loss of innocent lives and prayed for the survivors. Americans gave generously and sacrificially to aid the evacuees. Demonstrating countless acts of heroism and compassion, the American people showed their true greatness and grit. In addition to the outpourings of material donations from businesses, religious communities, and individuals nationwide, many kind souls opened their homes to provide shelter to their fellow citizens. Many physicians offered free medical service to tend to the sick.

There were countless acts of heroism and selflessness among the victims themselves, such as Mia, a native of New Orleans. Mia never thought of herself as heroic, but she certainly showed mettle at the time of crisis.

The first time she learned about Hurricane Katrina was on Saturday, two days before the disaster was to strike. She explains, "I was on my way to Jackson, Mississippi, to attend a meeting when I first heard about it from a friend who drove up with me. I immediately called my mother at home in New Orleans. When I alerted her about the oncoming hurricane, she refused to evacuate. I understand why she felt that way, because we had previously evacuated four times, and each time it had turned out to be unnecessary. Also, my mother's health was poor and I was concerned about how traveling would affect her condition. So I prayed and asked God for assistance and guidance."

For several years, Mia had been living in a diverse area in San Diego, California. She was a registered nurse and worked in a modern hospital in the city. She enjoyed her life, her friends, and the benefits a cosmopolitan city had to offer. However, in 1993, she sacrificed all of that to move back to her birthplace, New Orleans, to take care of her ailing father.

Mia says, "It was a very difficult transition for me. After the lifestyle I had enjoyed in San Diego for so many years, moving back to a segregated community and seeing so much poverty and despair made me feel as if I had entered a third world zone. As an African-American, I grew up in this environment and worked very hard to get out and leave it behind. But when I was living in California I learned about the Bahá'í Faith and became a Bahá'í. The prayers and the teachings of Bahá'u'lláh inspired my decision to move back to my hometown and take care of my parents. I had hoped in some way I could be useful in helping to better the community. I offered many prayers to make it so."

Mia took care of her father until he passed away in 2003. She stayed on to care for her mother, whose health was also frail, and she took jobs as a homecare nurse. She also became actively involved in a number of community service projects, advocating for children's education, health care, race unity, and other human rights issues. Mia said, "It was depressing to see drugs, alcohol, and crime everywhere on the streets. But I just kept praying and trusting in God and doing the best that I could do.

"I was always telling my friends, 'The prayers are my salvation!' The prayers gave me the strength and direction to stay where I was and try to do some good. I realized that a big problem is that most people who are educated and have a good career and nice homes don't want to give all that up to go to impoverished areas. But if we don't go to help, how are conditions ever going to improve? That is why I was committed to stay.

"Also my mother loved her house and her friends and her church— and I couldn't leave her there alone. That's why I was so conflicted when Hurricane Katrina was approaching. All the way home from my meeting in Jackson, I prayed for assistance. I became nervous when I saw the heavy traffic pouring out of New Orleans. People were already evacuating. Normally the drive from Jackson is three hours, but the traffic was so bad that it took ten hours to get back to New Orleans.

"My mother was determined to stay in the house and wait the storm out. I was still torn. I was concerned about whether my mother would be up to the long drive to Texas to stay with our relatives, as was the case whenever we evacuated. I was also concerned about my own health restrictions. And I was tired after just getting back from a ten-hour drive. The preparations for evacuation are exhausting.

"My mother was pleading for us not to go. But my instinct was to evacuate. I began packing our bags and preparing for evacuation, which made my mother upset. She was adamant that she would not take one step out of the house. I went upstairs and prayed most of the night. I recited repeatedly one of my favorite prayers: 'Say: God sufficeth all things above all things, and nothing in the heavens or in the earth but God sufficeth. Verily, He is in Himself the Knower, the Sustainer, the Omnipotent.'[149]

"I begged God to give me direction. finally, on Sunday morning, I told my mother I had been praying and that I sensed imminent danger. I told her that we were leaving. I packed food and as many belongings as possible, boarded up the house, and loaded the car. She was very unhappy but she got into the car and we were off.

"What happened after that was horrible. With everyone trying to get out of the city, the traffic was bumper to bumper, practically at a standstill. It was like a parking lot. Normally the drive to Dallas is nine hours, but it took us twenty-two hours. My mother was miserable, and I felt guilty for forcing her out of the house. It was awful seeing her so despondent, but I had prayed, I put my trust in God, and I felt spiritually guided. Of course, my mother continued to give me the silent treatment even days after the hurricane destroyed the city.

"My cousins and I were worried about our aunt and uncle who also lived in New Orleans. None of the family had heard from them. We were especially concerned because our aunt was diabetic and our uncle had Alzheimer's. And so, exactly one week after I had evacuated, I was in a car once again driving back to New Orleans with my cousins, hoping and praying to find our aunt and uncle. We drove more than twenty hours, and we prayed all during the trip.

"But just as we were about to enter the section of the city where my aunt and uncle lived, National Guardsmen stopped us at a checkpoint. Because we didn't have the proper identification tags, they ordered us to turn around. We took another route, but again we were not permitted to pass through the checkpoint. It was getting late, we were exhausted, and, unsure of what to do at that point, we drove to Baton Rouge to stay with some friends. The next morning we returned to New Orleans. This time we were determined to find our aunt and uncle. Before reaching the checkpoint this time, we said a round of prayers. We prayed fervently, beseeching God to assist us. We drove to the checkpoint, and no one was there. Not a guard in sight! We drove right through.

"The streets were very dangerous. They were mostly dry, but everywhere there were fallen trees, broken branches, electrical poles and wiring, and all kinds of objects all over the streets. It was a mess. finally, we managed to reach their house and knocked on the door. We heard from inside the house my aunt scream, 'Praise God! Thank God! Our prayers have been answered. I knew someone would come and rescue us!' My aunt opened the door, and when she saw us she was overjoyed. We all hugged and thanked and praised God, and my aunt said, 'I just kept praying to the Lord and I never gave up. I knew that someone was going to save us.'

"Before the storm had taken out the electricity, my aunt had wisely boiled a dozen eggs. They were down to the last two eggs, and that was basically all they had left to eat. Their house was mostly intact, but the power had been out all week and it was as hot as an oven in there. Being elderly and having serious medical problems, my aunt and uncle would have not been able to survive much longer on their own. We grabbed a bunch of their things, threw them in the car, and with our aunt and uncle in tow, our plan was to head back to Texas. However, first I needed to see my house, which was fairly close.

"It was a very emotional experience for me when I walked into my house. While there wasn't much damage done to the bottom floor, the entire roof of the house was gone. I walked up the steps to the second level and looked up at the sky and just cried. I realized at that moment that my mother and I never would have survived the hurricane if we had stayed. My mother and I lived in a split-level house, and the top level was where I had resided. Everything there was destroyed—my computer and all its files, my furniture, books, clothes, shoes, and photographs. I stood there crying and thanking God for His guidance and assistance. I felt amazingly detached about losing my material possessions, and I knew it was because of the prayers. But I cried when I saw this destruction because it was an affirmation that I had made the right decision to insist that my mother and I evacuate. We never would have survived in this house."

Mia and her aunt and uncle arrived safely in Texas. Mia's mother eventually began talking to Mia again, although somewhat begrudgingly. In reflection, Mia said, "It is interesting. Only days before the hurricane came, I heard several people in the community remark that the city had gone spiritually adrift. I know that some people feel that it wasn't a fluke that the city was hit by a disaster of 'biblical proportions.' So many people have lost everything. Our house was old and uninsured, and we don't have the money to repair it ourselves. I grew up in that house and now it is gone. I have no idea what is in store for me in the future. But I trust in God, and I feel very blessed and grateful that we are alive, safe and receiving tremendous support from family and friends.

"I truly believe there is a divine purpose in all of this. I just hope and pray that as we rebuild the cities that were destroyed, we also learn whatever it is that God wants us to learn."

Mia's insight reminds me of an invaluable piece of advice my mother gave me: "You can always learn to make the best of any situation, no matter how terrible it is, if you learn from it. You can turn anything negative into something good by learning from it and then taking positive steps to rebound."

My mother was not a Bahá'í, but the Bahá'í writings affirm the importance and benefits of learning from our trials and misfortunes. A passage from the Bahá'í writings explains:

[T]hese events have deeper reasons. Their object and purpose is to teach man certain lessons. . . . These events happen in order that man's faith may be increased and strengthened. Therefore, although we feel sad and disheartened, we must supplicate God to turn our hearts to the Kingdom and pray for these departed souls with faith in His infinite mercy so that, although they have been deprived of this earthly life, they may enjoy a new existence in the supreme mansions of the Heavenly Father.[150]

Bahá'í scripture tells us that as much as we might pray, the words of prayer alone are not sufficient if we do not have trust and true reliance in God. That trust opens a spiritual channel, helping us to be more receptive to assistance and direction from the heavenly realm in times of crisis. There is a prayer that Bahá'ís often say at times of difficulties: "I adjure Thee by Thy might, O my God! Let no harm beset me in times of tests, and in moments of heedlessness guide my steps aright through Thine inspiration. Thou art God, potent art Thou to do what Thou desirest. No one can withstand Thy Will or thwart Thy Purpose."[151]

When we are in crisis, it is easy to panic. Ironically, it is more important than ever in times of calamity to remain calm, clear thinking, and focused so that we can proceed wisely and beneficially in accord with the situation.

Marcia, another lady from New Orleans, also shared her evacuation story, which is a good example of how prayer can help people stay on task with fortitude and calm under chaotic circumstances.

She explains, "My husband, Curtis, and I first heard about Katrina on Saturday. We immediately began preparations to evacuate with our two sons, but we were concerned about transportation. Our car was old and in no condition to travel beyond the city. We decided to rent a car, but the first several car rental agencies we called were booked. I kept praying while my husband kept calling. finally he found a rental agency that still had cars available, and my husband arranged to pick the car up on Sunday, mid-afternoon. The next morning we awoke early and prayed, meditated, and consulted. Afterwards we both had a feeling that we should not wait until the afternoon to get the car. Curtis called the car rental company several times, but no one answered. So we drove out there, but the outer gate was locked and the place was completely deserted. Curtis called the rental company for more than thirty minutes while I continued to pray. finally, someone on the phone informed him that the car rental office at the airport was open.

"That drive to the airport was quite a trip. The traffic was a nightmare, and our car was overheated and smoking badly. We were not sure if we were ever going to make it. We knew that the worst thing would be to panic, so we prayed, and that helped us stay calm and clearheaded.

"All the way to the airport we prayed and put our trust in God. I remember feeling very detached about what was happening, and I knew it was the prayers. I felt that if God wanted us to get out of New Orleans safely, then the best that we could do was to pray, trust in Him, and do all that we needed to do with a clear head, and it would happen. But I also felt that if it was His will for us to stay, then that was okay too. What was most important to us was to trust in God's will.

"When we arrived at the airport car rental, there was a huge mob of people and a ghastly long line. Many people were there without reservations, but only those with reservations were served. My husband and I thanked God profoundly, not only because we had persevered on the phone in making a reservation, but also because after prayers and consultation, we both had a strong sense that we should get the car in the morning. We stood in front of the last person who was permitted to rent a car. After that, the office was closed. If we had waited until afternoon, we would have had no car. As it is, it was a miracle that our old car, with all its smoke and heat, made it to the airport."

Marcia and Curtis's drive back to their house took two and a half hours due to traffic. By the time they had completed their preparations to evacuate, it was nighttime. finally, after loading the car, they headed for Indiana, where their two daughters reside. They spent nearly three hours in the car moving at a snail's pace just to get out of the city.

Marcia says, "It was pretty chaotic. People were frantic to leave. We were barely moving, and we wondered if we were going to get out of danger before the hurricane hit.

"There is no question that without prayers the experience would have been traumatizing. The prayers kept our family united and calm. We never stopped praying, and we never stopped trusting in God. I have to say that meditation also was a big factor. The day and morning before we evacuated and we had so many important decisions to make, Curtis and I quietly meditated after our prayers. Through the combination of prayer and meditation, we felt spiritually guided, unified, cool-headed, and focused on our tasks ahead."

The family made it safely to Indiana and initially stayed with one of their daughters, then through the aid of the Red Cross, moved temporarily into a small apartment. On reflection, Marcia said, "We have lost our home and much of our possessions, but we feel blessed to be alive and safe. Our spirits feel rapturous, enthralled in God's love. It is wonderful.

"I have a clearer understanding now of how the attachment to material things interferes with our spirituality. When one lives in a materialistic society, it is difficult to be detached from materialism. But when our material possessions are taken away and we turn to God, suddenly there is a sense of freedom that is really quite wonderful. I feel as if I have crossed over into a new spiritual plane—as if I am in heaven on earth. I have never in my life felt closer to the spiritual kingdom."

Bahá'u'lláh assures us that whenever we give up our trials to God and trust wholly in Him, we are then, in essence, suffering in the path of God and thereby reap the spiritual fruits of our sacrifice. Bahá'í scripture asserts,

> And if thou art overtaken by affliction in My path, or degradation for My sake, be not thou troubled thereby. Rely upon God, thy God and the Lord of thy fathers. . . . By God! Should one who is in affliction or grief read this Tablet with absolute sincerity, God will dispel his sadness, solve his difficulties and remove his afflictions. Verily, He is the Merciful, the Compassionate. Praise be to God, the Lord of all the worlds.[152]

Naturally, Marcia and her family suffered pain not just for their own losses, but also for the suffering and losses of the other victims. The family also prayed and grieved for the loss of many precious lives. Yet, still, through prayer and faith, this family experienced a joy that Marcia described as "rapturous."

How is it that a soul can experience two opposite emotions such as pain and joy simultaneously? The Bahá'í writings explain this phenomenon:

> There is no human being untouched by these two influences; but all the sorrow and the grief that exist come from the world of matter—the spiritual world bestows only the joy!
>
> If we suffer it is the outcome of material things, and all the trials and troubles come from this world of illusion . . . all our sorrow, pain, shame and grief, are born in the world of matter; whereas the spiritual Kingdom never causes sadness. A man living with his thoughts in this Kingdom knows perpetual joy.
>
> Today, humanity is bowed down with trouble, sorrow and grief, no one escapes; the world is wet with tears; but, thank God, the remedy is at our doors. Let us turn our hearts away from the world of matter and live in the spiritual world! It alone can give us freedom! If we are hemmed in by difficulties we have only to call upon God, and by His great Mercy we shall be helped.
>
> If sorrow and adversity visit us, let us turn our faces to the Kingdom and heavenly consolation will be outpoured.
>
> If we are sick and in distress let us implore God's healing, and He will answer our prayer.
>
> When our thoughts are filled with the bitterness of this world, let us turn our eyes to the sweetness of God's compassion and He will send us heavenly calm! If we are imprisoned in the material world, our spirit can soar into the Heavens and we shall be free indeed!
>
> When our days are drawing to a close let us think of the eternal worlds, and we shall be full of joy![153]

Now, this is not to say that we should walk around with our heads in the clouds, waiting idly by for the angels of mercy to come down and make everything good for us. Rather, we should take practical steps and center our lives on our "spirituality combined with practical vision and purpose."[154]

At a time of crisis, while Bahá'í scripture prescribes prayer as a means to call upon the Holy Spirit for aid and assistance, the writings also stress that it behooves us to be aware of the situation and confront it with practical, positive action. It is essential for our happiness and well-being that we offer prayers to help us avoid dwelling on the negative aspects:

> O God! Refresh and gladden my spirit. Purify my heart. Illumine my powers. I lay all my affairs in Thy hand. Thou art my Guide and my Refuge. I will no longer be sorrowful and grieved; I will be a happy and joyful being. O God! I will no longer be full of anxiety, nor will I let trouble harass me. I will not dwell on the unpleasant things of life.
>
> O God! Thou art more friend to me than I am to myself. I dedicate myself to Thee, O Lord.[155]

To be able to sustain a spirit of joy, regardless of the severity of our trials and difficulties, requires detachment from all things but God. In other words, we should love God above all else and remember that what is most important to the development of our souls is our communion with our Creator, as testified in Bahá'í scripture: "Be swift in the path of holiness, and enter the heaven of communion with Me. Cleanse thy heart with the burnish of the spirit, and hasten to the court of the Most High,"[156]

Everything in the material world is fleeting. What we take with us to the next world are the spiritual qualities and traits we develop in this world, sustained by the infinite love of God. We can take solace in the fact that, even when it seems as if trials and tribulations have compassed us on every side, through prayer and trust in God, our souls are protected from all harm: "Armed with the power of Thy name nothing can ever hurt me, and with Thy love in my heart all the world's afflictions can in no wise alarm me."[157]

Kimberly and Sam, a married couple residing in a town outside of New Orleans, were already accustomed to certain hardships even before Katrina pummeled their area. Due to an unfortunate accident when he was a teenager, Sam is a paraplegic and diabetic who requires dialysis every few days in order to survive. He requires a wheelchair and is completely paralyzed from the waist down.

Kimberly and Sam are an interracial couple in a small town in the Deep South, and they have seen their share of prejudice and discrimination. But they are a very special couple. They pray every day and trust in God, illuminating their souls with His love, which strengthens their love for each other. Loving all humanity for the sake of God has enabled them to greet their trials with courageous detachment and with a sense of humor. These two shining souls are dearly loved by their friends, and despite their challenges, their lives are rich and happy. Many look upon them as an inspiration.

Kimberly and Sam believe it was through their prayers and faith that they received an abundance of spiritual guidance and assistance in their evacuation when Katrina was approaching. Kimberly says, "We had made reservations to stay at a small hotel in Jackson, Mississippi, and arrived there on Sunday evening after a very long, hot, and difficult drive from New Orleans. On Monday, although we weren't directly hit by the hurricane, there was a pretty bad storm outside, and we could hear the wind blowing.

"I was really worried about my husband. Our hotel had no power, and it was extremely hot in the room, and because of Sam's health, he needs to be in a cool environment. And the room, being without light, was somewhat dangerous because Sam requires medicines and certain procedures every day with his apparatus, but we couldn't see. Also, his chair would soon need to be charged, but there was no power. Cooped up in that little, dark, hot room without power was a test.

"We had little food, and our car needed gas, but it was impossible to find an open gas station. Sam never stopped praying. He said prayers specifically for the power to go on so that we could have light and a working air conditioner to cool the room. Sam has a very loving heart, and his prayers are offered with a pure, earnest spirit. Usually he doesn't pray for himself; he usually prayers for others. But that night, he prayed for a cool room and light, and his prayers were most definitely answered— just not in the way we expected.

"On Monday evening, right after Sam prayed for light, there was a knock on the door of our hotel room. With the awful storm outside, I couldn't imagine who it would be. I opened the door and it was the hotel manager asking if we would like some candles. The dear man was going room to room, knocking on doors, handing out candles to the hotel guests!

"And then that night, because of the rain, it was actually very cool and comfortable in our room, so that was the answer to Sam's other prayer. But what I was most worried about was getting Sam on dialysis. He would be due for a session on Tuesday. I was growing very concerned and nervous. But my husband remained amazingly calm throughout. Of course, he was praying all the time. He was praying for everything— even gas for the car.

"There were several prayers from the Bahá'í writings that we said. One was the prayer known as the Remover of Difficulties, which I think is extremely powerful: 'Is there any Remover of difficulties save God? Say: 'Praised be God! He is God! All are His servants, and all abide by His bidding!'[158]

"Also there were certain passages from the writings of Bahá'u'lláh that kept me grounded and helped to soothe me: 'My love is My stronghold; he that entereth therein is safe and secure, and he that turneth away shall surely stray and perish. Thou art My stronghold; enter therein that thou mayest abide in safety. My love is in thee, know it, that thou mayest find Me near unto thee.'[159]

"Meanwhile my friend Janet, who lives in Texas, was worried about us and was trying in vain to reach me on my cell phone, so she called my mother in Wisconsin. When I called to check in with my mother, she told me about the call from Janet. I called Janet, who sounded relieved to hear my voice and told me that she and all our friends had been praying for Sam and me. She also gave me the telephone number of a physician she knew in Jackson, who happened to specialize in the treatment of Sam's condition.

"By that time, I had already located a nearby hospital that would provide Sam with dialysis on Tuesday, but the power in our hotel room was still out, and it was very hot. Sam and I were seriously considering driving up to Wisconsin to stay with my family. But I went ahead and called the doctor, and I was able to reach him right away."

The doctor was a Bahá'í, and Kimberly found him to be caring and concerned. She learned that he was affiliated with four hospitals in Jackson. He said, "Normally, I would have not been at home at this time, but I was unable to find gas for my car. Thank God you got ahold of me. Let me make arrangements to check Sam into a room at the hospital and get proper care for him after the ordeal he's been through."

Kimberly says, "At first, Sam and I were unsure what to do because we were fairly set on driving to Wisconsin. It was difficult to think clearly, so Sam and I sat down and prayed and consulted about it, and it suddenly became clear to us that this doctor was an answer to our prayers. It would provide an opportunity for Sam to get the appropriate medical attention he needed. How could we not take advantage of it? So we called the doctor and accepted his kind offer."

The physician immediately made arrangements for Sam to have a room in a hospital in town, and he also arranged for Kimberly to stay there with him. For the next week, Sam received excellent medical care, restoring him to better health, and both of them were able to rest, wash and eat in a clean, safe, and air-conditioned environment. Kimberly even found an open gas station and filled her car's tank.

The doctor later arranged for Kimberly and Sam to stay at a friend's home in Jackson. It turned out that the friend's mother, who was deceased, was an old and dear friend of Kimberly's. When the daughter discovered who they were, she graciously opened her lovely, big home to them and told the couple they could stay there indefinitely.

While staying at their friend's home, Kimberly and Sam consulted about their future. Kimberly's family was hoping that they would relocate to Wisconsin. But in their hearts they longed to return to their home in Louisiana and prayed about it and put their trust in God. Once again, they felt their prayers were answered when they received news from friends that their house was in fairly good condition. In fact, at this writing, they are happy to be resettled in their home, which is now equipped with running water and electricity. Their trust in God never wavered, and they are profoundly grateful that their prayers were answered affirmatively.

Together, in the stronghold of God's undying love, they share an undying love for each other. And they both keep on praying.

Prayers do not necessarily prevent hardships, but through prayer and faith, we become attuned to our spiritual reality and draw blessings from the divine bounty, endowing us with the ability to endure trials and difficulties with a radiant and noble spirit. "Let it ever be borne in mind that we earn our victories through test and trial; Let us also remember that our blessings are equal to our challenges."[160]

CHAPTER 13

Spiritualizing Our Endeavors

Ann's utmost desire as a little girl was to learn to play the violin. When she was eight years old her two preschool-age brothers began studying with a violin teacher who had initiated a new Suzuki program in their town. Suzuki is a specialized method for teaching violin to children, and Ann, who was very hopeful to enter the program, was rejected because the teacher insisted that eight was too old.

Ann was heartbroken. Reflecting on that episode, she says, "I remember hiding behind a chair and crying because I wanted to play the violin so badly." Fortunately, her father intervened and was able to arrange for Ann to join the traditional strings class in her public school. Two years later when she was ten, they found another Suzuki teacher who accepted Ann in her program. Ann was delighted.

By the time she was thirteen years old, after demonstrating a love and talent for playing the instrument, Ann knew in her heart that the violin would always be a part of her life. She had an earnest desire to bring to children as much joy as the violin brought to her, and she made up her mind that someday she would be a Suzuki violin teacher. However, it would be many years later before her violin playing would become a spiritual endeavor—a means to give worship and praise and to express her love to God—as in prayer.

Ann had been brought up in the Roman Catholic Church and attended Mass every week. The Mass included a Communion, where bread and wine were consecrated and consumed in remembrance of the death of Christ. Catholics revere this ceremony as a sacred rite in their belief that the bread represents the body of Christ and the wine represents his blood.

Although Ann was moved by the enormity of the sufferings and trials of Christ, she possessed little understanding about Christ or the purpose of religion. She attended Mass every week because it was expected of her. She was told that it was a sin for her not to attend Mass, and she certainly had no desire to sin.

Even so, there were parts of the Mass that she greatly enjoyed, such as hearing the Gospel stories and listening to the interpretations of the priest, whom she considered especially erudite and wise. She wished to learn how to relate Christ's teachings and experiences on earth to her own life so that she could make sense out of the painful things that happened to her and to the people around her. She was inspired by the words in a prayer of Saint Francis of Assisi, "Lord, make me a means of Thy peace," and she aspired to understand how to rise above whatever difficulties and challenges she faced in life to make a positive difference in others' lives.

Ann was resolute in her belief that her religion was the one and only true faith, but as she grew older she became aware that something was missing in her spiritual life. She longed to walk in the path of God's love, but it wasn't clear to her exactly how to achieve that. She was asking herself, "How does one show God's love? What does forgiveness look like?" Looking back, she now realizes that she had not yet learned the true nature and significance of prayer as a means of personally communing with God and forming an intimate relationship with Him.

Ann says, "My prayers were offered in a passive, congregational manner in which I would join others in reciting prayers, such as saying grace with family members at the dinner table or prescribed prayers with fellow parishioners at Mass on Sunday morning service. I said all the words, but that's all the significance the prayers held for me. They were just words to me."

When she turned eighteen and began her freshman year of college, it became even more important to her to help humanity by exemplifying the teachings of Christ through her deeds. Her awareness of the social ills that plagued humanity pained her, and she felt a burning desire for justice and universal peace, which she demonstrated as a political activist.

She says, "Although engaging in such activity would certainly not be considered prayer in the formal sense, upon reflection, I see it as a personal expression of my relationship with God at the time."

Ann left the church after graduating from college with a bachelor of arts degree in music education and redirected her spiritual journey by seeking God in nature. She channeled her activism towards working in organizations that were committed to protecting the environment. Her prayers took the form of communing with nature and beholding and paying homage to God's marvelous creation.

In addition, she was deeply concerned about the deplorable state of the world's children and the apathy she saw all around her regarding this issue. More determined than ever to carry out the decision she had made back in the eighth grade to be a children's teacher, she soon found employment as a violin teacher. She seriously hoped to make a difference by enriching the lives of children and helping to maximize their potential through the music.

However, Ann's world crashed when she and her family were dealt a painful blow. "I was in a spiritual crisis when, after a valiant struggle against brain cancer, my father died at the age of forty-nine. Two months later, my grandpa passed. I was twenty-six years old at the time. Having never been convinced of the whole heaven and hell scenario, I didn't know where they were, which was very painful. 'Where are you?' I wailed!"

With all her good intentions and worthwhile endeavors, Ann continued to feel that something was missing in her life. She was an insatiable seeker, searching for answers and thirsting for spiritual knowledge. She was desperate for answers. She had thought that she might find what she was looking for by searching for something that would significantly better the condition of the peoples of the world. Still, the sense of a spiritual void in her life persisted and plagued her. She continued her search for that significant something—but what was it?

The following year, Ann was living in the town of Adams, Wisconsin, and was perusing the religion page of the local newspaper when she noticed an article that announced a talk to be given on "progressive revelation." The topic sounded interesting and, feeling somewhat isolated in such a small town, her attention was particularly heightened when she read that the speaker was from Chicago. This made it an exciting cultural event.

She attended the meeting, which was held outside a neighboring village and hosted by Bahá'ís. The speaker, also a Bahá'í, explained Bahá'u'lláh's teachings on progressive revelation, the belief that throughout history God has revealed His message to humanity through a series of divine messengers.

"That night I immediately recognized that I had found the 'significant something' that I'd been searching for," she says. "I learned how Bahá'u'lláh had suffered unspeakable wrongs for His teachings. The speaker proposed that either Bahá'u'lláh really was a messenger of God or he was 'just plain crazy' to put up with all the persecutions to which he and his followers were subjected. I decided the former was true because I knew that is exactly what happened to Christ."

She was fascinated to learn that Bahá'u'lláh had written the equivalent of more than one hundred books and that some of his writings were available at the public library in "even as remote a place as Adams."

Ann says, "When they told me about the books, I was reminded of my dad, a vocal artist and university arts program manager, who, in his characteristic way of challenging authority, would facetiously demand, 'Where is it written?' I would giggle at his remonstrations at the time, but his question became my personal watchword, because underlying the playful nature of his jest, I sensed a keen respect for the truth. He wasn't about to be convinced of anything on hearsay. Now I imagined he would be very pleased because I could show him, 'Here it is Dad! This is where it is written!'"

That meeting was the first time that Ann had learned about the Bahá'í Faith, and that very same night she became a Bahá'í. She was drawn to and wondrously inspired by the message and spirit of Bahá'u'lláh's teachings. She was also deeply touched when, upon hearing about her departed father, the Bahá'í hosts suggested that her father's soul had guided her to the meeting. Before she left they also presented Ann with a Bahá'í prayer book, which to Ann's solace, contained many prayers for the departed.

Ann was eager to learn more about the teachings of Bahá'u'lláh and understand the principles of the faith. However, the Bahá'í family who had hosted that first meeting soon left for China, and Ann, not living near or seeing any other Bahá'ís, felt terribly alone. She says, "I had found my spiritual family, those who nurtured my soul, my true being. How was I to learn about the teachings of Bahá'u'lláh in such isolation?"

Ann prayed for assistance and guidance. Soon after, she received an invitation to serve as a violin instructor at the American Suzuki Institute at the University of Wisconsin in Stevens Point, where she met and quickly became close friends with a visiting faculty member from New York State, who also happened to be a Bahá'í. For them both there was an immediate bond. Ann could not help noticing that when a request is in accordance with divine will, God can move very swiftly—and she felt overwhelmingly grateful, for it was abundantly clear that God was assisting her.

"God had graciously answered my prayer!" she says. "Here was a spiritual sister, someone whom I'd never met before, but whom I recognized immediately as family. I asked her about the topic most on my mind at the time—how does one pray? We spent many hours together during those two weeks as my friend shared with me the teachings of Bahá'u'lláh. As I studied the prayers and passages from Bahá'í scripture and listened to my friend explain the principles, I learned a little more about how to draw closer to God through my prayers. I also came to realize that I could be a more effective agent for the spiritual and material progress of the peoples of the world through the application of the Bahá'í teachings."

Ann was elated because she was finally beginning to understand that prayer was a personal and private conversation with God. She especially loved reading the prayers from Bahá'í scripture because she could feel their potency and the uplifting effect they had on her spirit. Not only did the prayers reinforce and deepen her understanding of her spiritual purpose in knowing and loving the Divine Creator, but they also helped her to feel a more intimate relationship with God.

Ann continued to pursue her education and graduated with a master of music education degree with a Suzuki emphasis from the University of Wisconsin. Following graduation, she moved to a larger, more diverse community in southern Wisconsin. After living in small towns nearly all of her life, and having had little exposure to people of different ethnicities and cultures, she prayed fervently to learn how to relate to diverse populations. An initial answer came when a friend encouraged her to join a local chapter of the One Human Family Workshop Choir.

Founded in the mid-1990s by three young African-American Bahá'ís, the choir was formed for the purpose of bringing singers together from different backgrounds and teaching them to sing gospel music and spirituals in the African-American tradition. Based on the Bahá'í principles of unity in diversity, the choir has evolved into a multifaith, multiethnic choir with chapters in cities nationwide. The choir has been extremely successful in fostering fellowship and understanding and promoting unity through uplifting, inspiring, and prayerful music. Joining this choir was a huge step for Ann, who had previously had little opportunity, in the small Midwestern towns where she had resided, to associate with people of different cultures.

She says, "Initially I thought I was joining the choir to get involved in singing music, but God obviously had more in store. He lovingly answered my prayers, confirmed even my most insignificant attempts to educate myself, and mercifully forgave my mistakes as I exposed my ignorance of my own racism. The Bahá'í teachings tell us that racism is the greatest challenge in the United States, and it was painful for me to confront my own prejudices, but I know now that it was necessary for me to recognize those prejudices in order to work towards uprooting them. It was a tremendous learning experience to sing with this choir."

Ann was now turning to God, beseeching Him in prayer for more guidance. It was her heartfelt desire to understand how best to use her unique talents and faculties as a violin instructor, combined with her new awareness of the necessity of unity in diversity. She was inspired by a movie that she had seen, *Music of the Heart,* featuring Meryl Streep playing the role of a Suzuki violin teacher who started a successful public school strings program in Harlem, New York. Ann declared, "That's what I want to do," and asked God for assistance.

Her prayer seemed answered when she was offered a position at a predominantly African-American elementary magnet school. Unsure of herself and lacking in confidence, she struggled at first with the decision of whether or not to take the position, but through prayer she was motivated to accept it. After working on the job for a few years, she feels thoroughly immersed in the culture of a most unique inner-city school and says joyfully, "I absolutely adore my students and their families, and I love what I am doing!"

Ann found her niche through prayer and learned how to spiritualize her talents and skills by offering them up to God to be used as a service to humanity. Ann has never been happier and more fulfilled in her life, and while she continues to press onward in her spiritual journey, she feels grateful and blessed with confirmations of the Holy Spirit. She is enjoying success with her students by helping them develop a multitude of skills— not merely violin skills, but also social skills, coordination, attentiveness, and positive self-esteem and confidence. The success of her endeavors is also a confirmation of the Bahá'í teachings that pertain to the benefits of educating children through music: "The latent talents with which the hearts of these children are endowed will find expression through the medium of music. . . . It is necessary that the schools teach it in order that the souls and hearts of the pupils may become vivified and exhilarated and their lives be brightened with enjoyment."[161]

Shortly after Ann started teaching at the school, she also began attending a series of courses offered to the public by the Bahá'í community called "study circles." The first used a book titled *Reflections on the Life of the Spirit,* which addresses the meaning and practice of prayer and the subject of life after death. She found the passages from Bahá'í scripture about life after death and the prayers for the departed to be particularly comforting, as well as fascinating and illuminating. She derived great solace in believing in the eternal soul of her father and took comfort in knowing that she will see him again in the next world.

She says, "I continue to pray for my father every day. Through these prayers, I feel closer to him now than when he was on this earthly plane. I pray for his spiritual progress and ask for his assistance and guidance. I know he is in a much better position to assist me now than he was in his earthly life."

Today, still an insatiable seeker, Ann continues to enjoy attending the study circle courses, which address various spiritual topics such as acquiring spiritual qualities, serving God through service to humanity, spiritual transformation, and the importance of educating and training children in morals and spiritual principles. She attributes the courses with inspired her towards taking an active role in serving the greater community by teaching at a performing arts camp for adolescents with developmental disabilities and initiating outreach projects that focus on educating young adolescents from a local housing project about spiritual virtues and values. And she continues to derive immeasurable pleasure and a multitude of rewards from teaching the violin to her beloved students at the public school.

She says, "For years I prayed for a way to help facilitate children's spiritual and material progress, and now through the application of the teachings of Bahá'u'lláh and through the help of the study circles, I feel that I finally have the tools and opportunities to fulfill that dream. I have direction and purpose and feel that I am fulfilling that purpose. What a gift from God! I feel truly very blessed!"

"At times, I feel an overpowering sense of gratitude when I'm playing the violin. It is as if God opens a channel directly to my soul and I can pour out my heart to Him, asking for guidance, begging forgiveness, offering thanksgiving and praise. At moments like this my soul delights in the pure and holy, the present and the eternal—as in a prayer."

CHAPTER 14

Music, a Ladder for the Soul

A little girl, Laura, had no friends, and all the other children made fun of her despite her loveliness and sweet disposition. She was never invited to birthday parties, and no one would play with her in the schoolyard or neighborhood playground. Laura had mild learning disabilities that delayed her social and academic development, so she lagged behind her peers. The children did not understand why Laura behaved so strangely and moved so awkwardly. They regarded her as odd and, unfortunately, found her an ideal target for their teasing and mischief. It made Laura very sad that none of the children seemed to like her, but there were two things that made her exceedingly happy. She loved praying to God, and she loved singing. Best of all, she loved combining the two, especially at church, where she would sing spirituals and hymns.

One day at church when she was about twelve years old, her pastor overheard her singing during the Sunday service and was touched by the beauty of her voice. He asked her if she would like to sing a solo at the next church service, and she enthusiastically accepted his offer. The following Sunday, the pastor told the congregation to expect a special treat and invited Laura to stand up in front of the pulpit and sing.

The parishioners were startled to see Laura stand up there because they regarded her as a slow, shy, and awkward child. But their jaws dropped in amazement as soon as they heard this little girl's exquisite voice sing out her first notes. With complete confidence and focus she sang "Amazing Grace" in heavenly tones. Her parents knew that Laura was blessed with a gorgeous singing voice, but she was normally so withdrawn and insecure that they had never imagined she would sing before a large audience.

Her high notes were as a clear as a bell, her tone was sweet, and her pitch was flawless. Tears streamed down the cheeks of church members, who were deeply moved by Laura's singing and the purity of her spirit.

Life was never again the same for the young girl. Encouraged by her performance at the church, her parents brought Laura's musical talents to the attention of her teacher at school, and soon Laura was singing before the entire school body in the auditorium. The children were enchanted, and when Laura finished her song the room exploded with applause.

Laura's parents found her a vocal coach, and through the years as she continued to take voice lessons her voice grew stronger and more assured. By the time she was in high school, Laura was performing in school musicals, talent pageants, and concerts, and she was a regular soloist in her school and church choirs. Laura vastly improved in her grades and self-esteem and made some very special friends.

What continued to astound people who knew Laura was the level of confidence and assurance she possessed as soon as she took stage and began singing. There was no evidence of shyness or clumsiness when she performed, and whenever people asked her "Where do you get all that confidence?" she always gave them the same reply: "I sing for God."

The essential role of music in devotions

From ancient times to the present, music has played an essential role in the expression of prayer and communion with God. In all parts of the world people have invoked and given honor, thanks, praise, and love to God through music. The Hebrew prophet David understood the divine power of music and joyously declared his love for God through song and dance. He articulated and promulgated spiritual teachings in his psalms and sang aloud: "Make a joyful noise unto God, all ye lands: Sing forth

the honor of his name: make his praise glorious."[162] The Hindu prophet
Krishna proclaimed, "We will sing thy praises, O God almighty. We will
now and evermore sing thy praises,"[163] and Hindu followers have long
offered their devotions through music and dance.

Citizens of ancient Greece saw music as a divine gift and regarded it as
such an indispensable tool for communication that it had become a
tradition for the Greek philosophers to incorporate song in their
presentations. In truth, the Greeks contributed tremendously to the
advancement of civilization in the development and knowledge of the
art of music.

Regardless of religion or culture, those who have offered heartfelt
devotions to God through music attest to its power and to the joy and
gladness it brings to the spirit. Bahá'í scripture tells us that when music is
recognized as a heavenly gift and used as a devotional supplication to
God, the soul is nourished and the spirit contented: "The art of music is
divine and effective. It is the food of the soul and spirit. Through the
power and charm of music the spirit of man is uplifted."[164]

There are, however, some religious cultures that forbid the use of music
and dance. Certain sects of Islam interpret Muḥammad's view towards
music as hostile, but in fact, the prophet himself instituted the chanting
of prayers, and there is other evidence to suggest that he did not oppose
the use of music. In the book *Muhammad and the Course of Islam*, religious
scholar H. M. Balyuzi writes, "Although there is not a single verse
condemnatory of music in the whole text of the Qur'án, all four Sunni
schools of jurisprudence forbade it, a ban which was largely ignored."[165]

There are also some Christian groups that have banned the use of
music, but, again, their opposition is based on their own interpretations
of religious values and concepts, which may stem, understandably, from
the manner in which people often use music to debase the soul. Perhaps
those who are opposed to music are unaware that it can be a means to
elevate the human soul. Instead of eliminating music and denying
ourselves this wonderful means to enrich our lives, we should strive to be
more thoughtful in the way we use it and recognize that it is a God-given
gift to cherish and appreciate as a "ladder for your souls." Bahá'u'lláh
writes, "We have made it lawful for you to listen to music and singing.

Take heed, however, lest listening thereto should cause you to overstep the bounds of propriety and dignity. . . . We, verily, have made music as a ladder for your souls, a means whereby they may be lifted up unto the realm on high; make it not, therefore, as wings to self and passion. Truly, We are loath to see you numbered with the foolish."[166]

When music is used to promote harmful practices, particularly to our children and youth, it is a transgression of Bahá'u'lláh's exhortation and a misuse of a divine gift. When we examine some of the music being produced today, we can see how it reflects the disorder, corruption, and decadence of a world sadly bereft of spiritual values.

The Bahá'í teachings affirm the true purpose of music as a means to uplift and gladden the soul:

Music is regarded as a praiseworthy science at the Threshold of the Almighty, so that thou mayest chant verses at large gatherings and congregations in a most wondrous melody. . . . By virtue of this, consider how much the art of music is admired and praised. Try, if thou canst, to use spiritual melodies, songs and tunes, and to bring the earthly music into harmony with the celestial melody. Then thou wilt notice what a great influence music hath and what heavenly joy and life it conferreth. Strike up such a melody and tune as to cause the nightingales of divine mysteries to be filled with joy and ecstasy.[167]

Elsewhere we read that "Music is one of the important arts. It has a great effect upon the human spirit. . . . In sooth, although music is a material affair, yet its tremendous effect is spiritual, and its greatest attachment is to the realm of the spirit."[168]

I can personally testify to the spiritual effect of music. I was on tour with a multiethnic gospel choir and standing on a church platform before a predominantly African-American audience at a Southern Baptist revival meeting in small town in Alabama. Our director, Eric Dozier, was about to lead us in our first song of the evening. Standing there, I remember feeling more aware than usual of my Eastern European background and Yankee roots.

Although the year was 1999, segregation was still practiced in this town's schools, restaurants, and other public facilities. We were aware that the church we were singing at had for more than fifty years maintained a policy to restrict attendance exclusively for African-Americans.

However, a newly hired pastor had adamantly refused to sign the pledge to uphold the restriction policy. After developing a close friendship with a local Bahá'í in the town, the pastor had taken the initiative to break the restriction code by inviting our choir, which at that time was comprised mostly of Bahá'ís, to sing at the church. So, not only was the choir an ethnic mix, but on top of that we were Bahá'ís.

Our being there was against the wishes of the elders, who made it clear that they were skeptical, if not horrified, to see our choir standing there in their church about to sing at the revival. Even so, some of the church members and the pastor who had invited us were warm and welcoming, if somewhat apprehensive.

The church elders sat directly in front of the pulpit, facing us with folded arms and stern faces, studying the diverse collection of singers in our choir. This was a revival, after all, and it was the job of the choir to uplift and exhilarate the spirits of the congregation by singing the praises of God through spirituals and gospel music in the Southern African-American tradition. In other words, the choir was expected to bring down the Holy Spirit while singing the roof off the building.

Although our director and about half of the forty members of our choir were themselves African-American, the elders continued to study us, frowning skeptically and seeming to have little faith in the ability of our choir. It was extremely important to their choir members not to disappoint the pastor, the congregation, or our director; we all wanted to sing our best that night.

We opened our mouths and belted out our first notes. Perhaps because we were trying to make a good impression, the sound came out like a boom. A good boom! The congregation was impressed. It did not take long for most of the congregation to rise to their feet, clapping, cheering, and singing along. It took the elders longer to openly acknowledge their pleasure, but when we saw their bodies swaying to the beat, their feet tapping, and their frowns turning into grins, we were overjoyed.

By the time we were midway into our second song every person in the church was on their feet. We were scheduled to sing only three or four songs, but the pastor and congregation would not let us stop, and we sang the night away in joyful praises and loving remembrance of God through the spiritual gift of music. People clapped, tapped their feet, and some danced in the aisles—all rendering thanks to the Lord.

At one point, the pastor was so excited by the overwhelming spirit of love and unity, which seemed to affect everyone in the room, that he asked the choir to stop singing in order for every person in the church to "walk over and hug a person of a different race."

There was already a small sprinkling of diversity among the people who sat in the pews, thanks to the attendance of some local Bahá'ís and their relatives, and after the choir members stepped down from the platform to add to the diversity, everyone at the church warmly exchanged hugs with another "of a different race." People laughed, shed tears of exuberant happiness, and rejoiced aloud, "Praise God! Thank you, God!" Many of the congregation members shouted, "Thank you, Jesus!" One church member hugged me tightly and said, "I prayed all my life to see this happen. I never thought I would live to see it, but today I see it with my own eyes. I will never forget this night! Praise God!"

The exhilarating spirit of the evening carried through to the next day when the choir, which was rehearsing at the local Bahá'í center, received a homemade loaf of bread accompanied by a letter. The bread was baked and the letter composed by a white Christian woman who had attended the revival the previous night. She explained in the letter that her daughter, who was a Bahá'í, had told her about this "wonderful choir," and because she enjoyed gospel music she had come to the church to hear us sing. She told us that she enjoyed the choir and the music was beautiful, but what most affected her was the spirit she felt through the music.

She explained that before that evening, although she had considered herself a good Christian, she had never thought much about racism, and it had never occurred to her to associate with people of different races. As for the Bahá'í Faith, she had not been interested in learning anything about it, and in fact had cursed it and despised it as she had been quite upset with her daughter for becoming a Bahá'í and, in her opinion, "straying from the path of God."

The woman further explained in the letter that she was now looking at everything differently after her experience at the church. She had never realized that such love and unity and joy could exist between people of diverse backgrounds. She came to the painful realization that racism is a disease, and she now felt impassioned to do whatever she could to eliminate all forms of prejudice in her own life and in the community.

She also wrote in the letter that she was eager to learn more about the Bahá'í Faith because she believed it was the spirit of the choir and the heavenly music, much of which had been set to Bahá'í prayers, that had generated the "miracle of unity" she had witnessed that night. She thanked the choir profoundly and hoped that we would enjoy her homemade bread, assuring us that she had baked it with an abundance of love and gratitude in her heart.

We were all deeply moved as we listened to one of the choir members read aloud the letter. The homemade bread was cut into small slices and everyone had a bite. It truly was the most delicious bread I ever had tasted.

Fostering spirituality through music

The teachings of the Bahá'í Faith tell us that music "helps us communicate with the soul,"[169] which we see exemplified when we look at oppressed peoples throughout the ages who have found comfort and strength in the blending of music and prayer. Even among those who were the most persecuted and subjugated, through devotional music they found it possible to preserve their dignity and humanity and to connect with their spirituality.

The African-American community has long understood and used the spiritual power of music as a means to quicken the soul and commune with the Holy Spirit. For four centuries African-Americans breathed and worked in this nation in bondage and were often denied the freedom to worship openly. Despite their chains and sufferings, and despite being robbed of their right to freely offer devotions—a right to which every human soul is entitled—their hearts were receptive to the knowledge and love of God and to the blessings of the Holy Spirit.

Though they were not allowed to speak the words of devotion, they sang the words in prayerful songs and gave up their hearts and praise to God through heavenly music as they labored in the fields. That is how the spirituals and gospel music became a cherished and significant tradition of their culture.

Regarding the significance of this music in the African-American community, historian and author Derrick Bell writes in his book *Gospel Choirs,* "Long ago, the slave singers by interweaving melody and lyric in songs of faith—the spirituals—were able to transcend the awful oppression that defined their lives. Embracing religion that was undergirded by this music helped slaves to be free in their minds."[170]

Likewise, music has traditionally played an important role for the Jewish people, particularly for the millions of European Jews who endured unspeakable crimes during the pogroms, and later in the concentration camps during the Holocaust. Many of the survivors have since conveyed stories that tell of the vital role music played for the Jews who continuously sang songs of prayer in the camps. They testified that the music aided and comforted them, helped to preserve their sense of humanness in remembering their love for God, and helped to maintain their sanity, ennobling them with the will to endure and stay alive.

"Ani Maamin," a song with a haunting melody, was sung by the Jews in the Warsaw Ghetto in Poland as they were marched away by the Nazi solders to their death. Thousands of Jewish men, women, and children prisoners sang the song over and over again, which expressed their confidence in God and their belief in the coming of the Messiah:

I believe, I believe,
With reassuring faith,
He will come, he will come,
I believe, Messiah, he will come,
I believe, although he may delay,
I believe he'll come,
I believe.

Those who have suffered oppression, persecution, and injustice have borne witness to finding courage, hope, and a measure of joy and comfort when turning their hearts to God through devotional music. They have found that the blending of music and prayer fortifies and illumines their souls and exalts their comprehension of God as well as their sense of nearness to Him and the eternal realm beyond. This has enabled them to persevere through their trials of subjugation and hardship with a bright and noble spirit.

In the Bahá'í writings we are told,

> Bahá'u'lláh, in this glorious period has revealed in Holy Tablets that singing and music are the spiritual food of the hearts and souls. In this dispensation, music is one of the arts that is highly approved and is considered to be the cause of the exaltation of sad and desponding hearts. . . . [S]et to music the verses and the divine words so that they may be sung with soul-stirring melody in the . . . gatherings, and that the hearts of the listeners may become tumultuous and rise towards the Kingdom.[171]

While there is no need to limit our musical tastes solely to hymnals and spirituals, it is most advantageous to the development of our souls and to the progress and welfare of humanity to create, perform, and listen to music that is spiritually inspiring and uplifting. While the lyrics need not necessarily be devotional in context, the message should be devotional in spirit, with lyrics that promote spiritual values and principles. Truly, the world will be a far more beautiful and happier place if we take advantage of this God-given gift of music and use it as a means to inspire, educate, and exalt the spirit of humanity.

CHAPTER 15

My Prayer . . . My Praise

As a young man, Eric Tyrone Dozier was taught by his family to worship and praise God through the African-American tradition of spirituals and gospel music. He was gifted with a beautiful baritone voice and a natural talent for playing the keyboard instruments. Music had not only become an essential part of his life, but to him his music was an offering of prayer in praise to God.

This feeling was nurtured after Eric became a Bahá'í in his early twenties. He was encouraged by passages from Bahá'í scripture such as the following that suggested the importance of incorporating music during devotions: "[S]ing out the holy words of God with wondrous tones in the gatherings of the friends, that the listener may be freed from chains of care and sorrow, and his soul may leap for joy and humble itself in prayer to the realm of Glory."[172]

Inspired and encouraged by the Bahá'í writings, he prayed and meditated about how to best use the music to foster unity. Eric shared his thoughts and vision with two close friends, Dilsey and Cara, who were both immensely talented singers and performing artists. The two young women had also recently become Bahá'ís after learning about the Faith from Eric, and now, through prayer and consultation, the three of them collaborated in constructing a plan to bring together singers of diverse populations for the purpose of forming a gospel choir.

More specifically, their shared vision was to promote Bahá'u'lláh's message of the oneness of humanity by teaching a diverse group of people to sing gospel music and spirituals. They recognized that if the choir was to succeed in its mission, it was of vital importance that the integrity of the music be preserved, honored, and truly indicative of African-American culture. Too often they had seen various aspects of their culture compromised by mainstream society. They wanted music that was spiritually uplifting, joyful, and healing—music that could help to break through racial barriers, fusing all hearts into one.

This genre of music is very joyful, not just because of its upbeat rhythm and melody, but because of the words, too. For example, the words of the song "The Spirit of the Lord Is Everywhere" remind us that wherever and whenever we turn to God, His spirit is always there to bless and uplift our souls. The simplicity of the words and the tune make the music very accessible, and everyone loves to sing this music, which makes it a wonderful point of contact for such a diversity of people. Perhaps that is why this genre of music has influenced so many other popular types of music, including jazz, blues, ragtime, and rock and roll.

Eric, Dilsey, and Cara established the One Human Family Workshop Choir in 1996. It is a multifaith, multicultural organization with chapters in cities around the country. The primary mission of the organization, which is founded on Bahá'í principles, is to assist communities in the development of models of unity for diverse populations in which issues of conflict are addressed through frank and honest dialogue, multimedia presentations, and artistic expression.

The National One Human Family Worship Choir has traveled on concert tours in the United States, Belgium, South Africa, Switzerland, and the Virgin Islands. Through candid and open dialogue, intimate fellowship, and by praying and offering their music as a service to the community, the members of the choir have become as united as a loving family. They share joy at special and happy occasions and provide support and prayers for each other during times of trials and difficulties.

For five years Eric has been leading the choir on a performance tour through various regions of the United States. He named the tour "The Harvest Tour," drawing inspiration for the name from a passage of Bahá'í scripture: "Because the ground is rich, the rain of the divine outpouring is descending. Now you must become heavenly farmers and scatter pure seeds in the prepared soil. The harvest of every other seed is limited, but the bounty and the blessing of the seed of the divine teachings is unlimited."[173] The mission of the Harvest Tour is to spread the fragrance of divine unity on the planet and, in the words of the choir's slogan, "To unite the world—one song at a time!"

Eric continues to study and find inspiration in Bahá'í scripture and regards the Bahá'í Faith, and life for that matter, as a workshop, which is precisely why it was important to him to name the choir the "One Human Family Worship Choir." He recognizes that spiritual growth is an ongoing process that requires prayer, meditation and prayerful action.

"Prayer is a vital and very personal aspect for spiritual progress," he says. "Through prayer we evoke the power of the Holy Spirit. Prayer fortifies our spiritual life and is essential and central to our spiritual transformation. I believe that the prayers from Bahá'í scripture are especially potent because they are in conformity with the will of God. These are prayers that ensure the good fortunes of the planet. They give us peace, hope, joy, and new life. These prayers are very important to me because they me give direction and rejuvenate my spirit to keep me doing what I can to help this planet. The prayers alone are not enough to generate change—we need to meditate on them and then strive that our efforts reflect our prayers. I strive to live my life as a prayer.

"Prayer is essential for motivating and inspiring the direction of our lives. Our life is a series of moments, and how we respond to each of those moments can greatly affect our lives. There is a song that I wrote, which the choir sings often, 'God is good! All the time! All the time, God is good!' Prayer helps us remember that God is good all the time. When we remember that God is good and turn to Him, even when we have trials and unhappy times, God will see us through. When we remember that God is good all the time, it strengthens our faith and we are inclined to pray more, and at some point, we remain in a state of conversation with God all the time. There are two kinds of prayer. One is the kind when we might open up our prayer book, get on our knees, and very consciously supplicate a prayer, and the other is living the prayer—where we find ourselves turning to God at every step. But that's not always easy to do. There are times when things get so difficult that we might not feel like we want to pray."

Eric knows personally how a painful experience can deter one from praying. While on a summer concert tour in 2001, he and the choir were in Philadelphia, where they had presented a concert the previous evening. Their next stop on the tour was Boston, but that morning, when they went out to load their buses, something was amiss—they spotted a drum sitting on the parking lot outside of the equipment truck.

To the choir's horror, the truck had been broken into, and more than $30,000 worth of equipment and five years' worth of master tapes, filled with original songs composed and arranged by Eric, were missing. The choir, which was on a mission to promote the message of the oneness of humankind, had been robbed. Eric was devastated. Not only was every bit of equipment needed for the rest of the tour stolen, but also, since music was Eric's sole means of livelihood, the equipment and instruments were the tools of his trade. It had taken Eric several years of dedicated work to accumulate the equipment and tapes, and now, as the result of a crime, those items were gone. And they were not insured. The choir reported the theft to the police, who could provide no assistance other than to take down the report and promise to try to find the thieves and stolen items.

Sadly, Eric had learned the day before the robbery that his beloved cousin, Tony, had passed away due to illness. She was the same age as Eric, and the two of them had always been extremely close. Her death was a painful shock for him, and it broke his heart to not be there for her funeral. This, combined with the theft of his equipment and musical instruments, was too much for him. Eric was hurting for the loss of his cousin. He was angry at the injustice of the robbery. He was torn and conflicted knowing that he was the leader of the choir and they relied on him to give them direction—not just in the music, but also in spirit. How could the choir continue the tour without equipment? A part of Eric knew that he should pray, but he lacked the desire and will to do so. He felt lost.

Eric's normal instinct under difficult situations was to retreat somewhere to pray, meditate, and regroup his emotions in solitude. But this time was different. He was in such a painful state that he felt paralyzed—as if all good feelings had been drawn out of him, and, worst of all, he lacked the inclination to pray. The members of the choir, who were suffering too, had collectively decided to push forward and continue the tour without the equipment. Eric had also agreed to carry on, but he remained inconsolable.

Seeing that Eric had fallen into an isolated and despondent condition, one particularly sensitive and compassionate member of the choir somehow managed to draw Eric out of his shell. The two of them conversed for a period of time in private, and suddenly the floodgates of Eric's soul burst open. Tears streamed down his face, and the release of the pain felt good. As soon as the pain began pouring out, his heart opened as well, and he turned to God with all his soul and prayed arduously. He said prayers from Bahá'í scripture and recited one of his very favorite Bahá'í verses: "God is sufficient unto me; He verily is the All-sufficing! In Him let the trusting trust."

More than a hundred and fifty years earlier, Bahá'u'lláh and his fellow prisoners had chanted that verse when they were confined in a notoriously wretched dungeon in Persia. Their crowded prison cell, which was four levels underground, was so dark, dank, and putrid that the dungeon was commonly known as the "Black Pit."

Eric was well familiar with the story, and it never failed to move him when he contemplated it. That day while on tour, as he recited the verse, he pondered on the immensity of Bahá'u'lláh's suffering and was able to acknowledge that his own personal plight in comparison was not nearly as devastating as it had first appeared to him. Through the prayers he became detached from the loss of his equipment and realized that they were material things that could be replaced. And he was not alone in his prayers. The entire choir was praying fervently. It became clear to all of them that what was most important about the choir and the tour was maintaining their spirit of unity—which had not been lost, but had in fact become stronger. The choir's collective prayers and steadfastness in faith had increased their unity, and their joyful enthusiasm for continuing the tour touched Eric to the core of his soul.

Reflecting on that difficult episode in his life, Eric says, "Our faith is shaken and tested during times of trials and tribulations, and sometimes when that happens we don't feel like praying. We just feel like giving up. That's how I initially felt. But that's when we need to take a leap of faith. Once I began to pray, my perspective on everything changed. I was reminded that there are always lessons to learn during times of crisis, providing opportunities for spiritual growth. And when you think about it, here we were a group of people traveling, working, and associating closely together from many different ethnic, religious, and cultural backgrounds—and we're calling ourselves a family. The realization dawned on us—how can we call ourselves a family and not expect to go through trials? This was a time for us to galvanize. The people on that tour demonstrated a spirit of selflessness—preferring the needs and wishes of others to those of their own selves—a spirit which has permeated and sustained the organization from the beginning.

"But it would have been impossible for us to cope with the ordeal and stay united without the prayers. What happened to us was a reminder that we can always look to God and know that as long as He is in our lives, that's all we need to get by. And through the collective prayers we remained united and supported each other as a family."

The choir did a lot more than pray, in fact. Soon after the robbery, they sent out e-mails and made telephone calls to family and friends back home. As soon as the American Bahá'í community got wind of what had happened, donations were sent from all over to help the choir. A good friend of Eric's rented the equipment and instruments the choir needed to complete the tour, and the tour turned out to be a huge success.

Eric says, "It was phenomenal the way Bahá'ís and other friends from all over the nation rallied around us—sending donations and letting us know that they were praying for us. It turned into a community effort, and so our trials not only brought the choir closer together, but they had a unifying effect on people all over the country."

During the tour, Eric felt further blessed when he had a dream about his cousin Tony. He had been unable to shake off his guilt and remorse for missing her funeral until he saw her in the dream riding in a brand new car and looking healthy and very happy. She conveyed to him in the dream that she was all right, that there was no need for him to worry about her, nor was there any need to be concerned about missing the funeral. Eric took this dream as a confirmation that he was where he was supposed to be, and he was able to move on with a more solaced heart.

"Everything positive happening at that time was a reaffirmation to me that life should be lived as a prayer," he says. "The way I see it there will always be struggles in our lives. But if we look at the world as a big classroom, then we are better able to see that those struggles help us to learn and grow spiritually. The prayer that I live and breathe everyday is to promote the message of unity. I don't believe that God desires a monolithic human race, but I do believe that He wants us to realize our oneness in a manner described in the Bahá'í writings as 'unity in diversity.' There are blessings in humanity's diversities, and I think the choir exemplifies that message. This is the prayer that I live—and I have come to accept that while even though there may be trials both big and small that I need to face on this path, as long as I turn to God and pray in both words and deeds, God will suffice and comfort my spirit, lighten my load, assist my endeavors, and help me be more detached from material hardships.

"There is a first line of a prayer that I like to say: 'Intone, O My servant, the verses of God that have been received by thee, as intoned by them who have drawn nigh unto Him, that the sweetness of thy melody may kindle thine own soul, and attract the hearts of all men.'[174] I love that line because it reminds me that our souls are transforming every time we pray. Every time we pray we are blessed."

It is pertinent to mention that the One Human Family Workshop Choir is the same gospel choir that has been mentioned in earlier chapters, so I can testify first hand that singing and touring in the choir has a transforming effect. There are no words to describe the joy and the ecstasy I have experienced in singing heavenly music with people of such glorious diversity. When we sing together we feel our hearts connect through the love of God. There is something truly extraordinary that happens to our souls and spirits when we blend beautiful, joyful music with prayer.

Prayer should not be offered exclusively through music, but it is significant to recognize that the divine art of music is a joyful and powerful means to express our love for God. Notwithstanding, all prayer, whether it is recited, chanted, or sung, enables us to know and love God and bask in the blessings of the Holy Spirit. And, as Bahá'í scripture indicates, the highest and most potent prayers are those offered in private to express our love and devotion to God.

Eric affirms, "The short obligatory prayer we say in private from the Bahá'í writings help us understand the purpose of prayer—as well as understanding the purpose for our very existence. The prayer says: 'I bear witness, O my God, that Thou hast created me to know Thee and to worship Thee. I testify, at this moment, to my powerlessness and to Thy might, to my poverty and to Thy wealth. There is none other God but Thee, the Help in Peril, the Self-Subsisting.'"[175]

"When I meditate on the words of this prayer it gives me the proper perspective of how important it is to turn our hearts and souls to God to be guided on a daily basis. I think, 'How do we know God?' 'What is our relationship with God?' So many answers are revealed in that one little prayer. When we say the prayer every day, the words gradually internalize, transforming our souls and enabling us to live, as it says in the Bahá'í writings, in a 'state of prayer.' The way I see it, while we are on earth our souls are attached to these physical bodies for the purpose of learning and growing spiritually. Through prayer we are guided on a purposeful journey."

"I am able to personally testify that the trials I have endured in my life have helped my spiritual growth. But it was through prayer and the blessings of the Holy Spirit that gave meaning and purpose to my tests and growth and happiness to my soul. More than ever I offer up my music as a prayer in praise to the Lord."

CHAPTER 16

The Purpose and Practice of Meditation

In 1978, before I began investigating the Bahá'í Faith, I experienced a rather interesting epiphany while on a Transcendental Meditation retreat at an old and rustic Catholic monastery in the mountains of western Maryland. It was late summer, and the weather was lovely—sunny, not too hot, and not too cool. On the last morning of the retreat, I awakened at early dawn, feeling unusually relaxed and healthy and in great spirits. After being there for three days of meditation and learning some new yoga postures, I felt an urge to take a brisk run outdoors before eating breakfast. No one else on the retreat seemed to be up yet, so I quietly put on my running shoes and tiptoed through the hall and out the heavy doors, making certain they closed with as little sound as possible.

Jogging around the courtyard of the monastery, which stood high and remote on the top of a hill, afforded me a breathtaking view of the surrounding mountains. I was in awe, struck with an enormous appreciation of God's creation of nature. I found something to sit on, closed my eyes, and began to meditate on a personal mantra (an incantation in Hinduism or Buddhism that is repeated in certain forms of meditation) that had been given to me by a Transcendental Meditation instructor the previous year. Falling into a deep state of meditation, my

171

breathing slowed, and for a while it was as if I had entered a valley of sweet nothingness. I felt as if I had not a care in the world. And then I began to think about God, and my love was so intense that I thought my heart would explode from sheer joy. I thought about the people in my life and all the people in the world, and I began to think of the animals and all living creatures, and the beauty of the earth. I thought about the sun and the moon and the stars and the planets.

I was overcome with a feeling of profound love for everything and everyone—and the sense of oneness that gripped my soul in connection with God and all of His creation filled my veins with a joy of such intensity that my spirit soared in utter delight. My eyes were closed, but tears seeped through and ran down my cheek. I wanted this feeling to last. I loved this sense of oneness and yearned to hold onto it and bask in the joy of it every day of my life. I silently prayed to God with praise and gratitude in my heart and asked Him to help me hold onto this glorious feeling of oneness.

During that period of my life, I had become fascinated with Eastern religions, particularly Hinduism and Buddhism, both of which prescribe the practice of daily meditation as a means of communing with God and of connecting with our spirituality by delving into a state of silent, contemplative prayer and reflection. These religions teach that we may attain a sense of peace, serenity, and true happiness through meditation by inwardly renouncing all attachment to material things and by desiring only what is good for the soul—the nearness of God and the acquisition of spiritual attributes.

The mantra that I had been given by the instructor was a meaningless two-syllable sound, which I would repeat in slow, even rhythm as I concentrated. The soothing rhythm of the mantra often reminded me of the calming lull of the ocean waves hitting the shore, and after a few minutes of meditation my breathing would slow to match the beat of the mantra. As my body relaxed, different thoughts entered my mind, none of which I resisted or felt particularly attached to. Often, in the beginning of my meditations, I would think about practical things such as what I needed to buy at the grocery store. And then another thought would pop into my mind—perhaps something that had happened in my childhood or an occurrence from earlier that day.

A telephone would ring, but I had learned not to resist the sounds around me, which enabled me to be detached from them. Through this process the sounds did not disturb my tranquillity. This particular form of meditation was helpful for me because I had always been somewhat restless and impatient. Through meditation I had learned to relax and slow down a bit. I had also observed that by entering into this deep state of relaxation, my inner thoughts and reason appeared clearer and more focused.

During meditation I would not concentrate on any particular subject. Thoughts would simply come and go. Through this process I found myself taking account of my deeds, which at times was painful but was nonetheless enlightening. At some point, my thoughts would turn to God, and then I would enter a state of bliss and a deeper level of silent discourse between my inner and outer consciousness. I had always enjoyed my meditations, but my experience on top of the hill at the old Catholic monastery was a turning point.

Very shortly after the retreat, I happened to meet two Bahá'ís, a married couple, who gave me some Bahá'í books to read. I was intrigued to discover that the fundamental teachings of the Bahá'í Faith were the recognition of one God, the oneness of humanity, and the oneness of religion. I felt this information was an affirmation of my experience at the monastery. I had already spent several years investigating many of the world's major religions and had observed several common threads that linked them. The laws and customs of the various religions were different, but the spiritual messages were the same, a truth that I discovered was also affirmed in Bahá'í scripture and in the talks and writings of 'Abdu'l-Bahá:

> Bahá'u'lláh has revoiced and reestablished the quintessence of the teachings of all the Prophets, setting aside the accessories and purifying religion from human interpretation. He has written a book entitled the Hidden Words. The preface announces that it contains the essences of the words of the Prophets of the past, clothed in the garment of brevity, for the teaching and spiritual guidance of the people of the world. Read it that you may understand the true foundations of religion and reflect upon the inspiration of the Messengers of God. It is light upon light.[176]

Abdu'l-Bahá further explains,

> let us try with heart and soul that unity may dwell in the world,
> that all the peoples may become one people, and that the whole
> surface of the earth may be like one country—for the Sun of Truth
> shines on all alike. . . . All the Prophets of God came for love of this
> one great aim.
>
> Look how Abraham strove to bring faith and love among the
> people; how Moses tried to unite the people by sound laws;
> how . . . Christ suffered unto death to bring the light of love and
> truth into a darkened world; how Muhammad sought to bring unity
> and peace between the various uncivilized tribes among whom he
> dwelt. And last of all, Bahá'u'lláh has suffered forty years for the
> same cause—the noble purpose of spreading love among the
> children of men—and for the peace and unity of the world the
> Báb gave up his life.[177]

As a result of my investigation of various world religions, I was intrigued
to discover the oneness of the spiritual truths that linked the sacred
scriptures. But I was also attracted to the progressive nature and different
aspects of the religions. I was fascinated with the mysticism of the Eastern
religions, the wisdom of Judaism, the spirituality of Christianity, and
the devotion of Islam. The more I studied Bahá'í scripture, the more I
was able to recognize all those components in its teachings and much
more. Nothing was missing.

I found the writings of Bahá'u'lláh especially moving, particularly the
prayers and a book titled the Hidden Words. For me it was peaceful as
well as enlightening to sit quietly and meditate on various passages of the
Hidden Words, my favorite verse being "Love Me, that I may love thee.
If thou lovest Me not, My love can in no wise reach thee. Know this, O
servant."[178]

I remember studying many of Bahá'u'lláh's writings back then and
not understanding most of what I was reading. Only after I took the
time to sit down and quietly ponder and reflect on the verses would I
discover, to my delight, new levels of insight and understanding. I was

aware, however, that what attracted me to the Bahá'í Faith—far more than my intellectual understanding of the scripture, which at that time was very limited—had more to do with the way the readings and meditations affected my spirit.

During that period I experienced a plethora of emotions—elation, intrigue, fascination, confusion, revelation, stimulation, excitement, and a curious awakening of my spiritual reality. One thing was certain: I was deeply attracted to teachings of Bahá'u'lláh, and the more I investigated Bahá'í scripture, the more my attraction grew.

In the course of my investigation I learned that Bahá'u'lláh had prescribed the daily practice of both prayer and meditation as tools for spiritual development: "Meditate profoundly, that the secret of things unseen may be revealed unto you, that you may inhale the sweetness of a spiritual and imperishable fragrance, and that you may acknowledge the truth . . . so that light may be distinguished from darkness, truth from falsehood, right from wrong, guidance from error, happiness from misery, and roses from thorns."[179]

The Bahá'í teachings on meditation, I discovered, were compatible with the spiritual teachings of the Eastern religions. For instance, the Bhagavad-Gita extols the importance of good deeds, attaining virtues, detachment from material things, and trust in God: "On heavenly meditation . . . want not! ask not! find full reward of doing right in right! Let right deeds be Thy motive, not the fruit which comes from them. And live in action! Labour! Make thine acts Thy piety, casting all self aside."[180] In another verse: "When a man surrenders all desires that come from the heart and by the grace of God finds the joy of God, then his soul has indeed found peace."[181]

The Buddhist scripture teaches that meditation "removes fears, and gives confidence . . . removes greed, hate and delusion; it slays pride, breaks up preoccupation . . . generates gladness . . . and brings exuberant joy, causes delight."[182] Buddhist scripture also stresses meditation as a means to achieve detachment from the material world: "[I]n the same way that rain breaks into a house with a bad roof, desire breaks into the mind that has not been practising meditation . . . While in the same way that rain cannot break into a well-roofed house, desire cannot break into

a mind that has been practising meditation well."[183] One of the fundamental tenets of Buddhist teaching is meditation on acquiring a virtuous
soul, "To live righteously, to give help to kindred, to follow a peaceful
calling—This is the greatest blessing."[184]

I had discovered that many other religions also prescribe the practice of
meditation, as in the Hebrew scripture of the Old Testament: "Blessed is
the man that walketh not in the counsel of the ungodly, nor standeth in the
way of sinners, nor sitteth in the seat of the scornful. . . . But his delight is in
the law of the Lord; and in his law doth he meditate day and night."[185]

Bahá'u'lláh urged His followers to meditate every day, however, he
specified no particular method for meditation. He prescribed no particular
form—such as sitting cross-legged in the lotus position, chanting a
mantra, or using special breathing techniques. Again, as in prayer, each
individual is free to choose his or her own form of meditation.

As for myself, after becoming a Bahá'í in the summer of 1979, I began to
explore various methods of meditation, and while there is no single
technique that I now practice regularly, daily meditation remains a very
important part of my life. I am certain that meditation played a significant
role in opening my heart and enabling me to be receptive to the Bahá'í
teachings.

How do we meditate?

In its simplest definition one may say that meditation is a silent exercise
of contemplation and reflection on spiritual or philosophical subjects.
From the Bahá'í perspective, meditation is a silent discourse of one's inner
senses and "is the key for opening the doors of mysteries."[186] Meditation
is often described as a silent prayer because it is a means to commune
with the Holy Spirit. It is also a time used for personal reflection and
taking account of one's deeds, actions, and purpose. Bahá'í teachings tell
us, "There is a sign (from God) in every phenomenon: the sign of the
intellect is contemplation and the sign of contemplation is silence, because
it is impossible for a man to do two things at one time—he cannot both
speak and meditate."[187]

Meditation enables us to comprehend spiritual realities: "It is an axiomatic fact that while you meditate you are speaking with your own spirit. In that state of mind you put certain questions to your spirit and the spirit answers: the light breaks forth and the reality is revealed."[188]

Through this faculty of meditation, as the cognitive powers become more aware of the spirit, the soul becomes more receptive to the breath of the Holy Spirit and more conscious of the reality of eternal life. The purpose and benefits of meditation are described in the following passages from Bahá'í writings:

> The spirit of man is itself informed and strengthened during meditation; through it affairs of which man knew nothing are unfolded before his view. Through it he receives Divine inspiration, through it he receives heavenly food.
>
> Meditation is the key for opening the doors of mysteries. In that state man abstracts himself: in that state man withdraws himself from all outside objects; in that subjective mood he is immersed in the ocean of spiritual life and can unfold the secrets of things-in-themselves. To illustrate this, think of man as endowed with two kinds of sight; when the power of insight is being used the outward power of vision does not see.
>
> This faculty of meditation frees man from the animal nature, discerns the reality of things, puts man in touch with God.
>
> This faculty brings forth from the invisible plane the sciences and arts. Through the meditative faculty inventions are made possible, colossal undertakings are carried out; through it governments can run smoothly. Through this faculty man enters into the very Kingdom of God.
>
> Nevertheless some thoughts are useless to man; they are like waves moving in the sea without result. But if the faculty of meditation is bathed in the inner light and characterized with divine attributes, the results will be confirmed.[189]

On what do we meditate?

Bahá'í scripture attests, "Meditate on that which We have, through the power of truth, revealed unto thee, and be thou of them that comprehend its meaning. . . . The purpose of God in creating man hath been, and will ever be, to enable him to know his Creator and to attain His Presence."[190]

Bahá'í scripture continually reminds us that the purpose of our creation is for us to know and love God and to attain spiritual attributes; therefore, the things we meditate on should help us fulfill that purpose. The meditative faculty, which is of the spirit, is like a mirror. If our thoughts are of God, our spirit will reflect the love and glory of God. The nature and quality of our meditation reflects the direction of our thoughts. When we turn our thoughts towards God and heavenly subjects, the bestowal of the Holy Spirit is given, and our meditation reflects that bestowal, opening our hearts to be more receptive to divine blessings:

> Therefore if the spirit of man is contemplating earthly subjects he will be informed of these.
>
> But if you turn the mirror of your spirits heavenwards, the heavenly constellations and the rays of the Sun of Reality will be reflected in your hearts, and the virtues of the Kingdom will be obtained.
>
> Therefore let us keep this faculty rightly directed turning it to the heavenly Sun and not to earthly objects—so that we may discover the secrets of the Kingdom, and comprehend the allegories of the Bible and the mysteries of the spirit.[191]

Bahá'í scripture encourages us to meditate on the things that will immerse us in the celestial love and sweet mysteries of the knowledge of God and stresses the importance of spending time each day in meditation. Specifically, Bahá'u'lláh stressed the importance of reflecting at the end of each day on our deeds and their worth: "Bring thyself to account each day ere thou art summoned to a reckoning; for death, unheralded, shall come upon thee and thou shalt be called to give account for thy deeds."[192]

Expanding our inner sight through meditation

There is an old saying that asks, "If a tree falls in the forest with no one around to hear it, does it still make a sound?" We know for a fact that the failure to comprehend something is not necessarily proof of its non-existence. A rock has no knowledge of the existence of humanity, but humanity comprehends the rock. A child in the womb has no knowledge of the world outside, but nevertheless, the mother comprehends the child's existence. "In the human world, if we do not understand the divine world, is that a proof that the world of God does not exist?" 'Abdu'l-Bahá asks. "When we view the universe we see it as endless space, for we cannot restrict the universe to the lower kingdoms and to man who is here for a few days only, then vanishes."[193]

Meditation enlarges our inner sight, enabling us to perceive and reflect upon the vastness of the universe and the miracle of creation. It allows us to ponder the infinite worlds and workings of God:

> This physical universe is infinite, and if material existence is endless, how much more so are the worlds of God! When we think of the visible worlds as infinite, how can we think that the worlds of God are limited? There is no beginning and no end to the material or spiritual worlds. Man passes through different phases and when in a lower consciousness he cannot comprehend the consciousness above. When we were in the state of the unborn child we had no knowledge of the world of man. If the vegetable kingdom could speak it would cry out, 'Where is the world of man?' We cry out, 'Where is the kingdom of the spirit?'[194]

Through meditation, when our thoughts are centered on God and heavenly subjects, we are as spiritual travelers, journeying through the universe of existence and becoming acquainted with new and wonderful significances. Through meditation our ability to comprehend inner and outer realities is intensified, our knowledge and powers of insight are increased, and our clarity of thought is sharpened. Our capacity and energy levels are enhanced. Meditation has also been known to improve health because it is an effective method of reducing stress. And when we are calmer and more focused, we make better decisions. Of course, the level of success in our meditations, like our prayers, is in accordance with the measure of our effort and sincerity.

Through daily prayer and meditation, we learn to spiritualize our lives and all of our endeavors so that our entire lives may be lived in a state of prayer.

CHAPTER 17

Can Prayer and Meditation Help Us Make Better Decisions?

People often dread having to make certain decisions because they are aware that the wrong decision can lead to disappointment and unhappiness, whereas the right decision can greatly transform a life and generate happiness, success, and prosperity. It is fascinating how certain decisions can result in a life-altering impact on a person's well being.

When I was growing up I knew a woman who had diabetes. She was told by her doctor not to eat sweets, and yet I would often see her eat ice cream sundaes, chocolates, and candy. Her family would get quite upset with her and warn her that she should not be so careless with her diet. She would respond, "I don't want to think about it. I just want to enjoy myself."

Another relative in her family also had diabetes, but this woman chose to keep in shape, eat healthy foods, and exercise. By the time the woman who consumed sweets was in her early forties, she had completely lost her eyesight, and she died before reaching fifty. The choice to eat the sweets was hers alone, but it was a decision that caused her much physical suffering, and in the end, shortened her life. But the other woman, who made choices in her life to be fit, is still vibrant, and active, and is amazingly youthful for a woman in her eighties.

Let's face it—there are times when it is much easier to just not confront certain issues. But when we do not take responsibility for the decisions in our lives, we indubitably suffer as a result. Making good decisions is a challenge, but identifying and weighing the pros and cons carefully, thinking them through and basing the decision on pure and selfless motives are signs of spiritual growth, and the rewards are many.

There is guidance offered in the Bahá'í teachings that has proven extremely beneficial to Bahá'ís worldwide in their decision-making efforts, which stresses foremost the need of more prayers and meditation. Individuals may also wish to consult with one or more persons in order to arrive at a collective decision.

Inspired by this guidance, the first step of a decision-making process that has proven through the years to be very successful for my own family begins with my husband and I meeting together in a quiet setting, and possibly joined by other family members and friends, and saying a round of prayers. When people gather together and pray, "Their eyes are opened, their hearts in tune with Thy love, and their ears in communion with Thy hidden mysteries."[195] Following the prayers, we do our best to identify the facts that pertain to the issue at hand; write out a pros and cons list; consult about our objectives and motives; and then again say a round of prayers.

The next part of the process is extremely important. Following prayers, my husband and I, and any others who may happen to be part of our decision-making group, then sit and quietly meditate. The effect is quite unifying and powerful. We may sit there five, ten, or twenty minutes—no-one ever really keeps track of the time. Following our meditations, we share our reflections and through the process of consultation we find unity and make our decision. Bahá'í scripture assures us that through the power of divine unity "the truth will be revealed and the wrong made right."[196]

Another vital aspect of the consultation process is to carry out the decision once it has been made. The Bahá'í teachings stress the value of action: "Prayer and meditation are very important factors in deepening the spiritual life of the individual, but with them must go also action and example, as these are the tangible result of the former. Both are essential."[197]

We use this process to make important decisions, whether it concerns our careers, our children, our finances, or whether or not to buy a new car. Not only has this process helped us tremendously in making decisions, but also it has greatly benefited and strengthened the unity of our marriage and family.

While there is certain potency in prayer that endows us with guidance and assistance, it is through meditation that our inner sight is clearer and more cognitive of those blessings. Guidance and assistance might be right in front of us, but if we are not spiritually cognizant, we are less receptive to them. Meditation helps us to internalize our prayer and, through contemplation, helps us to manifest prayer into action.

Meditation provides us with practical benefits as well as spiritual ones. Decisions are so incredibly important because they affect all aspects of our lives. Meditation helps us to make better decisions because it enables our body and soul to share in a debriefing of information. Meditation brings us in tune with our spirit and divine realities and creates a sense of unity, balance and peace within us. It gives us clarity of thought and enables us to make decisions and choices in our lives that benefit us both physically and spiritually.

What is prayerful consultation?

The art of prayerful consultation is an essential component in the decision-making process. It is a distinctive method of nonadversarial decision making that is prescribed in the Bahá'í writings, and Bahá'ís have found this process to be useful in virtually any area where group decision making and cooperation is required. 'Abdu'l-Bahá explains: "[C]onsultation is of vital importance, but that its purpose and intent are to meet in a spiritual conference, which is not the mere voicing of personal view."[198]

Prayer in words alone does not make a "spiritual conference." Rather, when we recognize the spiritual reality of all humanity, it stands to reason that ties with our fellow human beings will be more unified and productive when our communications exemplify spiritual traits. This includes not only our speech, but also our actions, such as demonstrating courtesy, mutual respect, equity, humility, and kindness. Bahá'í scripture affirms, "[T]he spiritual message is fruitful and effective. . . . without it communication is useless."[199]

The Bahá'í writings further explain that the objective of consultation should be to search for truth, which requires the participants to come into the consultation with an open mind and a receptiveness to learn: "[C]onsultation must have for its object the investigation of truth. He who expresses an opinion should not voice it as correct and right but set it forth as a contribution to the consensus of opinion, for the light of reality becomes apparent when two opinions coincide."[200]

While each person has the right to fully express his or her views, it is counterproductive to insist upon one's opinions:

> Man should weigh his opinions with the utmost serenity, calmness and composure. Before expressing his own views he should carefully consider the views already advanced by others. If he finds that a previously expressed opinion is more true and worthy, he should accept it immediately and not willfully hold to an opinion of his own. By this excellent method he endeavors to arrive at unity and truth.[201]

This does not imply that in consultation an individual should restrain from expressing an opposing opinion. On the contrary, "The shining spark of truth cometh forth only after the clash of differing opinions."[202]

When prayer is used to begin the discourse, and the behaviors and goals of the individuals involved are based on spiritual motives, free of prejudice and biasness, conflicts are often quite wonderfully resolved, leading to mutual understanding and agreement.

When some measure of meditation is also incorporated, the hearts are united, the thoughts are clearer, and the spiritual channel is purer, enabling the souls to draw assistance from the Holy Spirit, resulting in productive and beneficial decisions. Of course, not everyone is amenable to incorporating prayer and meditation in consultation, such as in the workplace, but in those cases, we ourselves can take the initiative to pray and meditate privately before entering the meeting.

Several years ago I was having a very difficult time getting along with a coworker. This woman seemed to dislike me intensely, and I wracked my brain in trying to understand what I had done to offend her. Both serving on the same task force, we were expected to collaborate closely in developing a proposal for a very important project. But every time we met, I found her to be curt, distant, and unfriendly, if not outright hostile. It seemed that we were completely incompatible and the situation, which I found extremely stressful and tense, was interfering with our productivity. It was not a pleasant environment.

And so I prayed and meditated about it. I analyzed the situation. Perhaps I had said or done something to offend her without knowing it. Or perhaps we just had a personality clash. I continued to pray and meditate. In my meditation, I made the decision to phone her and ask if we could meet outside of work and talk. When I called her, she sounded very surprised. "Why?" she asked. I explained that because we were working on such an important project together, perhaps it might be beneficial for us to meet outside of the work setting, and just talk. She sounded confused but agreed to meet with me. We agreed to meet at her place.

Not knowing how she would feel about prayers, I made sure to pray and meditate in my home before going to see her. For months I had sensed a negative tension building between us, and for me, saying the prayers before the meeting was very important. I prayed for unity and I asked God to please erase all the feelings of animosity that were in my heart so that I would enter the meeting without prejudice.

After my arrival, I sat down and asked my coworker if she would be agreeable to say some prayers with me before we began our talk. I was pleasantly taken aback when she not only agreed to pray with me, but also seemed very happy to do so. We both said some prayers, followed by a brief and silent, meditative interlude. I then immediately asked her if I had said or done something to offend her—because if I did, I wanted her to know that I was sorry and that it was never my intent to offend. She looked at me as if I had just spoken in a different language. "What are you talking about?" she asked. "You have done nothing to offend me. Why do you think you did?"

"Well," I said, "I have the feeling that you dislike me. You always seem so annoyed and impatient with me. To be frank, I feel that our incapability is interfering with our productivity at work. Perhaps we just have a personality clash. I thought that if we meet today and consult about it, we could work it out."

My coworker sat in her chair, very still. Clearly, genuinely surprised by my comments, she asked, "Why do you feel this way? What is that I have done to make you feel that I dislike you?"

I felt both boosted and protected by the spiritual atmosphere that had been created by our prayers, and decided to be forthright. "Well, sometimes I feel as if you are about to bite my head off. You never smile and, I truly don't want to hurt your feelings when I say this, but you always seem so curt and stoic around me. You never even say 'hello' to me when I enter your office. I get the sense that you are very unhappy to work with me."

My coworker burst into tears. I sat there motionless as she left to get some tissues. I thought to myself, "Uh oh. Did I go too far in my honesty?"

She returned to the room holding a tissue box, and said, "I am so sorry! Please forgive me! I had no idea that I was treating you rudely. It's not you. Honestly, it has nothing to do with you! My husband left me for another woman several months ago and it broke my heart. On top of that, my father died. I have been a mess. I am so glad that you came today so that we could talk. I've been so unhappy and alone! I've been walking around in a fog, just trying to get from one day to the next."

Ah, the bliss that comes from understanding. One moment I was praying to God to not feel animosity for this woman, and now, all I wanted to do was to console her. Instantly, my heart melted and I felt nothing but compassion for her. Instinctively I offered her comfort and friendship. Because of the spiritual environment that had been created through our prayers and meditation, a safe place had been established where we could speak candidly and openly. Together we found truth and understanding and our hearts were unified.

As a result of our consultation that day, we ended up being the best of friends. We became the best of coworkers too. Our project was such a success that we continued to work on more projects together. We continued to pray and meditate together at the start of our meetings, even at work, and we felt that we derived tremendous assistance.

We now live in different states and it has been some years since I have seen my dear friend. But I can honestly say that I have never had a coworker whom I enjoyed working with more. Our story is a testimony of the power of prayer, meditation and spiritual consultation.

Personally, in my own life, I have found it extremely helpful and unifying before beginning a consultation to recite and meditate upon the words of the following prayer for unity:

O my God! O my God! Unite the hearts of Thy servants, and reveal to them Thy great purpose. May they follow Thy commandments and abide in Thy law. Help them, O God, in their endeavor, and grant them strength to serve Thee. O God! Leave them not to themselves, but guide their steps by the light of Thy knowledge, and cheer their hearts by Thy love. Verily, Thou art their Helper and their Lord.[203]

The First to Arise

Kevin Locke, of the Hunkpapa Band of Lakota Sioux (Sitting Bull's people), was raised and lived most of his life on the Standing Rock Reservation, a territory bordering the eastern side of the Dakotas, west of the Missouri River. As a descendent of the Native American Indians of the northern plains, Kevin dwelled on the land of his ancestors and was inspired by the teachings of his family and community to respect the ancient customs of his culture. His Lakota name, Tokeya Inajin, "The First to Arise," was given to him by his maternal great-aunt.

These indigenous people, commonly known to the outside world as the Sioux Nation, are a confederacy known historically as the Oceti Sakowin ("the Seven Council fires"), which existed on the northern plains. Today the people of this confederacy, comprised of seven bands (or tribes) prefer to identify themselves as the Dakota and Lakota, for these are the names that most accurately represent the groups' different dialects, regions, beliefs, economy, and genealogy. Both "Dakota" and "Lakota" can be interpreted to mean "Spiritual Unity" or "People Who are Unified in Spiritual Peace" in a dialect of the language shared between the two peoples.

The Lakota Nation was also known as the People of the Prairie and the Pte Oyate ("Buffalo People"). A profoundly spiritual people, the Lakota were known and recognized as the caretakers and protectors of the Black Hills in Southwest Dakota. The traditional belief, particularly among the Lakota, is that the Black Hills region has a strong religious significance and is the birthplace of their nation.

Their traditions speak of a holy prophet, known as Ptehincala Ska Win or, in English, "White Buffalo Calf Woman," who made her presence known in the southern Black Hills. It is said that White Buffalo Calf Woman revealed the message of Wankan Tanka ("God"), and enlightened the people regarding their spiritual reality. It is told through the oral traditions that White Buffalo Calf Woman brought divine teachings, prayers, and values to the people, giving them religion and guiding them to become a spiritual, powerful, and more advanced, independent nation. Even today, despite the many challenges the people have faced in more than a century to preserve their heritage, the prayers, stories, and teachings of White Buffalo Calf Woman continue to be honored by many of the indigenous people of the northern plains.

The entire Black Hills region is known to the Lakota as "the heart of everything that is." It is regarded as sacred ground for praying, fasting, and meditating for spiritual enlightenment, guidance, and healing. This, the people believe, is the area in which White Buffalo Calf Woman came to reveal the message of God and establish their nation. Today, many of the Lakota still participate in a spiritual ceremony called the Ghost Dance on the Standing Rock Reservation. This dance is a prayer for the return of the messenger of God, as promised many centuries ago by White Buffalo Calf Woman.

Kevin grew up on the Standing Rock Reservation, exposed to this culture. As a boy he did not yet fully appreciate its spiritual significance, though he understood on some level that the Lakota maintained a direct link to the past by passing on from generation to generation the oral tradition of prayers, beliefs, and anecdotes of local activities of the tribe. He had often seen these traditions practiced at various gatherings, such as in *wacipis* ("powwows"), where prayers were expressed through sacred music, ceremonial dance, and storytelling. The focal point of the powwow was to pray and to promote unity. In essence, it was a devotional gathering that included both a spiritual and a social component.

Kevin was strongly influenced by the customs and values of his heritage, but he had no formal training in religion as a child, and it struck him when he was a teenager that there was a spiritual void in his life. His soul hungered for an understanding of the purpose of his being, and he sensed that there was greater meaning to life than the physical realities existing before him in his everyday world. He yearned for spiritual truth.

He began asking questions of his family and of the community elders, who explained to him that it was the Lakota way to seek a spiritual path by going out alone in the wilderness to fast and pray. In accord with the sacred tradition of the indigenous people of the northern plains, there had been a time in the past when it was common practice for the spiritual leaders to train children in the spiritual customs. After reaching puberty, a boy would be sent out to the wilderness in complete solitude without food and water for four days and four nights. This sacred rite, known as a vision quest, was part of a number of coming-of-age ceremonies that not only stressed the value of detachment from the physical world, but also encouraged the youth to understand the importance of prayer and individual search for spiritual truth and guidance.

While this experience was a rite of passage and a sign of spiritual maturity for the youth, journeying out to the wilderness alone to fast and pray was an activity intrinsic to the Lakota religion, and it was practiced by people of all ages. It was no longer commonly practiced among the young adolescents on the reservation, but Kevin, searching for spiritual truth and understanding, decided to try following this path. How to do so, however, was unclear to him, so he turned to an elder in the tribe, Charles Kills Enemy, for answers. Because the sense of kinship among the Lakota people is often expressed through familial terms, Kevin called him "Uncle Charles," although they were not blood relations.

Kevin approached Uncle Charles and told him that he was on a quest for spiritual understanding and hoped to find it by fasting in the wilderness. He asked how to go about this. The man studied the teenager, looked him in the eye, and asked, "Why do you want to do this?"

Kevin responded, "Because I want to learn to pray and find a spiritual path." Uncle Charles continued with his queries, "What are you going to do when you get there? How are going to pray? What are you going to pray for?"

Kevin answered, "I will pray for my family."

This answer did not fully appease Uncle Charles, who said, "We sing our prayers. I will not help you unless you know what words to pray and learn how to sing them." And so, for the next year, in following Uncle Charles's directions, Kevin adhered to a strict discipline in preparation for his time of praying and fasting in the wilderness. He endeavored to memorize the words and sing the appropriate prayers for fasting in the Lakota language and tradition. He studied the customs and learned their spiritual meanings. Through the process, he began to gain a greater appreciation for his culture, particularly its sacred music. Through his training he also gained an understanding of the spiritual significance of fasting.

Kevin says, "The law of fasting is universal, and I think that it must be well pleasing to God. Fasting is not merely depriving oneself of food and water. It is a symbolic gesture of detachment from the physical world. The divine revealers of all the major religions have renewed the sacred law of fasting since time immemorial."

Kevin had learned that fasting for four days and four nights was significant as well because four is regarded by the Lakota as a sacred number, designating the four seasons, the four elements (earth, wind, fire and water), the four directions, and, among other things, the four colors of the human race.

Kevin additionally gained a new respect and appreciation for the Lakota language. He learned that the language was vital to his culture. He discovered that everything in the Lakota perspective has a sacred connotation, including the language, which is referred to as *wakan,* meaning "sacred" or "mystery." Like most Native American Indian languages, Lakota was not originally a written language and therefore it is taught by the elders that for one to speak it in its purest form, one must learn the language through the oral tradition.

During his training Kevin began to comprehend the immense power of language. He came to realize that language could be used to harm or to honor and bless. He learned that language could be used to injure peoples' feelings or to praise, encourage, and lift people's spirits. He learned that language is a powerful tool that can be used to educate and promote unity, or to destroy and cause dissension, and therefore the language must be used with respect—and not with heedless carelessness. Most importantly, he came to understand that language enables one to talk to God—to pray.

Reverence for language as a sacred tool reflected the mores of the Lakota people, as their every thought and action were hedged or bolstered by spiritual beliefs. The Lakota language is itself a language of prayer. From the traditional Lakota perspective, every word that is uttered should be reverent and thoughtful, as in a prayer. The people of the northern plains made no distinctions between the natural and the spiritual; they perceived that everyone and everything in the universe was created by God and therefore is sacred and entitled to respect. The Lakota believed that living in harmony with nature was a sacred duty. In adhering to the teachings of the White Buffalo Calf Woman, the Lakota people recognized their very existence as a gift from God and could see and appreciate the divine in all created life and things.

After one year of immersing himself in studying the prayers in the Lakota language and learning many of the traditions of his ancestors, Kevin believed himself ready to journey deep into the wilderness alone with nothing more than the clothes on his body and one blanket. He would stay there in complete isolation for four days and four nights out in the open Dakota plains to face the elements, hunger, thirst, snakes, and other potentially deadly creatures. There would be no water for washing, no weapons for protection, no shelter, and no amenities for comfort other than the one thin blanket.

Out alone in the hilly, barren plains, often under a mercilessly hot sun, several miles from civilization, Kevin sang and chanted the prayers that he had learned during his year of training. He supplicated to God in the Lakota tradition, often referring to Him as "Grandfather," and sang the words of the sacred songs, beseeching the Creator to help him find his spiritual path.

Kevin says, "Physically I suffered a lot. But when you are out there all alone without food and water for days, it's just you and God. Everything you say and do is between you and God, and you feel that you can talk to Him about anything."

For the next several years Kevin continued to pursue this endeavor of fasting and praying in the wilderness. He had learned to speak Lakota and practiced many of the customs of his culture, including mastering the Lakota flute and Hoop Dance. Notwithstanding, while he had become proficient in the observance of his ancestral traditions, a lack of spiritual fulfillment and dissatisfaction persisted within him. With all of his years of praying and fasting, his soul cried out for deeper understanding. He was desperate for answers and concluded that without knowing the purpose for existence there was nothing to justify his life on earth. He returned again to the wilderness to fast and pray.

The sun was relentless, with temperatures reaching 110 degrees. By the fourth day, Kevin was literally baking from the heat. Looking back at that time, he says, "This law of fasting came from a people who led a very strenuous lifestyle. This method of fasting—going out in the wilderness alone with no food and water for days at a time reflected their hard life. That last time that I went, I knew that it was a life-threatening situation because of the unusual heat. But I was so hungry for a purpose and meaning to my life, and I felt at that time that if I did not find what I was looking for, then life wasn't worth living. I was at the bottom of my spiritual well."

While Kevin's physical hunger and thirst matched his urgent need for spiritual sustenance, something wondrous happened. He explains, "When you fast in the wilderness you throw away all social conventions and tend to be more reliant on God. This time, however, with the temperature so high and having no water for days, and being in such a physically weakened state, I became more aware of the significance of my personal relationship with God. I realized that what was most important in my life was this relationship. I realized that without a strong relationship with God, my life meant nothing. I was still looking for something—a purpose and meaning for my life. But now my heart had opened—and I felt compelled to look beyond."

While his ancestral prayers were extremely meaningful to Kevin, he came to a realization that prayer from the heart offered in private communion with complete trust and reliance on God was what spiritually awakened his soul. He still yearned for deeper understanding, but he sensed that he was now closer on the path to finding answers by opening up his heart to God. Kevin had discovered the power of inner prayer, and he was enthralled in the love of the Holy Spirit.

Kevin said, "There was a Bahá'í family that had been living on the reservation, and although I attended a few gatherings at their home, I never really had much of an interest in learning about the Bahá'í Faith. However, after my recent experience in the wilderness, I felt compelled to look at this religion more seriously. I went to visit them, and they gave me a Bahá'í prayer book. The first prayer I opened to immediately caught my eye because it spoke of a 'highway,' a common metaphor found in many of the Lakota prayers."

O Lord, my God! Praise and thanksgiving be unto Thee for Thou hast guided me to the highway of the kingdom, suffered me to walk in this straight and far-stretching path, illumined my eye by beholding the splendors of Thy light, inclined my ear to the melodies of the birds of holiness from the kingdom of mysteries and attracted my heart with Thy love among the righteous.

O Lord! Confirm me with the Holy Spirit, so that I may call in Thy Name amongst the nations and give the glad tidings of the manifestation of Thy kingdom amongst mankind.

O Lord! I am weak, strengthen me with Thy power and potency. My tongue falters, suffer me to utter Thy commemoration and praise. I am lowly, honor me through admitting me into Thy kingdom. I am remote, cause me to approach the threshold of Thy mercifulness. O Lord! Make me a brilliant lamp, a shining star and a bless tree, adorned with fruit, its branches overshadowing all these regions. Verily, Thou art the Mighty, the Powerful and Unconstrained.[204]

Kevin said, "This prayer was the perfect answer for all my questions! This is what the Lakota people had been praying for—for generations! All the answers were in this single prayer. It captured the beautiful springtime and visions of spiritual transformation described in many of the Lakota prayers."

As Kevin continued to pursue his investigation of the Bahá'í Faith, he discovered many other common threads linking his ancestral spiritual beliefs with this young religion. He discovered numerous passages in Bahá'í scripture that affirm the importance of fasting: "Even though outwardly the Fast is difficult and toilsome, yet inwardly it is bounty and tranquility. Purification and training are conditioned and dependent only on such rigorous exercises as are in accord with the Book of God and sanctioned by Divine law. . . . Whatsoever God hath revealed is beloved of the soul."[205]

He observed that, similar to the teachings of the Lakota, passages in Bahá'í scripture testify to the power of speech as a tool that can be used for both harmful or noble purposes: "[R]efrain from idle talk. For the tongue is a smoldering fire, and excess of speech a deadly poison . . . inasmuch as backbiting quencheth the light of the heart, and extinguisheth the life of the soul."[206] And he observed that Bahá'í scripture emphasized the importance of prayer: "At the dawn of every day he should commune with God, and, with all his soul, persevere in the quest of his Beloved."[207]

Kevin was especially attracted to Bahá'u'lláh's teachings on the oneness of humanity:

> Know ye not why We created you all from the same dust? That no one should exalt himself over the other. Ponder at all times in your hearts how ye were created. Since We have created you all from one same substance it is incumbent on you to be even as one soul, to walk with the same feet, eat with the same mouth and dwell in the same land, that from your inmost being, by your deeds and actions, the signs of oneness and the essence of detachment may be made manifest.[208]

Kevin, who became a Bahá'í in his twenties, said, "I came to a realization of the truth of the Bahá'í Faith because of the prophetic elements implicit within Lakota spiritual traditions. As I read the writings of Bahá'u'lláh, I realized it was a message from God, a renewal of the eternal principles. It is significant to me that I found the Bahá'í Faith through fasting and praying on a spiritual journey of suffering and hardship. In the Lakota tradition, those are the means to find the true path of God. Also, it is meaningful to me to have become the first Bahá'í in my family because of my Lakota name, which is 'The first to Arise.'"

Kevin continued, "I believe that the relationship between God and humankind is and has been binding over all peoples, and that all peoples have been informed of its existence and parameters either through major prophets and messengers of God such as Krishna, Abraham, Moses, Zoroaster, Buddha, Jesus, Muhammad, the Báb, Bahá'u'lláh, or through other holy souls who established spiritual pathways within unique cultures worldwide, such as among my people, the Lakota."

It was important to Kevin that there was no demand or expectation for him to assimilate into a mainstream culture. On the contrary, he felt encouraged to freely express his individuality and to explore his heritage more deeply. He was delighted to see that Bahá'ís from all over the world, from widely diverse backgrounds, in recognition of the global dimensions of the human family, have been working for nearly a century towards the elimination of prejudices in their efforts to promote unity and peace among peoples of diverse populations.

Kevin was awakened to a new purpose and mission. He was inspired to share his culture with the world community in the cause to promote greater awareness of the oneness of the human race. In the years that followed, Kevin achieved his mission and traveled to countries all around the globe and became internationally renowned and beloved as an educator, folk artist, and popular recording artist.

For more than two decades, Kevin has delighted audiences worldwide by performing the intricate dances and ceremonies of the Lakota. He has become world famous for his exquisitely soulful music on the flute; and he has captivated, as well as educated, countless audiences with his ancestral tradition of storytelling and explanations of the spiritual metaphors of his presentations. Through these endeavors he has not only entertained and inspired audiences of all ages, but also has succeeded in dispelling myths and helped to cast away prejudices, promoting unity and opening hearts to new ideas and concepts.

Frequently people are surprised to learn that Kevin, who honors and perpetuates the traditions, values, and culture of the Lakota Nation, is a member of the Bahá'í Faith. But from his perspective, becoming a Bahá'í has reinforced his cultural identity. At the same time it reinforces his belief in the oneness of the human spirit. Although he normally makes no reference to the Bahá'í Faith in his presentations, his performances exemplify the teachings found in Bahá'í scripture as well as in the sacred texts of all the world religions.

Kevin and his wife, Danielle, who is of the Cree Nation from Saskatchewan, are grateful for many bounties, including their seven children and seven grandchildren. Extremely devoted to his family, Kevin manages to divide his time by spending as much quality time with them as possible while continuing to fulfill engagements by popular demand that require him to travel the world, singing the prayers, telling the stories, playing the flute, and performing the dances of the Lakota culture with respect, honor, and artistic expertise.

Even so, while he has a deep appreciation for the spiritual significance of his ancestral traditions, he learned several years ago while fasting in the wilderness, removed from all the physical trappings of religion and conventions of society, that what is most important in life is his personal relationship with God. Alone and fasting in the wilderness, he realized that prayer is the simple act of talking to God from the heart, which requires no ceremonies or special attire.

As a Lakota he had already understood in principle that life should be lived in a state of prayer. But he believes that he has learned through the prayers and teachings of Bahá'u'lláh how to strive to attain that state every day of his life.

CHAPTER 19

A Prayer for Keisha

Keisha went to live with her grandmother when she was eight years old, after her mother, a prostitute, died of a heroin overdose. Keisha had never met her father, and she grew up in a neighborhood of prostitutes, drug dealers, and addicts. This was the wretched environment to which Keisha had been exposed for the first eight years of her life.

Keisha's grandmother lived in a predominantly African-American residential area consisting of hardworking, churchgoing families whose children played in the nearby neighborhood park. It was unquestionably an improved environment for the little girl. Her grandmother loved her very much and dearly hoped to provide Keisha with a good home and a new and better life, but the child was so full of anger and resentment that the older woman found her incorrigible.

The child spat profanities at her grandmother and displayed her belligerence through frequent tantrums. She refused to interact with the children in her school and neighborhood, and although her teacher believed the little girl to be extremely intelligent, she reported with distress to the grandmother that the child was verbally hostile, ill behaved, and uncooperative. Even with counseling, the invisible wall that Keisha had built around herself was impenetrable.

Keisha's grandmother, a Bahá'í, sought assistance from the Bahá'ís in her community for help with her granddaughter. It was early summer,

and Keisha had turned nine years old. A Bahá'í family in the community
offered to take Keisha and her grandmother to the Green Acre Bahá'í
School in Eliot, Maine. The grandmother, an elderly woman, was not
physically up to the trip but agreed to let Keisha travel with the family to
stay at the school for one week.

Green Acre is located in a lovely area in southwestern Maine, not far
from Portsmouth, New Hampshire. The main facility at Green Acre is a
large, rustic inn perched on a hill and surrounded by plush tree-shaded
grounds overlooking a large river. Visitors from all over the world have
for many decades come to Green Acre to relax, vacation, and spiritually
reenergize while attending classes that present a wide spectrum of topics
relating to Bahá'í principles.

I met Keisha there while I was teaching the children's class for Keisha's
age group. The school offered a series of different sessions and courses
that rarely lasted more than seven days, so basically every week I was
greeted by new faces in my classroom. The week that Keisha was there
we had about twelve children in the class. It was a small class, but it was
ethnically and culturally diverse. Although most of my students were
from Bahá'í families from different parts of the U.S., including one from
Alaska, there were also two children from Canada, one from Argentina,
and one whose family came from Iran.

I am a strong believer in educating children through the arts, and,
with my background in performing arts, I enjoyed putting together plays
and musical activities with the children. I have seen tremendous successes
through the years in using the arts to help children learn and achieve an
array of skills, in addition to helping them learn and acquire spiritual
principles and values and raise their self-esteem and confidence. Also,
the children always had great fun, especially at the end of each session
when they performed before an audience.

And so, here it was, the first day of a new class. Following introductions
and prayers, many of which were recited or sung by the students, I
informed the students about the play they would be doing. Everyone's
eyes lit up with excitement—that is, everyone except Keisha. The pain
and anger in her eyes drew my attention; I sensed she was a troubled girl.

That first day, from the get-go, Keisha asserted her rebellious nature
and made it clear that she would present a challenge. She was unco-

operative, unfriendly, and ill-mannered. She used language that shocked the other students. She let it be known that she was not happy to be in the class, nor was she going to make any attempt to be friendly with anyone, even though it was evident that she was going out of her way to draw attention.

Knowing nothing about her background, I could nevertheless see that this child was in deep pain, but even so, it was unacceptable for her to disrupt the class and expose the students to hostile and other inappropriate behaviors. I asked one of the older students to watch the class as I took Keisha outside with me. When I was alone with her, we sat down on the grass, and I asked her why she was so unhappy. She made no reply.

I asked her if she ever prayed. She shook her head. I asked, "Never?" Defiantly she responded, "Never!"

I asked her if she would mind if I said a prayer for her. She stared at me curiously and asked, "Why do you want to pray for me?"

I responded, striving with all my heart to convey sincerity, "Because you are a precious child, and I know that God loves you very much. He loves all His children. Well, I love God very much, and knowing how much He loves you—that makes me want to love you too. So, I would like to say a prayer for you."

She shrugged as if it really didn't matter to her what I did, and said, nonchalantly, "Okay."

I recited one of my favorite prayers:

O Thou kind Lord! These lovely children are the handiwork of the fingers of Thy might and the wondrous signs of Thy greatness. O God! Protect these children, graciously assist them to be educated and enable them to render service to the world of humanity. O God! These children are pearls, cause them to be nurtured within the shell of Thy loving-kindness.
Thou art the Bountiful, the All-Loving.[209]

I looked at Keisha, curious to see a reaction. She sat there motionless and quiet. I looked into her eyes. The anger seemed to be dulled, but the pain was still there. There was also something new—a look of confusion and pensiveness. I asked her if she wanted to say a prayer. She shook her head and said nothing. I asked her if she wanted to come back to class. She agreed, and we walked into the classroom together.

I was delighted to see the children well behaved and busy. For the play, each child had chosen a country to represent, and now they were designing and coloring their flags. Everyone but Keisha had already decided what country to represent for the play. I turned to Keisha and asked her what country she would like to represent. She looked around the room, looked at the children, threw a crayon across the room, and ran out of the building. I did not see her again until later in the afternoon.

At lunchtime, the family who had brought her to Green Acre sought me out and filled me in about her background. When I heard about this little girl's past, my heart broke. I went off to be alone and turned to God and prayed. I asked God to please assist me in doing whatever it required as her teacher in this class to help this child. I knew that I could not help her alone. I put my trust in God and prayed to become as a hollow reed so that the Holy Spirit might work through me. With all my heart I prayed for guidance, patience, and insight. I prayed for all of the students in my class.

Overall, it truly was a wonderful, fun class. The other children were delightful—very smart and eager to carry out their assigned tasks. In the late afternoon on that first day, hours after Keisha had stormed out of the classroom, she returned to her seat carrying a smug and defiant attitude. When I asked her if she had decided what country she wanted to represent, she surprised me. She answered, "China." Her response was so readily offered that it was apparent she had given it some thought. I was encouraged. She also seemed to take an interest in art because she spent the rest of the afternoon quietly and productively, carefully crafting her flag. Still, she maintained an unfriendly and distant attitude to the other students.

The next few days Keisha had her ups and downs. She was very smart and learned her lines for the play quickly. But every morning when the children recited and sang a round of prayers, she never participated, but instead sat quietly. Following prayers, though, her outbursts were unpredictable, particularly when I began talking to the class about the spiritual principles and message in the play and then encouraging them to consult about it. Whenever her behaviors became unacceptable, I would give the other children a task to work on and then take Keisha outside for ten or twenty minutes to spend time alone with her.

She seemed to enjoy it when it was just the two of us. It was during those brief times we spent outside together that she began to ask me questions about the Bahá'í Faith. She never seemed interested in hearing about God or faith in the classroom, but when it was just the two of us, she appeared more attentive. It was apparent that she enjoyed it when I said prayers for her. This became a regular routine at least twice a day. Each time after I said a prayer, I would invite her to do the same. She always refused and, while she made a great effort to show disinterest, her eyes told a different story. They were still wracked with pain, but they were inquisitive, intelligent eyes, and the spark of curiosity glimmered through. My affection for the child grew steadily, and my heart, while feeling much love for her, ached.

I developed an especially warm affection for all the children in my class, and I was exceedingly grateful that the other students were well-behaved, bright, enthusiastic, loving, and eager to please. They quickly bonded with each other and became close friends. In the beginning of the class they tried to befriend Keisha and showed her kindness. However, children, like adults, have their limitations, and they began to show their annoyance with her conduct.

The end of the week arrived, and my class prepared to perform their play for the adults and other children and youth at the school in midafternoon. The plan was for us to have a dress rehearsal right after lunch. It was a relief to me that Keisha knew her lines and that her flag was completed, but she was the only student who had not yet made a costume, which concerned me. I had brought with me a large box filled with old clothes, fake jewelry, hats, and other paraphernalia, which worked nicely as costumes for the children. In addition, the school had lent us an assorted collection of clothing that could also be used, so the children had plenty from which to concoct their outfits.

That morning, following class devotions, I told Keisha to look through the items and begin making her costume. She responded with insolence and shouting and ran out of the building. The other children were upset. They were concerned that Keisha would ruin the play. I encouraged them to consult over this, and I presided over their discourse. They unanimously agreed that Keisha did not deserve to be in the play because she was "mean" to everyone and her costume wasn't even made yet. Plus, as they pointed out, she might not even show up for the play. Yes, they concluded, Keisha should not be in the play. They would perform it without her.

"But," I interjected, "what about Keisha's lines?"

The children briefly mulled this over and decided that they could perform the play quite nicely without her and without her lines. I empathized. They had worked very diligently all week to prepare for the play, and it was understandable for them to have grown weary of Keisha's surliness and tantrums.

Very gently, and carefully omitting specific details, I explained to the class that Keisha's mother had died and the heartbreaking truth was that she now was an orphan. I told them that she was very sad and lonely, and what she needed more than anything in the world was to feel loved. I told them that the Bahá'í teachings tell us that when someone is unlovable it is because that person needs more love than anyone else. I told them that it is very difficult to be lovable when you feel that no one loves you. I then read to the class some passages from the Bahá'í teachings about love: "The more love is expressed among mankind and the stronger the power of unity, the greater will be this reflection and revelation, for the greatest bestowal of God is love. Love is the source of all the bestowals of God. Until love takes possession of the heart, no other divine bounty can be revealed in it."[210]

It never ceases to amaze me how remarkably receptive and perceptive children are in their understanding of spiritual teachings. I asked the children if they had any ideas as to how we could help Keisha feel more loved. One student suggested that we pray for her. The other students concurred, and we said a round of prayers.

Following the prayers, I asked the class if they had any other ideas about helping Keisha feel that we loved her. After a few moments of silent thought, one child said with excitement, "I know! Let's make Keisha's costume!"

Another child added, "Yeah! That's a great idea! But let's make it really pretty!"

The children all loved the idea, and with my approval they went off to carry out their new assignment. They went through the boxes, pulling out shiny fabrics, fake jewelry, and hair ornaments. I heard one child say, "Let's make her a Chinese princess!" This suggestion was greeted by affirmative cheers, and so, while some of the children worked on finishing their flags or memorizing their lines, the rest of the class very meticulously worked on putting Keisha's costume together.

Keisha returned to class after lunch. The children were beaming with excitement. I said, "Keisha, the children have a surprise for you." One of the girl students, hardly able to contain her delight, exclaimed, "Come with us, Keisha," and all the girls in the class went over to her, gently taking her hands and arms. Keisha, perhaps surprised by all this positive attention from the other children, allowed them to lead her to the girls' bathroom.

When Keisha returned to the class, she was beautiful! The girls had dressed her in a gold, shiny, long dress with a mandarin color. She wore long, beaded necklaces, a silky, navy blue shawl wrapped around her shoulders, and garnishing her upswept hair were sheer pink and blue butterfly ornaments, delicately trimmed with gold. Also, the girls had put makeup on her—exotic black eyeliner, blue eye shadow, and lipstick.

The authenticity of her costume as a Chinese princess may have been questionable, especially since her flag design was that of Communist China—but it mattered little. The class had created the most beautiful costume in the play for her. She looked lovely—and absolutely bewildered.

We quickly went through a dress rehearsal, said some final prayers, and then I led the class to the building where they would perform their play before an audience. Every seat in the room was taken. I said a quick prayer under my breath, and then it was show time and the children made their entrance on stage. The children marched out single file, each holding the stick of the flag up against his or her shoulder, like a soldier carrying a rifle. The children, wearing their makeshift costumes, marched out on stage. Standing at attention, they faced the audience and announced in loud and angry voices the name of each of their respective countries, adding, "My country is the best country in the world!"

Each child made a little speech, insisting that his or her country was superior to all other countries, which led to a shouting match and the children all turning to each other, holding their flags aimed as if readying guns for war. Of, course the play had a happy ending. A child representing no particular country came out and demanded the attention of the others on the stage. This mysterious person explained that there was one God and that all of humanity belonged to one human family. At first the characters were unreceptive to this message, but the speaker persevered and told them about the different messengers of God and the oneness of religion, quoting passages from the Bahá'í teachings: "All are the servants of God and members of one human family. God has created all, and all are His children."[211] "Ye are the fruits of one tree, and the leaves of one branch. Deal ye one with another with the utmost love and harmony, with friendliness and fellowship. He Who is the Daystar of Truth beareth Me witness! So powerful is the light of unity that it can illuminate the whole earth."[212]

The speaker managed to convince the others on stage to pray and consult with each other, which led to their realization that not only did the people of all nations have a lot in common, but they could also learn from each other! Everyone on stage proceeded to shake hands, and the play ended with a song and dance. Ah, if only global peace could be achieved so easily!

Keisha and the other children recited their lines perfectly, and the play was a smashing success. The children were excellent, and at the end of the play they radiated a genuine spirit of love and unity towards one another. The spirit of unity that shone from the children was very powerful, permeating the room, and captivating and moving the audience. The play ended with the children forming a circle, holding hands, and dancing to a song that played in the background on the tape recorder.

The audience stood up, clapped and cheered, and shouted out their praise and accolades. The children took their bows and were thrilled and elated by the response of the audience. I looked at the children and beheld a new and memorable sight. Keisha was smiling! It was the first time I had seen her smile. She was radiantly happy! She wasn't just grinning—she had a huge, wide-opened, gorgeous ear-to-ear smile, and she was glowing!

After the play, the children ran outside, giggling, happy, and hugging each other—with Keisha right in the center of their embraces. I stood there watching them, moved beyond words. Keisha turned to me and left the huddle of her peers. She ran to me and threw her arms around my waist, buried her head against my chest, and cried her heart out. I held her tightly, and my own tears drenched my face. I felt such an abundance of love for this child, and my gratitude to God was profound. I thanked God again and again and begged Him to bless and protect this precious, dear child.

We stood there embracing for quite a while, and after we found tissues and wiped our faces, I told Keisha how very proud I was of her. Just at the moment when I thought I was finally composed, Keisha looked up at me and said in the sweetest, most earnest of tones, "I love you." I was completely done for, and the floodgates reopened. I bawled like a baby. I told her that I loved her too and that I would never forget her, nor would I ever stop praying for her.

That evening, the people who had brought Keisha to Green Acre told me of their shock and amazement at Keisha's transformation. Her grandmother had told them that Keisha had never cried—not even after her mother's death. They warmly thanked me, but I told them to thank God. He was the Overseer of the miracle. Keisha was a great blessing to me. She had been a great challenge, but because of her the entire class had benefited.

The following day, the children came to my class for one last time, which would only be for a short morning session. As usual the children recited or sang prayers. I almost fell off my chair when Keisha opened her mouth and recited from memory a Bahá'í prayer: "O God, guide me, protect me, make of me a shining lamp and a brilliant star. Thou art the Mighty and the Powerful."[213]

I knew from the start that she was bright, but it was never clear to me how much she had been absorbing from the class or from our times alone together. But I had prayed for her every day and had been determined not to give up on her. The other children prayed for her as well, and their loving and selfless actions played a key role in Keisha's transformation. And now here she was: happy, beloved by her classmates, and reciting a prayer! It is always very hard for me to bid farewell to my classes, but this one was especially difficult.

About ten years later, I ran into some Bahá'í friends who lived in Keisha's area. They told me that Keisha was a Bahá'í and a full-time student at a local university. They assured me that she had grown into a charming, lovely young woman. I feel sad for those who live their lives motivated by material rewards alone, because I know of nothing in this physical world that could have brought me greater joy than I felt in that moment upon hearing about Keisha's success.

CHAPTER 20

The Spiritual Education of Children

Several years ago I served as artistic director for the Children's Education Program for the Performing Arts. Although sponsored by a Bahá'í Local Spiritual Assembly, the project was open to the general public, and its purpose was to train young people from ages seven to twenty-one in morals and virtues through use of the performing arts. A fascinating aspect of the project was that the forty or so children and teenagers in this project came from suburban neighborhoods as well as from the impoverished inner city area. They were of extremely diverse backgrounds, not only ethnically and religiously, but also in social and economic status. These were kids who attended different schools and probably never would have associated with each other in any other context, let alone become close friends.

We were working on a musical play I had written that focused on promoting race unity. It was a play with a great deal of singing, dancing, and funny lines. The students loved it. However, not all of them were performers. Some preferred to work behind the scenes, helping to build sets or make costumes. There was a lot of talent there, and the program was very successful. But far more important than the theatrical production itself was the exquisite unity that was created among those young people.

What developed among them was a solid, loving friendship. Actually, it was more than a friendship—they became like a family. There is no question in my mind that prayers played an integral role in their unity, especially considering the vastly different backgrounds they came from and the differences in their ages.

We met every Saturday morning in the basement at the local Bahá'í center, where we would begin the workshop with a round of prayers. Any child or teen was welcome to share a prayer. They were free to say prayers from any Bahá'í texts or other scriptures or to simply offer a spontaneous prayer from the heart. Sometimes a young person would sing or chant a prayer. The children were always eager to offer prayers, and many of them had memorized prayers from Bahá'í scripture. Because prayer is such a vital component for creating a spiritual environment, I never set a time limit for the amount of prayers being offered during our devotions. On the other hand, no one was pressured to say a prayer. If someone wished to offer one, they were welcome to do so—and if not, that was okay too, as long as all sat silently and respectfully while others prayed.

I was always struck by the enthusiasm of the group to say prayers, and I was doubly awed by the quiet reverence they demonstrated during prayers. Most of the time, there was little or no fidgeting, even from the younger children. On the rare occasions when I saw fidgeting, it would almost always be from beginners who were coming to our workshop for the first time and were perhaps unaccustomed to this type of devotional. But gradually, after a few weeks of attending these workshops, they too would begin to relax and breathe deeply, inhaling the sweet fragrances of the love of the Holy Spirit. These children's hearts were so pure and receptive to the knowledge of God. As for me, being in a room of sweet children praying together, particularly when the color of their skins were as diverse as different flowers in a beautiful garden, was a celestial experience. Heavenly sweetness, happiness, and pure joy permeated the air.

Bahá'í scripture affirms, "Every day at first light, ye gather the Bahá'í children together and teach them the communes and prayers. This is a most praiseworthy act, and bringeth joy to the children's hearts: that they should, at every morn, turn their faces toward the Kingdom and make mention of the Lord and praise His Name, and in the sweetest of voices, chant and recite."[214]

The intent of this project was not religious conversion, nor was it a platform for preaching. Its purpose was to use the arts to educate and train young people in spiritual values and virtues such as kindness, generosity, compassion, truthfulness, selflessness, trustworthiness, fair-mindedness, and respect. At the beginning of every class, following prayers, I would read a passage from the Bahá'í writings that addressed a particular theme or virtue. Because of the play's theme, I read passages from the Bahá'í writings pertaining to race unity, such as, "Let all associate, therefore, in this great human garden even as flowers grow and blend together side by side without discord or disagreement between them."[215]

After reading the passages, I would facilitate a group discussion about the passage, using game-type exercises to elicit participation from all the young people, including the younger children. Sometimes we would split up the groups by age for the discussions. But again, it never ceased to amaze me how patient, loving, and helpful the teens could be with the younger children. I discovered that teenagers are natural role models to children. The younger children adore them and look up to them and want to copy everything they do. For that very reason, teenagers are often more successful in winning the cooperation of children. This can be potentially a good thing or a bad thing. Teenagers who are morally astray are often the ones who lure children into gangs, drugs, and crime. On the other hand, a teenager who is a positive role model can be a very effective teacher to a young child.

The prayers and discussions of virtues in the beginning of each of our classes had a profoundly unifying effect on all the students in the project, regardless of their age. It seemed to inspire the older ones to help and teach the younger ones. And the spiritual environment the prayers created appeared to give all the students more confidence in themselves. Perhaps it was because the prayers brought to light the truth of their spiritual nobility, as affirmed in Bahá'í scripture: "O Son of Spirit! Noble have I created thee, yet thou hast abased thyself. Rise then unto that for which thou wast created."[216]

Also, the arts—particularly music—combined with spiritual purpose in an environment steeped in the love of God, are a very powerful medium to educate young people:

> The latent talents with which the hearts of these children are endowed will find expression through the medium of music. Therefore, you must exert yourselves to make them proficient; teach them to sing with excellence and effect. . . . teach it in order that the souls and hearts of the pupils may become vivified and exhilarated and their lives be brightened with enjoyment.[217]

One of the students in the class was David, who was fourteen years old. He was a handsome boy with blue eyes and shaggy blond hair, but he never smiled and rarely talked. He was extremely shy, and when he spoke it was often in a murmur. When the students auditioned for the play, I assigned David to work backstage. When I saw that he was disappointed, I took him aside to talk to him alone. We sat down, and I asked him why he seemed unhappy, and he mumbled incoherently. I asked him to speak up, and he just looked at me with his sad, blue eyes.

Now I knew that David was capable of speaking clearly, because during devotions he was always quick to volunteer to recite a prayer and he even had memorized some prayers from Bahá'í scripture. When he prayed, his words were articulate and heartfelt, so I asked him if he would like to say some prayers with me, and he quietly nodded his head. We each said a prayer, and then I asked him if he would like to tell me what was troubling him.

"I want to be in the play," he said.

I was surprised. I found that generally young people who suffered from extreme shyness preferred not to be in the spotlight. I asked, "Are you sure? What do you want to do in the play?"

He responded without hesitation, "I want to act. I want to sing. I want to be in the play."

I said, "But I have already cast all the parts in the play. I think you'll have a lot of fun working backstage, painting and building sets. Perhaps you can be in a play next time."

"No!" He said, with pleading eyes. "I want to be in this play. I don't want to work backstage. I want to act." His eyes were becoming teary, and he seemed filled with a sense of urgency.

It was late and it was time to pack up. I told David I would think about it. I drove home feeling confused and mulling it over in my head. I had assumed that David would prefer working backstage because of his extreme shyness. Also, I was concerned about the quality of the production. But I also thought about David's disappointment. On the surface he seemed withdrawn, but after our prayers together and consultation, I sensed there was hidden depth. The thought of causing him sadness and not helping him to realize his latent potential weighed heavily on my mind and in my heart.

I decided that I should learn something about his background and talk to his mother, but his mother beat me to the punch and telephoned me that evening. She explained that David had been diagnosed with mild learning disabilities and was in a special education class. She said that because of his learning disabilities he had very low self-esteem and usually kept to himself. His psychologist and teachers recognized that he had the potential to do much better in school, but his low self-esteem was keeping him down. She said that David wanted more than anything to be an actor, and he was also a good singer. She let me know in no uncertain terms how heartbroken he was to not be in the play. I told her that I would give this some thought.

I sat down, prayed, and meditated. During meditation I made a decision. I rushed to my computer and created a new role for David to be in the play. The role did not require many lines, but it was one of the leading roles, and it included singing. I had not seen David act or sing, and I was taking a chance. But here was a young soul who wanted with all his heart to be in this play. I put my trust in God and wrote out his new part.

A few days later, I called his home and told him about the new role that I had written just for him, and he was thrilled. I told him that I was going to drive to his house to deliver the script so that he could begin memorizing his lines. My heart lightened when I could hear his excitement over the phone, but I remained somewhat apprehensive. My thoughts vacillated. Was I was doing the right thing? How was this act of compassion going to affect the play? I offered a quick prayer and put my trust in God.

The following Saturday, we held our first rehearsal of the play. I was impressed because David was one of the few actors to have memorized all of his lines. But he muttered his lines at such a low volume that it was impossible to hear what he was saying beyond the stage. The same thing happened when he sang. The other instructors and I had given the cast some vocal exercises, but I had the sense that David's weak, timid voice was not due to lack of physical ability. It was his lack of confidence, made worse by the fact that he kept his head and eyes downward.

We took a break for lunch, and I pondered how to help him. I took him aside and asked him why it was difficult for him to speak in a louder voice. He shrugged and offered no verbal response and looked at me with those sad, blue eyes. I asked him if he would like to say prayers with me, and he brightened up. After we each said some prayers, I said, "David, are you aware that when you recite prayers, you speak in a beautiful, strong, clear voice?"

He looked at me and just shrugged again. I asked, "Why do you think that you can recite prayers in a strong voice, but not so with your stage lines?"

He paused, thought it over, and responded, "I guess it's because when I pray, I'm talking to God. When I pray I can feel God's love. The prayers make me feel happy."

"Well, when you say your lines in the play, why don't you say them for God?" I suggested. "The Bahá'í writings tell us that it is a spiritual principle to advance the arts. Also, this play is all about promoting race unity—and you know that God wants all of humanity to love each other as members of one human family. In this play you are helping people understand that, David. You have the opportunity in this play to promote two spiritual principles—the advancement of the arts and race unity. So, each time before you go on stage, say a prayer in your head asking for God's assistance to promote these spiritual principles. And when you say your lines in the play, say them for God. Think about God. Say your lines for the love of God. Say your lines as if they are a prayer." I also reminded him to keep his chin up and look at his cast members when he was speaking to them instead of to the ground.

David smiled and said, "I'll try."

David was amazing at the next rehearsal. He was focused, followed stage directions, kept his head upright, and he spoke in the same clear, strong voice that I heard when he prayed. His cast mates were impressed. And his mother was right—he really could act and sing! He was one of the best actors in the play. The production, held that spring, was a smashing triumph, and his talents and spirit contributed greatly to its success. No longer sad, David's blue eyes truly sparkled.

At the beginning of the next school year his mother called to share with me marvelous news, her voice bubbling with pride and happiness. David's teachers reported that they had noticed a remarkable difference in his schoolwork, and he was being placed in regular classes at his high school. He was improving in all the academics, particularly in mathematics, and the teachers raved. He was a different person. He seemed more confident and outgoing, and he was making friends.

After graduating from high school, David was accepted into a prestigious dramatic arts college and now works as a professional actor with a theater company. It has been several years since I last spoke to David, but knowing of his success brings much delight to my heart. He is such a shining example of how the power of prayer can affect our precious youth.

Who is responsible for the spiritual education and training of children?

The Bahá'í teachings assert, "Children are the most precious treasure a community can possess, for in them are the promise and guarantee of the future. They bear the seeds of the character of future society which is largely shaped by what the adults constituting the community do or fail to do with respect to children. They are a trust no community can neglect with impunity."[218]

From that perspective, all of society is responsible for the development of our children, but, more specifically, Bahá'í scripture tells us that it is the supreme duty of the parents to educate and train their children, emphasizing that this is a commandment from God. It is "obligatory and not voluntary."[219] The Bahá'í writings stress the crucial need for parents to create a spiritual and loving environment for their children:

> Independent of the level of their education, parents are in a critical position to shape the spiritual development of their children. They should not ever underestimate their capacity to mold their children's moral character. For they exercise indispensable influence through the home environment they consciously create by their love of God, their striving to adhere to His laws, their spirit of service to His Cause, their lack of fanaticism, and their freedom from the corrosive effects of backbiting.[220]

This, above all else, is the first duty of the parents: "Ye should consider the question of goodly character as of the first importance. It is incumbent upon every father and mother to counsel their children over a long period, and guide them unto those things which lead to everlasting honor."[221]

Spiritual education begins in the home by simply praying for and with our children. It was apparent that David had a spiritual upbringing because the importance of regular prayer was already instilled in him before he began the workshop. Through prayer he had the advantage of being in tune with his spiritual reality. Once he learned to regard his endeavors as a form of worship, combined with the services provided at school and through his love of the arts, he was able to overcome his awkwardness and shyness and circumvent his learning disabilities.

Bahá'í scripture encourages parents to nurture their children through prayer and spiritual education from infancy "and rear them so that from their earliest days, within their inmost heart, their very nature, a way of life will be firmly established that will conform to the divine Teachings in all things."[222]

A beautiful prayer from Bahá'í scripture reads,

> O God! Rear this little babe in the bosom of Thy love, and give it milk from the breast of Thy Providence. Cultivate this fresh plant

in the rose garden of Thy love and aid it to grow through the showers of Thy bounty. Make it a child of the kingdom, and lead it to Thy heavenly realm. Thou art powerful and kind, and Thou art the Bestower, the Generous, the Lord of surpassing bounty.[223]

There are also numerous prayers from Bahá'í scripture that are short and very easy even for young children to memorize, such as these two:

O God, guide me, protect me, make of me a shining lamp and a brilliant star. Thou art the Mighty and the Powerful.[224]

O God! Educate these children. These children are the plants of Thine orchard, the flowers of Thy meadow, the roses of Thy garden. Let Thy rain fall upon them; let the Sun of Reality shine upon them with Thy love. Let Thy breeze refresh them in order that they may be trained, grow and develop, and appear in the utmost beauty. Thou art the Giver. Thou art the Compassionate.[225]

While society may still have a long way to go in building a safe and nurturing child-oriented community, parents can create such an environment in their own home. They can initiate family prayers together and designate special times every week for family consultations that begin with prayer. Through family prayers and prayerful consultation, parents can create an atmosphere in which the child feels unconditional love.

What is the role of the community in the spiritual education of children?

Many years ago a reporter asked a foreign leader to express her thoughts about achieving peace, and to paraphrase the leader's response, "When we all learn to love our children more than we hate each other—that is the day when we will have peace in the world." Such an idea is worth pondering. Just imagine a world in which we all love our children more than we hate each other. War would be utterly inconceivable in such a world.

Such a familial attitude towards others, no matter where in the world we may be, is reminiscent of an old African proverb that reminds us that "it takes a whole village to raise a child." There is much wisdom in that adage, for in truth the world in which the child lives is a big classroom, and all the adults in it are, in essence, teachers. Children learn by observing the people and things around them; thus it is critical for young people to be exposed to positive role models and good examples of spiritual behavior. They watch us, emulate us, and learn from everything that we do in front of them. But children are not automatons, and they often dislike it when they hear adults preach at them, especially when those adults fail to practice what they preach. Children learn best through the dynamic force of example. From that perspective, each of us is a potential role model for our children.

In truth, whatever we want for our children to learn and do, we need to demonstrate by example. If we want our children to be truthful, courteous, compassionate, and respectful of others, then we must strive to exemplify those virtues in our daily lives. If we wish to teach our children not to be prejudiced and to avoid backbiting, then it is critical that we strive to demonstrate the desired behaviors and attitudes. And if we want to teach our children to love God and to pray—they need to see us pray. They need to see us pray for them and with them, without being preachy, forceful, or rigid about it. They need to learn to associate prayer and spiritual teachings as a means to bring joy and gladness to their hearts.

Children need to be taught that God helps those who turn to Him in prayer, not only in words but also through good deeds and spiritual virtues. They need to learn this in a loving environment that is safe and supportive. These teachings are so strongly emphasized in the Bahá'í writings that in the last few years a growing number of Bahá'ís have been initiating classes in communities all over the world that emphasize the importance of moral development and spiritual qualities. These classes are established and usually sponsored by Bahá'ís, but they are open to all children and are often held in churches, schools, or public centers.

These classes are not a substitute for academic schools but supplement them, for the advancement of academic education is very strongly advocated in the Bahá'í teachings as well: "The education and training of children is among the most meritorious acts of humankind and draweth down the grace and favor of the All-Merciful, for education is the indispensable foundation of all human excellence and alloweth man to work his way to the heights of abiding glory."[226]

The children's virtues classes provide opportunities for young people of diverse populations to pray together and to participate in fun, fellowship, and educational activities that are age-appropriate and focused on a variety of spiritual themes. In some communities, the parents benefit as well. I know a Bahá'í man in Texas of Latin heritage who travels with his son to a border village in Mexico every weekend to teach a Spanish-speaking children's virtues class. The classes there are popular and continue to multiply.

He explains, "Because the villagers see how much the children enjoy coming to our classes and see the positive impact the classes have on their children's behaviors, more and more parents keep bringing their children to the classes. We needed to recruit more teachers to increase the number of classes and make them more age-appropriate. But we also became aware of another need. It is a very poor village, and most of the parents are illiterate. The mothers usually just sit on the grass outside waiting for the children, so we started up literacy classes for the adults, which are held simultaneously while the children's classes are in session. Now the adult classes are packed too."

The teachers of these children's classes strive to create a spiritual and loving environment, which is why they always begin the classes with prayer. The adult literacy classes also begin with prayer because the parents are eager to read the beautiful Bahá'í prayers their children have learned to recite in children's class. Through prayer, the children become more receptive to the knowledge of God and to training in spiritual teachings, and this helps them learn right from wrong:

> The root cause of wrongdoing is ignorance, and we must therefore hold fast to the tools of perception and knowledge. Good character must be taught. Light must be spread afar, so that, in the school of humanity, all may acquire the heavenly characteristics of the spirit,

and see for themselves beyond any doubt that there is no fiercer hell, no more fiery abyss, than to possess a character that is evil and unsound; no more darksome pit nor loathsome torment than to show forth qualities which deserve to be condemned.[227]

How do we spiritually educate our children?

Bahá'í scripture tells us that "Every child is potentially the light of the world—and at the same time its darkness; wherefore must the question of education be accounted as of primary importance."[228]

It is imperative for a child's development and happiness to receive a spiritual education as well as academic learning:

Training in morals and good conduct is far more important than book learning. A child that is cleanly, agreeable, of good character, well-behaved—even though he be ignorant—is preferable to a child that is rude, unwashed, ill-natured, and yet becoming deeply versed in all the sciences and arts. The reason for this is that the child who conducts himself well, even though he be ignorant, is of benefit to others, while an ill-natured, ill-behaved child is corrupted and harmful to others, even though he be learned. If, however, the child be trained to be both learned and good, the result is light upon light.[229]

Children need to be taught that God is loving, forgiving, merciful, and compassionate. They need to be taught about prayer as a means of talking to God in a loving spirit. They need to know that they can talk privately to God whenever their heart desires, because God is always there for them, always loving them. God created all of humanity as members of one human family, and children need to learn to love everyone for the sake of God. Children are inherently receptive to this message because their hearts are pure and innocent. Bahá'í scripture asserts the importance of this spiritual education: "That which is of paramount importance for the children, that which must precede all else, is to teach them the oneness of God and the laws of God."[230]

Children also need to be taught spiritual principles and concepts in a manner untainted by prejudice, hatred, and superstition. These things are not inherent—they are taught. Teaching religion from a prejudiced perspective defeats its purpose, which is to unite people's hearts through the love of God.

Bahá'í scripture attests to the benefits of fostering our children, beginning in their earliest years, in the embrace of prayer and spiritual education: "Thus shall these tender infants be nurtured at the breast of the knowledge of God and His love. Thus shall they grow and flourish, and be taught righteousness and the dignity of humankind, resolution and the will to strive and to endure. Thus shall they learn perseverance in all things, the will to advance, high mindedness and high resolve, chastity and purity of life. Thus shall they be enabled to carry to a successful conclusion whatsoever they undertake."[231]

The Bahá'í teachings also place great importance on educating both boys and girls about the importance of the equality of women and men: "The world of humanity has two wings, as it were: One is the female; the other is the male. If one wing be defective, the strong perfect wing will not be capable of flight."[232]

The best we can do as parents, friends, and fellow human beings, is to gently guide our children to walk a spiritual path. Happy and blessed are the children who dwell in a loving home with a family who lives and functions together in peaceful and harmonious accord. And the happiest and most confident of all children are those who are nurtured in a spiritual home in which they are loved for the sake of God and are taught the knowledge of God. Children who learn to pray will be able to find their own spiritual path.

CHAPTER 21

Journey from Persecution to Freedom

Fariba was only a small child at the time of the 1979 Islamic Revolution in Iran, when Ayatollah Khomeini, the Iranian Shiite leader, became head of state after the overthrow of the regime ruled by Shah Mohammed Reza Pahlavi. Under the shah, the nation had made significant strides in the advancement of education and the economy. Following the fall of the Pahlavi regime, Iran reentered a dark age of prejudice, violence, and oppression. The Ayatollah established a new constitution, empowering himself with supreme powers and marking a return to strict observance of fundamentalist interpretations of Islamic law. The new government prohibited the equality of women, banned music, and ordered the arrest, imprisonment, and murder of thousands of its citizens, including many Bahá'ís, who were considered heretics under the regime and had no rights of citizenship.

Before the revolution, the Bahá'í community in Iran had emerged as a well-educated, hardworking, and prosperous group of people. Many Bahá'ís achieved wide recognition for scholarly achievements, some held important appointed posts in the government, and many others worked in the fields of medicine, research, and education. However, when the shah's government was overthrown, the Bahá'ís were among the first to be targeted for persecution. Many lost their jobs and homes, their children were banned from attending schools and universities, and many Bahá'ís were beaten, abducted, imprisoned, and even killed.

Young Fariba was born into a Bahá'í family and knew Bahá'ís who had been dragged out of their homes to be abused and arrested, and it saddened her that many of her Muslim neighbors and relatives demonstrated blatant hatred for the Bahá'ís. They jeered at her and her family, calling them unpleasant names, and she was even forbidden to enter the house of her neighborhood playmate. Fariba says, "She was supposed to be my friend, but I wasn't even allowed to drink a glass of water from her home."

The persecutions escalated in the years following the revolution. The Bahá'í community in Iran was the largest religious minority in the country, but its members were now on the brink of poverty, and many Bahá'ís were in hiding or were attempting to escape the country. By 1985, conditions had grown dismal. All females age twelve and older were ordered to cover their hair, arms, and legs by wearing the black chador, which is a loose robe that covers the body from head to toe, including the forehead. In addition to the chador, they wore long dresses, long pants, and thick, high socks, regardless of the weather. If a woman was seen in a public place and a strand of hair or a bit of arm or leg should happen to peek out accidentally, she could be beaten or sent to jail.

The nine elected members of the National Spiritual Assembly of the Bahá'ís of Iran, the elected administrative body of the Iranian Bahá'í community, were arrested by the government and murdered. More assassinations of Bahá'ís followed, and the Universal House of Justice, the international Bahá'í governing council, intervened and called for a halt of Bahá'í administrative activities in Iran. Nevertheless, the Iranian Bahá'í community managed to remain connected and unified through their love of God and their prayers. Despite oppression and danger, they endeavored to help and support each other in whatever ways were possible. In obedience to the Bahá'í teachings, they espoused no words of hatred or scorn towards the government.

In accordance with the Bahá'í law that enjoins believers to be obedient and respectful to the government of the nation in which they live, the Bahá'ís dressed in the required attire, and although they were treated with disdain and shunned or even assaulted, they quietly and unobtrusively adhered to the restrictions, displaying neither violence nor contempt, never showing even a hint of rebellion or subversive activity. Obeying the teachings of their religion, they persevered through their hardships in constant remembrance of the love of God, with faith and the blessings of the Holy Spirit consoling their hearts.

One of the things that most troubled the Bahá'ís was the persecution of their children. They were denied the right to be educated. Fariba had made it to the ninth grade in the public school, but her life came to a sudden halt on the day when she and the other Bahá'í students in the school were called to the principal's office. The principal announced that they were expelled because, as she stated bluntly, "You are Bahá'ís!"

The principal explained, "There are two things I want to say about Bahá'ís. All Bahá'ís are very nice. But the only reason you are nice is because you want to capture people into your faith. Second, Bahá'ís are very smart. We have fifty Bahá'ís in our school, and all of you are the best students in my school. But I want you to know that I am very happy that I am losing my best students in the school because you are Bahá'ís, and there is no place in this school or in the Muslim world for you!"

With that speech, she dismissed the students and told them never to return to the building. Fariba was devastated. It was unthinkable for her to be forbidden to finish school and get her degree. The other students were in shock as well.

The next day, Fariba's mother, a tiny little woman with a strong and determined spirit, took her daughter with her to the school and headed directly to the principal's office. Her mother faced the principal and asked, "How can you not allow my daughter to be educated?"

The principal responded, "You should be very happy for this decision. This is a Muslim land, and there is no place here for your daughter. You should be very happy that we even let you breathe in this country."

Defeated and heartbroken, Fariba returned home with her mother, went into her bedroom, and burst into tears.

When the Muslim students in Fariba's school realized that all the Bahá'ís had been expelled, they were confused, and many of them protested in the schoolyard, insisting that they would not return to class until the

Bahá'í students were also allowed to return. The faculty told the students that the Bahá'ís were bad people and warned them that if they associated with them, they, too, would be expelled from school.

Fariba says, "It was a very painful time for me. I was very unhappy and I just couldn't understand why this was happening. It just didn't make any sense. I was very worried about my future. In the Bahá'í Faith we are told that education is very important. What was my future without an education? My Muslim friends were told to stay away from me, and it was too dangerous for Bahá'í youth to socialize, because if we were seen together as a group we would be at risk for persecution. I had no school, and I had no friends. My future looked very bleak and frightening. I must admit that it was a terrible time for me."

An idea came about in the Bahá'í community for the Bahá'í children to each write a personal letter to Ayatollah Khomeini with a request that they be permitted to return to school. Fariba was among the many Bahá'í youth throughout the nation who wrote and sent letters to the Ayatollah with this request. Amazingly, he granted the request, and the following year after Fariba had been expelled, she and other Bahá'í students in all parts of Iran were readmitted to school.

The Bahá'í students were only allowed to go to school, however, if they agreed to follow certain stipulations. They were not permitted to discuss with the Muslim students the reason why they were expelled from school, and they were told not to mention a word to the other students about the Bahá'í Faith. Also, though they were permitted to go to elementary and high schools, they would not be allowed to attend the universities or pursue higher academic learning.

Fariba says, "The teachers told the students to ignore us and that we were bad people. Many of the students called us bad names, and some students would say to me before I was about to take an exam, 'I hope you get a zero on the test! I hope you fail!' Or else they would say, 'You are a really bad person! I hope you die!' And the teachers would never call on me in class. They ignored me and acted as if I wasn't there. This was very hurtful, and I would go home and cry and cry."

After having spent more than a year of praying and hoping that she would be allowed to return to school, Fariba now dreaded being there. She cried to her mother, "I don't want to go school!"

Her mother responded, "You need this education. Don't listen to what they say to you. Don't let them see you be weak, because that is what they want. They want to break your spirit. Don't let them. Be strong. Trust in God. Pray. You need to go to school!"

The cruelty inflicted upon her by her teachers and peers never stopped causing pain and sadness to her heart, but Fariba learned to endure in order to complete her education. She learned to tolerate the threats, name-calling, sneers, and shunning from the other students. Through her love of God and prayer, and through the loving support and guidance she received at home, she persevered, even at times when she felt as if her heart was seared by the scourging pain of injustice. The blatant acts of bigotry caused her much suffering, but she coped with her trials radiantly and with dignity. Her parents taught her to treat everyone with kindness and good manners, and she managed to respond in that fashion even towards the school custodian who went out of his way to treat her cruelly, letting his contempt for Bahá'ís be known.

The family's concerns intensified even more when they discovered that the lives of Fariba's two older sisters were in great danger. Several Bahá'í females in the town where they lived were arrested, abused, and imprisoned. Ten of them were murdered, including one girl who was only seventeen years old. Their "crime" was that they were active in the Bahá'í community, assisting the many families who were in need of food, shelter, and financial assistance, and they had been teaching classes to Bahá'í children who were banned from attending the public schools. Fariba was among the students who attended the home schools in order to keep up with her academic studies. To her horror and grief, two of her teachers were among the young women arrested and killed.

It was a time of mourning, extreme sadness, and immense suffering for the Bahá'í community. The Bahá'ís recognized more than ever that it was vitally important to pray and trust in God. It was incomprehensible to them and totally against the principles of their gentle religion that any child could be denied an education, and it was beyond their reasoning to comprehend how any people could possess such a degree of blind hatred that teenage girls would be sentenced to death simply because they were providing an academic education to the children—a service certainly the government should have been providing in the first place.

Fariba's sisters, who were also teaching the children's classes, learned from a source that they were next in line to be arrested. The girls, their lives now in great peril, made arrangements to flee the country and managed to escape to Pakistan and then went to the United States, where their two older brothers had emigrated before the revolution.

Reflecting on that harrowing episode, Fariba says, "I was very lonely for my sisters. It was such a difficult time. And not being able to go to school, I kept worrying about my future. My grandmother really helped me. She told me, 'You have a very good future. Trust in God. Pray. Everything will turn out good.' I know that I never would have gotten through that ordeal without prayers."

She adds, "My parents helped me a lot too. They were very strong and supportive—and I knew that it was their love and faith in God that made them the way they were. It was very difficult for them when my sisters left, especially because the escape route was dangerous, but my parents would not show their concern in front of my sisters because they wanted to be strong for them. That's how my parents were—they always thought of their children first. I felt very sad and suffered a lot of pain, but I never stopped praying and trusting in God. The future looked scary, but I never lost hope."

"I feel very grateful that my parents were so nurturing and supportive. They always made me feel loved and gave me a strong spiritual foundation. The prayers from Bahá'í scripture played an extremely important role in my home, and it was an important part of my upbringing. My parents loved God very much, and they taught me to love God. No matter how difficult things got, they would wake up at dawn every morning to begin their prayers, and prayers were always being recited or chanted in my home. I never would have been able to get through all that I did without the prayers and trusting in God and the support from my family."

In addition to the prayers, Fariba derived sustenance from the writings of Bahá'u'lláh, especially from the book known as the Hidden Words. She memorized all of its verses, and one in particular never failed to lighten her heart and soothe her soul, bringing her an outpouring of comfort and solace: "In the garden of thy heart plant naught but the rose of love, and from the nightingale of affection and desire loosen not thy hold. Treasure the companionship of the righteous and eschew all fellowship with the ungodly."[233]

Despite the discrimination, Fariba received good grades and made it through high school. In 1988, the year before Ayatollah Khomeini died, some of the strict ordinances such as the ban on music eased a bit. Fariba was familiar with the Bahá'í writings on the importance of music and was very eager to learn to play a musical instrument. She had always enjoyed the sound of the tombak, a Persian drum, and wanted to study it. At first, her parents were vehemently against this. The drum was regarded as a masculine instrument. They feared it could be very dangerous for her in the Muslim society to learn to play the drum. But Fariba reminded them of Bahá'u'lláh's teachings about the equality of women and men. She saw no reason why the drums should be an instrument only for men. Her parents could not argue against this and gave their consent, but, even so, they worried that this would present a danger for their daughter.

To Fariba's delight, she selected the wood from a cherry tree for the drum maker, who carefully crafted a tombak for her. She was thrilled to have her own drum and attended music lessons with other Bahá'í youth, instructed by a Bahá'í music teacher. She learned to read music and play her drum in the traditional style.

She loved the music, and she loved playing her drum, but she especially enjoyed playing her drum as an accompaniment when she sang verses from Bahá'í scripture to the enchanting traditional Persian melodies. After years of seemingly endless suffering, she found something in her young life to enrich her soul with boundless measures of happiness, joy, and fun! It was also a very spiritual experience for her. When she played her drum, it was the same as talking to God. She expressed her love and praise of God through her music. She created music and played her drum in a state of prayer.

Fariba learned to be a proficient drummer. However, her parents had been correct in their view that it would be a dangerous instrument for her to play. When Fariba took her drum outside the house for music lessons, she had to hide it inside a large, thick sock. And when she practiced at home, which was a townhouse unit divided by thin walls, she had to place a piece of cloth inside the drum to mute the sound. Furthermore, while it was permissible for a female to sing with a group, it was forbidden for a female voice to be heard singing alone. During those hours when she practiced at home, she sang in a hushed voice—but in her heart she sang out to the rooftops.

Meanwhile, due to the discrimination order, Fariba's father, had been fired from his job and, having no work, applied for a passport in 1985 for the family to leave Iran. They waited nine years before they heard a response from the passport office. But after those nine years it was only Fariba's father who received the passport document. Initially it was unthinkable for him to leave his wife and youngest child. His dear wife and Fariba put on their bravest faces and both insisted that it was best for him to go. They assured him that they would soon get their papers and join him in the United States. The mother knew that she must be stoic, for if she shed even one tear, he would not leave. They reminded him that it was sixteen years since he had seen his sons. They pleaded with him to go.

Although their hearts were saddened and they knew that they would miss him terribly, Fariba and her mother took him to the airport, smiling and showing great happiness and excitement about his journey. His own heart was heavy with concern for his beloved wife and child, whom he was leaving behind in this dangerous country, but he promised that he would return for them.

Nine months later, Fariba's mother received her papers to leave for the United States. It pained her terribly to consider leaving Fariba behind, and she experienced grave doubt. Fariba's grandmother had died, and it would mean that Fariba would be completely alone in the house with no one to care for or protect her. But, Fariba, smiling and doing her best to show jubilation, encouraged her mother to go. She reminded her that she had not seen her other children for several years.

When Fariba was alone with her Bahá'í friends, she no longer hid her tears, and she shared with them her great sorrow that her mother would be leaving. But she made her friends promise not to reveal this, knowing that her mother would never leave the country if Fariba showed any sign of fear or sadness.

The mother left, albeit reluctantly, and now it was Fariba, still a youth, living all alone in a house within the borders of a country that was hostile to her simply because of her beliefs. She was not permitted to study at a university, nor would she be allowed to find employment. Fariba, all alone, had no idea what to do with her life. Her worried family talked to her on the telephone and told her that she needed to consider escaping the country.

Escaping the country? Alone? The very thought terrified her. But what were her alternatives? She was not allowed to make any real life for herself in Iran, and she missed her family terribly. She also thought about her brothers and sisters who had gone on to further their education and advance in their careers. Her sisters had obtained their degrees and worked at a hospital as registered nurses. Fariba wondered what would become of her, left all alone in Iran.

Some friends had given her the name of a guide who helped Iranian Bahá'ís and Jews escape into Pakistan. She debated with herself. What to do? The guide was not a Bahá'í. Was he safe? Could he be trusted? She was terrified to take this trip alone. She was warned that the underground escape route was very dangerous.

She was invited to the home of a Bahá'í friend of her parents who advised her to take a week and spend it in a vigil of prayer and meditation. The friend advised Fariba to turn completely to God and beseech Him for guidance and assistance. Fariba returned home and spent the entire week in prayer and meditation, and by the end of the week it was clear to her that there was no more time for vacillation. She had made her decision. She was going to make her escape.

She looked at the number she had been given, mustered all her courage, called the guide on the telephone, and they set up an appointment. The day when he and another man came to her house, she was almost paralyzed with fear. It was the first time that she had ever met with a stranger alone in her home, let alone two male strangers. The guide told her to take one change of clothes, the minimum of necessities, money, and some food and water in one small bag. It was going to be an arduous trip, and there was little room in their traveling vehicle. He told her to pack and said that he would give her a call to inform her when it was time to depart—which could be anytime.

When Fariba's father learned that she was going to attempt an escape, he immediately flew out to be with her. It meant a lot to her that her father was there, as she derived strength and comfort from his presence. Aware of the potential danger of her plans, he was deeply concerned and uncertain about whether his daughter was making the right decision.

Soon the call came from the guide; it was time to leave. She needed to take a long bus ride to meet the guide and the group. The father escorted her on the bus to the designated location. From there they hugged and painfully broke away from each other's embrace as they shared their teary farewells. The father assured her that he and the family would be praying for her. Although he tried his best not to show it, inside he trembled with fear for his beloved daughter and prayed to God with all his heart for her safety.

Fariba began her journey with a group of eight Bahá'ís, counting herself and two Jews, none of whom previously knew each other, led by a Muslim guide. They were told that the trip would be no more than a few days, but it lasted two weeks. There were soldiers looking for them, and the group had to leave the vehicle and main road and hike through the wilderness, crossing over the mountains in the dark of night so as not to be seen. They were told not to make a sound, and it was so dark that they all had to hold on to each other so that no one would accidentally stray and get lost. Frequently, they would hear the sound of snipers, and the guide would lead them off in roundabout paths or caves to hide.

They went days without water and food. The nights were cold and the days were hot. Fariba, a petite girl under five feet tall, had insisted on bringing her drum despite the guide's protests. She slung the strap of the case that held the drum around her shoulder while her knapsack hung on her back. She also carried a blanket, which was essential for the chilly mountain nights.

Her drum was too dear to her to be left behind. It represented more than a material thing. The drum had brought her great joy and happiness at a time when the world around her was filled with sorrow and gloom. Not only did it represent the beauty of the traditional Persian culture, but the music of the drum uplifted her spirit, affirming to her the words of Bahá'u'lláh, who said, "We, verily, have made music as a ladder for your souls, a means whereby they may be lifted up unto the realm on high."[234]

After the first week of crossing the mountains, having had little to eat and drink, she was exhausted, dehydrated, and hot. The guide seemed genuinely touched by her love for her drum, but it was clear to him that little Fariba would not make it if she continued to carry this load. He promised her that if she allowed him to give it to one of his friends, she could trust him that the drum would be safely delivered to her in Pakistan. He said, "You treat your drum as a child. I know how much it means to you. But carrying the drum is slowing us down and impairing everyone's safety. Trust me, and I promise that the next group of people who are escaping will bring it to you because they will be going by car and the road and conditions will be safer. It will be easier for them. I promise that they will treat this drum as a child."

Fariba knew that she had reached her physical limit and apprehensively agreed to place the drum in the care of strangers. But as the guide promised, two weeks after she arrived in Pakistan, a Bahá'í family returned the drum to her. They smiled and said, "We were told to treat this as a child. Here is your child." Fariba was elated.

Fariba and the others were taken to a place near Islamabad, the capital of Pakistan. Unable to find a way out of the country, she remained in the town for six months. During her time there she enjoyed the freedom to play her drum and sing—and the Bahá'ís loved her music and asked her to play at all their various gatherings. She played with a group of musicians who exuberantly played the traditional music of Persia and the Middle East, often singing verses from Bahá'í scripture or verses that had been written by Bahá'ís. Her playing enchanted everyone. For her, each time she played it was a celebration of the glory of God. The playing made her very happy, and the Bahá'ís in the community were very loving and kind, but still she yearned desperately to be reunited with her family.

An international agency that helps persecuted refugees finally came to Fariba's aid and arranged for her to leave Pakistan. She arrived in the United States in the late autumn of 1996. At last Fariba was united with her entire family—her sisters, her brothers, and her beloved parents. They were together in a nation where there was light and joy, love of music, laughter of children, and freedom—freedom to be individuals, freedom to pursue education, freedom to be gainfully employed, and freedom to worship God without persecution, prejudice, or fanatical constraints.

Today, Fariba and her family are dearly loved and cherished in their local Bahá'í community. They are also admired and respected by their coworkers and neighbors. They went through extraordinary trials and tribulations, but their exuberantly radiant spirits, the genuine kindness and warm courtesy they show to all, and their humility and selflessness are exemplary behaviors of those who walk in the pathway of the knowledge of God's love. They humbly thank God for allowing them to be safe and together.

Fariba now dresses as she likes, enjoys her work, and appreciates the fact that she is able to sing and play her drum as loudly and as often as she pleases. She is a happy young woman with a generous, beautiful smile that makes others around her want to smile as well. Many things have changed in her life. But one thing that has not changed is her relationship with God. No matter how many freedoms were taken away from her in Iran, the one thing that could not be stolen, weakened, or tainted was her personal relationship with God. Her relationship with God was impregnable because she loved and trusted Him even in her darkest, most troublesome hours. Her spirit continues to be emboldened by her love of God, and her prayers are as much a part of her life as the air she breathes.

In the United States Fariba faces new tests. The culture is very different from that of Iran, and it is a more materialistic society. Compared to most American women, Fariba is reserved, soft-spoken, and shy. She still has some challenges with the English language and understanding American culture, but even so, she very much enjoys her life, and every day she recognizes her religious freedom as a precious blessing and gift.

When she was a youth she was very worried about her future. But she sees clearly now that what is most important about her life, in the present and in the future, is her relationship with God and her continuing effort to attain the nearness of the Holy Spirit. She is extremely grateful for her educational and career opportunities and for so many things that have brought her immeasurable happiness. Nevertheless, she recognizes that all of it—even playing the drum—would mean nothing without having the love of God in her life.

CHAPTER 22

What Is the Inner Reality
of Prayer?

In an earlier chapter I wrote about the brilliant, courageous, and beautiful Bábí heroine Ṭáhirih. As a symbolic gesture, Ṭáhirih boldly removed her veil at a public gathering, defying the Islamic law mandating that women's faces be covered. This was no small act of defiance. For challenging the established order and embracing the cause of the Báb, she was executed by the Muslim authorities. Emboldened by her certitude that all human souls are equal in His eyes regardless of gender, race, and class, she nobly sacrificed her life for the emancipation of women. How is it that a woman who lived under what were arguably the most extreme, oppressive conditions for females managed to break free of the chains of oppression in mind and spirit?

Ṭáhirih was born in 1817, the daughter of Haji Mulla Salih, a prominent mujtahid (Muslim doctor of law) in Qazvín, Persia. She grew up in a male-dominated society in which women were regarded as inferior. Even women born to the upper classes were not permitted to dine at the same table with men. They received a minimum of education, their freedom was nil, and they were forced to cover their faces with a black chador whenever they were in public. Not only did men expect the women to be obedient and docile to their command, but it was commonly believed that women were incapable of great intellectual thought and spiritual comprehension. The religious leaders of the time prohibited females from studying the Koran and denied them opportunities to advance in academic education and career. This was not a law based on text found in the Koran, but rather it was an ordinance devised by the priests based on their own interpretations of Muslim teachings.

As a young girl, however, Ṭáhirih, showed such extraordinary intelligence and such an intense curiosity for learning that her father could not ignore her brilliance. He selected a teacher who taught her various branches of knowledge and the arts, and she achieved remarkable ability in her literary pursuits. But she also sought a spiritual education. Prayer and her relationship with God were extremely important to her, and in her desire to search for spiritual truth she pleaded with her father to allow her to study the Koran. Her father relented, allowing her to sit behind a curtain while he would teach his class of male students in the parlor of his home.

She was looked upon as a child prodigy in intelligence and beauty alike. She was highly esteemed by some of the most haughty and learned scholars of her country for the brilliance and novelty of the views she propounded. When father and daughter were alone together discussing various portions of the Koran, she never failed to amaze him with her astounding insight and comprehension. She surpassed all of his students, and such was the degree of her scholarship and attainments that her father often expressed his disappointment, saying, "Would that she had been a boy, for he would have shed illumination upon my household, and would have succeeded me!"[235]

As a young woman, in a quest for spiritual truth, Ṭáhirih left her home and family, a most courageous feat for a young woman in that milieu, and set out to the city of Karbila to meet the spiritual teacher and writer Siyyid Káẓim. Intrigued by his writings and unconventional perspective, Ṭáhirih had been corresponding by mail with him for some time. To her dismay, he passed away before her arrival, but she discovered that before his death he had shared with his disciples his belief that the "promised one," a new messenger of God, would soon be proclaimed. Among his last words were "Go forth and seek out your Lord."[236]

Inspired by this final message, Ṭáhirih entered a period in which she fasted by day and engaged in vigils of prayer and meditation by night. She prayed fervently for spiritual truth and awakening. One night when it was nearing dawn, she laid her head on her pillow, lost all awareness of this earthly life, and dreamed of a youth wearing a black cloak and a green turban. He appeared to her in the heavens, standing in the air, reciting verses and praying with his hands upraised. At once, she memorized one of those verses, and wrote it down in her notebook when she awoke.[237]

It was a most extraordinary and powerful dream, and Ṭáhirih prayed and meditated about its significance. She had heard about the Báb, who had proclaimed his mission on May 23, 1844, and she was curious to read his writings. She was enthralled when she happened to come across a section of the Báb's text and read with her own eyes the exact verse from her dream. Instantly offering thanks to the Almighty God, she fell to her knees and bowed her forehead to the ground, convinced that the Báb's message was the truth.

She sent the Báb a message, which said, "The effulgence of Thy face flashed forth, and the rays of Thy visage arose on high. Then speak the word, 'Am I not your Lord?' and 'Thou art, Thou art!' We will all reply."[238]

Even though they had never met, the Báb recognized her as a pure soul upon receiving her note, and enrolled her as the only woman to serve as one of his nineteen apostles. Ṭáhirih's spirit was on fire. She traveled from village to village translating and expounding the teachings of the Báb by composing beauteous odes and lyrics, and humbly practicing her devotions. She eloquently promoted the emancipation of women and heralded the dawn of a new, more progressive age not just in words, but also in action, for the role she chose as a spiritual teacher and public presenter was breaking the strictest of taboos. Wherever she went she encouraged people to remove the veils of prejudice, superstition, and religious trappings of the past. She urged them to seek for themselves the inner truth of their relationship with God through the purity of prayer and virtuous deeds.

She had become widely renowned as a brilliant poet, a great scholar and teacher, and a courageous emancipator of women. To the Muslim clergy, however, she was dangerous. They regarded this woman's audacity as an abomination and viewed the teachings she espoused as heresy. The governor, responding to the demands of the clergy, ordered Ṭáhirih's arrest in Karbila. Although her life was in danger, her concerns were never for herself but for her companions, many of whom had also been arrested. She boldly sent a message to the governor, which said, "I am at your disposal. Do not harm any other."[239]

After three months of confinement, the governor finally gave her leave to go, which allowed her to travel and spread the teachings of the Báb. At nearly every village and city she visited, people admired her and celebrated her for her poetry, intelligence, and eloquence. Her popularity caused a great uproar among the authorities, and the authorities persisted in persecuting and arresting her. Her life was in grave danger when Bahá'u'lláh came to her rescue by arranging to bring her to his family's mansion in Tehran, where she stayed in an upper apartment. When word spread that she was in the city, the authorities hunted for her in every corner. At the same time, many supporters flocked in a steady stream to Bahá'u'lláh's home to visit her. Regardless of her brilliance and fame, to maintain propriety with respect to the customs of the time, she sat behind a curtain from where she would converse with the many people who came to speak with her. After listening to one visitor who carried on with obvious learning and piety, she responded: "Let deeds, not words, testify to thy faith, if thou art a man of true learning. Cease idly repeating the traditions of the past, for the day of service, of steadfast action, is come. Now is the time to show forth the true signs of God, to rend asunder the veils of idle fancy, to promote the Word of God, and to sacrifice ourselves in His path. Let deeds, not words, be our adorning!"[240]

It was the early summer of 1848 when the Báb, confined in prison, called a gathering of eighty-one of his followers to be held in the hamlet of Badasht, Persia. It was there, at the Conference of Badasht, where Ṭáhirih made clear to all that a new dispensation was established by appearing before the gathering with her face unveiled. Despite the outrage and fury of the men around her, she smiled calmly and said, "The great Trump is blown! The universal Advent is now proclaimed!" Horrified, many men ran away in panic, and one man was so overcome that he slashed his own throat.

Ṭáhirih had torn asunder ancient traditions through her heroic gesture. Removing the veil from her face symbolized the abrogation of the veils of ancestral laws and customs of the past in a new dispensation. How significant it was that the trumpeter of a new revelation of God, in a land that denigrated the female gender, was in fact, a female.

Ṭáhirih was later arrested again, this time confined for some time in the home of the mayor of Tehran. Although the government issued an order for her death, Ṭáhirih was aflame with the love of God and could not be stilled in her efforts to advance the cause of the emancipation of women. The wife of the mayor and some of the wives of the most elite families of Tehran adored Ṭáhirih, and on one pretext or another, literally besieged her place of confinement, crowding around her to seek the benefit of her knowledge. They were enchanted by her poetry and brilliance, her radiance, elegance, and beauty, and by her warmth, kindness, and generosity.

They were inspired and captivated by her message that women had untapped intellectual capacities and possessed the same potential as men to learn and achieve and comprehend spiritual knowledge. She offered them proofs in the Koran that there was nothing in the teachings of Muḥammad that exhorted the prohibition of education for the female gender. She advocated the renunciation of backward traditions that prevented the advancement of women. She shared with them the Báb's teachings about prayer: "The most acceptable prayer is the one offered with the utmost spirituality and radiance; its prolongation hath not been and is not beloved by God."[241]

On August 18, 1852, the prime minister's attendants came to remove Ṭáhirih from the house, for her day of execution had arrived. The mayor's wife relates an account of what took place prior to that occurrence:

One night, whilst Ṭáhirih was staying in my home, I was summoned to her presence and found her fully adorned, dressed in a gown of snow-white silk. Her room was redolent with the choicest perfume. I expressed to her my surprise at so unusual a sight. "I am preparing to meet my Beloved," she said, "and wish to free you from the cares and anxieties of my imprisonment." I was much startled at first, and wept at the thought of separation from her. "Weep not," she sought to reassure me. "The time of your lamentation is not yet come. I wish to share with you my last wishes, for the hour when I shall be arrested and condemned to suffer martyrdom is fast approaching. I would request you to allow your son to accompany me to the scene of my death and to ensure that the guards and executioner into whose hands I shall be delivered will not compel me to divest myself of this attire. It is also my wish that my body be thrown into a pit, and that that pit be filled with earth and stones. . . . My last request is that you permit no one henceforth to enter my chamber. From now until the time when I shall be summoned to leave this house, let no one be allowed to disturb my devotions. This day I intend to fast—a fast which I shall not break until I am brought face to face with my Beloved." She bade me, with these words, lock the door of her chamber and not open it until the hour of her departure should strike. She also urged me to keep secret the tidings of her death until such time as her enemies should themselves disclose it.[242]

And so in the last hours before this young woman was to be executed, she directed her soul to the heavenly light through prayer, meditation, and fasting. Four hours after sunset a group of men, sent by the prime minister of Tehran, the same man who had issued her death sentence, came to remove Ṭáhirih from the mayor's house. She kissed the mayor's wife and presented her with the key to her chest, which held whatever few possessions she owned. Ṭáhirih told her, "Whenever you open this chest and behold the things it contains, you will, I hope, remember me and rejoice in my gladness."[243]

She bade the woman her last farewell, and left with the men, accompanied by the woman's son. The men took her to a garden outside of Tehran where the prime minister and his attendants awaited her. They were drunk, besotted and roaring with laughter. Ṭáhirih called to the woman's son and said, "They apparently wish to strangle me. . . . I set aside, long ago, a silken kerchief which I hoped would be used for this purpose. I deliver it into your hands and wish you to induce that dissolute drunkard to use it as a means whereby he can take my life."[244]

It had already been the decision of the prime minister to kill Ṭáhirih by strangulation, and the young man had no difficulty persuading the executioner to grant Ṭáhirih's request. She turned to the prime minister and boldly declared: "You can kill me as soon as you like, but you cannot stop the emancipation of women."[245]

Ṭáhirih was strangled with the silk kerchief, and then her executioners lifted up her body and flung it into a well, there in the garden, and covered it with earth and stones, thus ending the life of this great heroine. Ṭáhirih is mentioned frequently in the Baháʼí writings, and the following passage attests to her purity of spirit, devotion and certitude of faith in the last moments before her execution: "But Ṭáhirih rejoiced; she had heard with a light heart the tidings of her martyrdom; she set her eyes on the supernal Kingdom and offered up her life."[246]

Another passage in the Baháʼí writings pays her the following tribute:

A poetess, less than thirty years of age, of distinguished birth, of bewitching charm, of captivating eloquence, indomitable in spirit, unorthodox in her views, audacious in her acts, immortalized as Ṭáhirih (the Pure One) . . . she had, in consequence of the appearance of the Báb to her in a dream, received the first intimation of a Cause which was destined to exalt her to the fairest heights of fame, and on which she, through her bold heroism, was to shed such imperishable luster.[247]

Living in a state of prayer

Ṭáhirih's life exemplifies the inner reality of prayer. She sacrificed, persevered, and struggled with purity of character and radiance of spirit until finally and courageously she gave up her life. She offered her talents, her knowledge, her skills, and her very being to serve the cause of God. She exemplified the saintlike qualities of modesty, chastity, selflessness, and humble piety. She learned to maximize her talents and abilities without compromising her values. Her death was not in vain.

This is not to imply that one must seek a martyr's death for the nearness of God, but a life that is offered for the selfless and noble purpose of contributing to the happiness, progress, and unity of humankind is a shining example of a soul who is aflame with the love of God.

Bahá'í scripture exhorts us not to seek to glorify ourselves but to glorify God. Those who glory in their own words and deeds as an example of righteousness and exalt their religious beliefs over the beliefs of others not only exhibit a sense of superiority, creating dissension and injury to others, but their false and vain imaginings result in the abasement of their own souls. Bahá'u'lláh testified in his writings:

> Hear no evil, and see no evil, abase not thyself, neither sigh and weep. Speak no evil, that thou mayest not hear it spoken unto thee, and magnify not the faults of others that thine own faults may not appear great; and wish not the abasement of anyone, that thine own abasement be not exposed. Live then the days of thy life, that are less than a fleeting moment, with thy mind stainless, thy heart unsullied, thy thoughts pure, and thy nature sanctified, so that, free and content, thou mayest put away this mortal frame, and repair unto the mystic paradise and abide in the eternal kingdom for evermore.[248]

Our aim should be to glorify God with humility and meekness. Regardless of our accomplishments, we are all equal in the sight of God. The short obligatory prayer from Bahá'í scripture reminds us of our human frailty and shortcomings, as well as the noble purpose for which were created: "I bear witness, O my God, that Thou hast created me to know Thee and to worship Thee. I testify, at this moment, to my powerlessness and to Thy might, to my poverty and to Thy wealth. There is none other God but Thee, the Help in Peril, the Self-Subsisting."[249]

When we recognize that the purpose for which we were created is to know and love God, we will have no wish to exalt ourselves over another, nor will we wish any harm on another soul. God created us to be noble, and we exemplify that nobility when we recognize the nobility in the spirit of all humanity, loving them for the sake of God: "Let your eyes be directed toward the kingdom of truth and not toward the world of creation. Love the creatures for the sake of God and not for themselves. You will never become angry or impatient if you love them for the sake of God."[250]

Perhaps it is only natural to sometimes feel frustrated with our fellow humans, but that is all the more reason to pray for each other and learn to forgive and love one another for the sake of God. While we strive to offer our prayers for the love of God, we also need to think about how to manifest those prayers in action in our everyday lives.

Praying for certitude

Ṭáhirih's certitude in her love for God is a wonderful example of sustainable faith. From the Baháʼí perspective, there is a fundamental difference between certitude and blind faith. Certitude is nurtured through prayer, search for truth, and the wellspring of divine confirmation. Blind faith, which emerges from factors like unquestioning adherence to tradition or from beliefs founded on superstition, shortchanges our inherent capacity for divine knowledge.

Through personal, heartfelt prayer, we foster an intimate relationship with God. Through the independent search for truth, when we break free of our attachment to the material world and rid ourselves of preset ideas and cultural conditionings, our spiritual channel is cleansed and our hearts are made more receptive to the blessings of God.

Through certitude our souls are sanctified by divine bounty. However, such certitude does not come to us through our attachment to inherited traditions or beliefs. It is attained through prayer, through open minds seeking truth, and through a love for, and trust in, God so firm that our faith is unshakable, regardless of what befalls us. Baháʼuʼlláh writes,

> Sanctify your souls, O ye peoples of the world. . . . The essence of these words is this: they that tread the path of faith, they that thirst for the wine of certitude, must cleanse themselves of all that

is earthly—their ears from idle talk, their minds from vain imaginings, their hearts from worldly affections, their eyes from that which perisheth. They should put their trust in God, and, holding fast unto Him, follow in His way. Then will they be made worthy of the effulgent glories of the sun of divine knowledge and understanding, and become the recipients of a grace that is infinite and unseen, inasmuch as man can never hope to attain unto the knowledge of the All-Glorious, can never quaff from the stream of divine knowledge and wisdom, can never enter the abode of immortality, nor partake of the cup of divine nearness and favour, unless and until he ceases to regard the words and deeds of mortal men as a standard for the true understanding and recognition of God and His Prophets.[251]

Souls with such certitude live in a state of inner prayer. Their certitude in God's love is so firm and steadfast that they see the good in all events, even in times of tests and tribulations. Through their fervent prayers and their love for God, their inner eyes are opened to see beauty and light where before there was darkness.

Bahá'í scripture affirms that a soul in this state will "come out of doubt into certitude, and turn from the darkness of illusion to the guiding light. . . . His inner eyes will open and he will privily converse with his Beloved; he will set ajar the gate of truth and piety, and shut the doors of vain imaginings. He in this station is content with the decree of God."[252]

This certitude is the inner reality of prayer and the purpose and very essence of faith. It is our love-line to God. Through such certitude we submit to the will of God and joyfully exalt in His love for us:

Those who had eyes to see rejoiced at the glad tidings and cried out: "O blessed, blessed are we!" and they witnessed the inner reality of all things, and uncovered the mysteries of the Kingdom. Delivered then from their fancies and their doubts, they beheld the light of truth, and so exhilarated did they become from draining the chalice of God's love, that they utterly forgot the world and their own selves.[253]

The search for truth and the inner reality of religion

The search for truth is a never-ending road for the spiritual seeker. God enabled our souls to have physical bodies so that we might endeavor on a journey in this physical world to learn, grow, and develop in preparation for the next world. All things in the physical world are transient, and our eternal reality is of the spiritual world. It is easy to become attached to the physical world, and without prayer and faith, one easily becomes heedless of the remembrance of God and veiled to the reality and purpose of the creation of the human soul. A seeker's quest for truth is infinite, just as the ocean of God's knowledge is fathomless, the sheltering haven of His love eternal, and the protective shield of His might is omnipotent and eternal.

Though God's love for us is absolute, an imperfect humanity will always be striving to comprehend that love; it is a never-ending quest. The writings of Bahá'u'lláh affirm that while the search for truth is infinite, the blessings showered upon the soul who journeys on such a quest is immeasurable:

> Be an ornament to the countenance of truth, a crown to the brow of fidelity, a pillar of the temple of righteousness, a breath of life to the body of mankind, an ensign of the hosts of justice, a luminary above the horizon of virtue, a dew to the soil of the human heart, an ark on the ocean of knowledge, a sun in the heaven of bounty, a gem on the diadem of wisdom, a shining light in the firmament of thy generation, a fruit upon the tree of humility. We pray God to protect thee. . . . He verily is nigh, ready to answer.[254]

We will always need to pray for the eternal love of God to sustain our spiritual hunger, and we will always need to search for the knowledge of God to quench our spiritual thirst with the ocean of the knowledge of God: "It is the duty of every seeker to bestir himself and strive to attain the shores of this ocean, so that he may, in proportion to the eagerness of his search and the efforts he hath exerted, partake of such benefits as have been pre-ordained in God's irrevocable and hidden Tablets."[255]

Bahá'í scripture tells us that there is one God, one human race, and that truth is one. However, that truth may manifest itself in different

sizes, shapes, colors, names, and packages. But the appearance of differences need not be the cause of division and dissension. When we embrace
the glorious diversity of the human family and seek truth with a pure,
radiant heart, we can delight in the reality of the oneness of humanity
and the oneness of religion.

'Abdu'l-Bahá tells us,

> God has sent religion for the purpose of establishing fellowship among
> humankind and not to create strife and discord, for all religion is
> founded upon the love of humanity. Abraham promulgated this
> principle, Moses summoned all to its recognition, Christ established
> it, and Muhammad directed mankind to its standard. This is the
> reality of religion. If we abandon hearsay and investigate the reality
> and inner significance of the heavenly teachings, we will find the same
> divine foundation of love for humanity.[256]

So important is the establishment of unity for the spiritual progress of
humankind that Bahá'u'lláh attested it would be better to have no religion
at all if it is the cause of dissension and strife:

> The purport is that religion is intended to be the cause of unity,
> love and fellowship and not discord, enmity and estrangement. Man
> has forsaken the foundation of divine religion and adhered to blind
> imitations. Each nation has clung to its own imitations, and because
> these are at variance, warfare, bloodshed and destruction of the
> foundation of humanity have resulted. True religion is based upon
> love and agreement. Bahá'u'lláh has said, "If religion and faith are
> the causes of enmity and sedition, it is far better to be nonreligious,
> and the absence of religion would be preferable; for we desire religion
> to be the cause of amity and fellowship. If enmity and hatred exist,
> irreligion is preferable." Therefore, the removal of this dissension
> has been specialized in Bahá'u'lláh, for religion is the divine remedy
> for human antagonism and discord. But when we make the remedy
> the cause of the disease, it would be better to do without the
> remedy.[257]

Our initiative to seek truth independenty and to investigate reality and study the sacred scriptures helps us avoid dogmatic adherence to tradition, but it is also through prayer, meditation, and an attitude of detachment that we can succeed in our search for truth. 'Abdu'l-Bahá explains,

> Man must cut himself free from all prejudice and from the result of his own imagination, so that he may be able to search for truth unhindered. Truth is one in all religions, and by means of it the unity of the world can be realized.
>
> All the peoples have a fundamental belief in common. Being one, truth cannot be divided, and the differences that appear to exist among the nations only result from their attachment to prejudice. If only men would search out truth, they would find themselves united.[258]

Shortly after Ṭáhirih's life was taken, Bahá'u'lláh was arrested in Tehran, chained, abused, and imprisoned in the infamous "Black Pit." He remained there, his body in chains, for four months. He lived in imprisonment and exile for forty years until the end of his life. Simply because they followed his teachings, thousands of Bahá'ís were killed and maltreated, and persecution of Bahá'ís continues in a number of countries today.

Why were the Muslim clergy so threatened by the teachings of Bahá'u'lláh? Why was Christ persecuted and crucified? Why were masses of Christians sent to the lions' dens? Why were the Báb and thousands of Bábís massacred? Why was Ṭáhirih strangled to death? Why was the prophet Abraham banished from his homeland in Mesopotamia, sanctioned by his own father?

The cause of these wrongdoings is and has always been the result of ignorance, prejudice, and superstition:

> Therefore it is imperative that we should renounce our own particular prejudices and superstitions if we earnestly desire to seek the truth. Unless we make a distinction in our minds between

dogma, superstition and prejudice on the one hand, and truth on the other, we cannot succeed. When we are in earnest in our search for anything we look for it everywhere. This principle we must carry out in our search for truth.

. . . Light is good in whatsoever lamp it is burning! A rose is beautiful in whatsoever garden it may bloom! A star has the same radiance if it shines from the East or from the West. Be free from prejudice, so will you love the Sun of Truth from whatsoever point in the horizon it may arise! You will realize that if the Divine light of truth shone in Jesus Christ it also shone in Moses and in Buddha. The earnest seeker will arrive at this truth. This is what is meant by the "Search after Truth."

It means, also, that we must be willing to clear away all that we have previously learned, all that would clog our steps on the way to truth; we must not shrink if necessary from beginning our education all over again. We must not allow our love for any one religion or any one personality to so blind our eyes that we become fettered by superstition! When we are freed from all these bonds, seeking with liberated minds, then shall we be able to arrive at our goal.

"Seek the truth, the truth shall make you free." So shall we see the truth in all religions, for truth is in all and truth is one![259]

When I look at my two younger children, Alex and Ben, who are both mentally impaired, I am aware that their analytical abilities to search for the truth are debilitated by their intellectual deficiencies. But I doubt that they have a prejudiced bone in their bodies; they are willing to accept anyone who shows genuine kindness and warmth to them, and it is so apparent that their hearts are pure and radiantly receptive to the love of God.

For most of us, however, our quest to draw nearer to God requires effort, which Bahá'í scripture tells us must be sustained through daily prayer, faith, individual investigation of the truth, and striving to make our thoughts, actions, and deeds motivated by our love for God. This is an ongoing process. The inner reality of prayer is how we view God and how we establish and maintain our relationship with God. Living in a prayerful state occurs when every decision we make, every action we take, every word we say, is motivated by the remembrance of God.

Epilogue

And so, dear reader, we come to the end of this book, but not to end of our quest for truth, because that is an ongoing spiritual journey. Bahá'í scripture refers to the first stage of spiritual seeking as "The Valley of Search," explaining, "The steed of this Valley is patience; without patience the wayfarer on this journey will reach nowhere and attain no goal."[260]

May God bless you with a patient, radiant, and happy heart and shower you with heavenly confirmations in your endeavors to travel the highway to the Kingdom of God. Enjoy your journey, unburden your soul, never lose hope, and be assured that all of your prayers are indeed answered by God.

Make a joyful noise, dearest reader! Sing out your praises to God and render thanks and joyful tidings to Him. Pray for forgiveness and have trust in His tender mercy. Have faith, seek the truth, and pray for your loved ones and friends. In your remembrance of God, be assured that your soul will delight and grow in the embrace of the Holy Spirit. God created you because He loves you. Pray for the love of God so that your soul may be filled with the heavenly fragrance of His love for you, which is eternal.

I give thanks to Thee, O my God, that Thou hast suffered me to remember Thee. What else but remembrance of Thee can give delight to my soul or gladness to my heart? Communion with Thee enableth me to dispense with the remembrance of all Thy creatures, and my love for Thee empowereth me to endure the harm which my oppressors inflict upon me.

Send, therefore, unto my loved ones, O my God, what will cheer their hearts, and illumine their faces, and delight their souls. Thou knowest, O my Lord, that their joy is to behold the exaltation of Thy Cause and the glorification of Thy word. Do Thou unveil, therefore, O my God, what will gladden their eyes, and ordain for them the good of this world and of the world which is to come.

Thou art, verily, the God of power, of strength and of bounty.[261]

Notes

Introduction

1. 'Abdu'l-Bahá, *Paris Talks,* no. 41.7–10.
2. Bahá'u'lláh, in *Bahá'í Prayers,* p. 163.
3. 'Abdu'l-Bahá, *Promulgation of Universal Peace,* p. 48.
4. 'Abdu'l-Bahá, in *Bahá'í Prayers,* p. 28.
5. 'Abdu'l-Bahá, *Selections from the Writings of 'Abdu'l-Bahá,* no. 103.5.
6. 'Abdu'l-Bahá, *Paris Talks,* no. 27.6.

Chapter 1

7. 1 Corinthians 13:1 (KJV).
8. Report of 'Abdu'l-Bahá's words, quoted in J.E. Esslemont, *Bahá'u'lláh and the New Era,* p. 94.
9. Bahá'u'lláh, Hidden Words, Arabic, nos. 3–5.
10. Bhagavad-Gita, Edwin Arnold, trans., 7:104.
11. Deuteronomy 11:13 (KJV).
12. Matthew 22:37 (KJV).
13. Koran 2:165 (Yusuf Ali trans.).
14. Attributed to 'Abdu'l-Bahá, quoted in Marzieh Gail, *Summon Up Remembrance,* p. 254.
15. Ibid., p. 255.
16. Shoghi Effendi, *Directives from the Guardian,* p. 87.
17. 'Abdu'l-Bahá, *Selections from the Writings of 'Abdu'l-Bahá,* p. 89.
18. 'Abdu'l-Bahá, cited in *Star of the West,* vol. 7, no. 4, p. 41.

19. Bahá'u'lláh, *Gleanings,* no. 125.3.
20. The Báb, *Selections from the Writings of the Báb,* p. 78.
21. Bahá'u'lláh, *Gleanings,* no. 136.2.
22. The Báb, *Selections from the Writings of the Báb,* p. 93–4.
23. Universal House of Justice, Introduction, *The Kitáb-i-Aqdas: The Most Holy Book,* pp. 2–3.
24. Bahá'u'lláh, *Prayers and Meditations,* p. 261.
25. Bahá'u'lláh, *Gleanings,* no. 134.12.
26. 'Abdu'l-Bahá, *Paris Talks,* no. 55.1.
27. Ibid., 2.3–6.
28. Bahá'u'lláh, *Prayers and Meditations,* p. 262.
29. Psalms 66:1–2 (KJV).

Chapter 2

30. The Báb, as reported in Nabíl-i-A'zam, *The Dawn-Breakers,* p. 30.
31. Nabíl-i-A'zam, *The Dawn-Breakers,* p. 30.
32. The Báb, *Selections from the Writings of the Báb,* p. 78.
33. 'Abdu'l-Bahá, *A Traveller's Narrative,* p. 4.
34. Shoghi Effendi, *God Passes By,* pp. 6–7.
35. 'Abdu'l-Bahá, *Memorials of the Faithful,* p. 188.
36. Shoghi Effendi, *God Passes By,* p. 31.
37. 'Abdu'l-Bahá, *Memorials of the Faithful,* pp. 198–9.
38. Shoghi Effendi, *God Passes By,* p, 32.
39. Ibid.
40. Shoghi Effendi, *God Passes By,* p. 31.
41. 'Abdu'l-Bahá, *Paris Talks,* pp. 41.7–8.
42. The Báb, as recorded in *God Passes By,* p. 52.
43. Ibid.
44. Bahá'u'lláh, as recorded in Nabíl-i-A'zam, *The Dawn-Breakers,* pp. 631–2.
45. Bahá'u'lláh, *Summons of the Lord of Hosts,* p. 98.
46. Bahá'u'lláh, as recorded in Nabíl-i-A'zam, *The Dawn-Breakers,* p. 632.
47. Bahá'u'lláh, *Gleanings,* no. 54.

48. Ibid., no. 132.3.
49. Ibid., no. 130.
50. Bahá'u'lláh, in *Bahá'í Prayers*, p. 4.
51. Ibid., pp. 7–8.
52. Bahá'u'lláh, *Gleanings*, no. 1.5.
53. 'Abdu'l-Bahá, *Promulgation of Universal Peace*, p. 142.
54. Bahá'u'lláh, cited in *The Importance of Obligatory Prayer and Fasting*, no. 26.
55. 'Abdu'l-Bahá, *Paris Talks*, no. 40.8.
56. Ibid., no. 11.4.
57. Bahá'u'lláh, *Gleanings*, no. 110.
58. The Báb, *Selections from the Writings of the Báb*, p. 78.
59. Bahá'u'lláh, Kitáb-i-Aqdas, ¶149.
60. 'Abdu'l-Bahá, in *Bahá'í Prayers*, p. 70.
61. 'Abdu'l-Bahá, *Paris Talks*, no. 35.14–15.
62. 'Abdu'l-Bahá, *Selections from the Writings of 'Abdu'l-Bahá*, no. 172.
63. Ibid., no. 82.
64. Bahá'u'lláh, Hidden Words, Arabic, no. 13.

Chapter 3

65. Bahá'u'lláh, *Prayers and Meditations*, p. 208.
66. 'Abdu'l-Bahá, *Tablets of the Divine Plan*, p. 64.
67. 'Abdu'l-Bahá, *Promulgation of Universal Peace*, pp. 213–4.

Chapter 4

68. Babylonian Talmud, Tractate Shabbat, trans. Rabbi Dr. H. Freedman, folio 31a.
69. Bahá'u'lláh, *Gleanings*, no. 125.3.
70. Bahá'u'lláh, *Tablets of Bahá'u'lláh*, pp. 24–5.
41. Bhagavad-Gita 7:104.
72. Muhammad, cited in J.E. Esslemont, *Bahá'u'lláh and the New Era*, p. 88.

73. 'Abdu'l-Bahá, *Selections of the Writings of 'Abdu'l-Bahá*, p. 27.

74. Report of 'Abdu'l-Bahá's words, quoted in J.E. Esslemont, *Bahá'u'lláh and the New Era*, p. 94.

75. Bahá'u'lláh, in *Bahá'í Prayers*, pp. 19–20.

Chapter 5

76. Bahá'u'lláh, in *Bahá'í Prayers*, pp. 309.

77. The Báb, in *Bahá'í Prayers*, p. 226.

Chapter 6

78. Bahá'u'lláh, *Prayers and Meditations*, pp. 262–3.

79. Bahá'u'lláh, *Gleanings*, no. 29.1.

80. 'Abdu'l-Bahá, *Some Answered Questions*, p. 210.

81. Ibid.

82. 'Abdu'l-Bahá, *Paris Talks*, no. 11.5.

83. Ibid., nos. 11.4, 11.11.

84. Ibid., no. 11.13.

85. Ibid., no. 31.6.

86. 'Abdu'l-Bahá, *Promulgation of Universal Peace*, p. 226.

87. The Báb, in *Bahá'í Prayers*, p. 226.

88. 'Abdu'l-Bahá, *Selections from the Writings of 'Abdu'l-Bahá*, no. 110.2.

89. 'Abdu'l-Bahá, *Foundations of World Unity*, p. 51.

Chapter 7

90. 'Abdu'l-Bahá, *Paris Talks*, no. 6.12.

91. Letter written on behalf of Shoghi Effendi, cited in "The Importance of Prayer, Meditation, and the Devotional Attitude," *Compilation of Compilations*, vol. 2, p. 240.

92. Bahá'u'lláh, Kitáb-i-Aqdas, ¶76.

93. 'Abdu'l-Bahá, in *Bahá'í Prayers*, p. 23.

94. 'Abdu'l-Bahá, cited in "The Importance of Prayer, Meditation, and the Devotional Attitude," *Compilation of Compilations*, vol. 2, p. 231.

95. Bahá'u'lláh, *Tablets of Bahá'u'lláh*, p. 24.

96. Bahá'u'lláh, cited in Shoghi Effendi, *God Passes By*, p. 215.

97. 'Abdu'l-Bahá, *Promulgation of Universal Peace*, p. 328

98. Bahá'u'lláh, Hidden Words, Arabic, no. 31.

99. 'Abdu'l-Bahá, *Promulgation of Universal Peace*, p. 453.

100. 'Abdu'l-Bahá, *Some Answered Questions*, p. 232.

101. 'Abdu'l-Bahá, quoted in J.E. Esslemont, *Bahá'u'lláh and the New Era*, p. 94.

102. 'Abdu'l-Bahá, *Selections from the Writings of 'Abdu'l-Bahá*, no. 59.3.

103. Bahá'u'lláh, Kitáb-i-Íqán, ¶164.

104. Bahá'u'lláh, Hidden Words, Arabic, no. 5.

105. 'Abdu'l-Bahá, *Promulgation of Universal Peace*, p. 93.

106. Bahá'u'lláh, in *Bahá'í Prayers*, p. 169.

Chapter 8

107. Bahá'u'lláh, in *Bahá'í Prayers*, p. 102.

108. 'Abdu'l-Bahá, *Paris Talks*, no. 3.1.

109. Quoted sections are taken from 'Abdu'l-Bahá, *Paris Talks*, no. 55.1.

Chapter 9

110. Bahá'u'lláh, in *Bahá'í Prayers*, p. 169.

111. Bahá'u'lláh, *Prayers and Meditations*, p. 247.

112. Bahá'u'lláh, *Gleanings*, nos. 66.11, 66.10.

113. Ibid., no. 66.10.

114. 'Abdu'l-Bahá, *Selections from the Writings of 'Abdu'l-Bahá*, no. 86.1.

115. Abdu'l-Bahá, in *Bahá'í Prayers*, pp. 65.

116. Luke 6:38 (KJV).

117. 'Abdu'l-Bahá, *Promulgation of Universal Peace*, p. 247.

118. Ibid., p. 246.

119. Ibid., p. 247.

120. 'Abdu'l-Bahá, *Selections from the Writings of 'Abdu'l-Bahá*, no. 139.7–8.

121. 'Abdu'l-Bahá, *Some Answered Questions*, p. 224.

122. 'Abdu'l-Bahá, *Paris Talks*, no. 14.8–9.

123. Bahá'u'lláh, cited in "Health, Healing, Nutrition, and Related Matters," *Compilation of Compilations,* vol. 1, p. 458.

124. 'Abdu'l-Bahá, *Selections from the Writings of 'Abdu'l-Bahá,* no. 133.1–2.

125. 'Abdu'l-Bahá, *Paris Talks,* no. 35.1–7.

Chapter 10

126. Bahá'u'lláh, in *Bahá'í Prayers,* p. i.

Chapter 11

127. 'Abdu'l-Bahá, *Promulgation of Universal Peace,* pp. 46–7.

128. The Universal House of Justice, letter to an individual, April 8, 1982.

129. Bahá'u'lláh, *Epistle to the Son of the Wolf,* p. 14.

130. Ibid., p. 93.

131. 'Abdu'l-Bahá, in *Bahá'í Prayers,* p. 26.

132. The Universal House of Justice, *The Promise of World Peace,* p. 1.

133. Psalms 133:1 (KJV).

134. 'Abdu'l-Bahá, *Selections from the Writings of 'Abdu'l-Bahá,* no. 58.

135. Bahá'u'lláh, *Gleanings,* no. 131.2.

136. 'Abdu'l-Bahá, *Promulgation of Universal Peace,* p. 214.

137. Ibid., p. 402.

138. 'Abdu'l-Bahá, *Selections from the Writings of 'Abdu'l-Bahá,* no. 60.

139. Ibid., no. 56.

140. 'Abdu'l-Bahá, *Selections from the Writings of 'Abdu'l-Bahá,* no. 58.

141. Shoghi Effendi, *Directives from the Guardian,* p. 78.

142. Written on behalf of the Universal House of Justice, letter dated 8 April 1982 to an individual.

143. 'Abdu'l-Bahá, *Selections from the Writings of 'Abdu'l-Bahá,* no. 55.

144. Shoghi Effendi, cited in a letter written on behalf of the Universal House of Justice, in *Lights of Guidance,* no. 1503.

145. Written on behalf of the Universal House of Justice, letter dated 27 June 2001 to an individual.

146. 'Abdu'l-Bahá, *Selections from the Writings of 'Abdu'l-Bahá,* no. 74.1.

147. Ibid., no. 58.
148. 'Abdu'l-Bahá, *Promulgation of Universal Peace*, pp. 144–5.

Chapter 12
149. The Báb, in *Bahá'í Prayers*, p. 56.
150. 'Abdu'l-Bahá, *Promulgation of Universal Peace*, p. 48.
151. The Báb, in *Bahá'í Prayers*, p. 227.
152. Bahá'u'lláh, in *Bahá'í Prayers*, pp. 309–10.
153. 'Abdu'l-Bahá, *Paris Talks*, no. 35.3–11.
154. Shoghi Effendi, *Bahá'í Administration*, p. 53.
155. 'Abdu'l-Bahá, in *Bahá'í Prayers*, pp. 174–5.
156. Bahá'u'lláh, Hidden Words, Persian, no. 8.
157. Bahá'u'lláh, *Prayers and Meditations*, p. 208.
158. The Báb, in *Bahá'í Prayers*, p. 226.
159. Bahá'u'lláh, Hidden Words, Arabic, no. 9.
160. The Universal House of Justice, Riḍván message to the Bahá'ís of the World, April 21, 1993.

Chapter 13
161. 'Abdu'l-Bahá, *Promulgation of Universal Peace*, p. 52.

Chapter 14
162. Psalms, 66:1–2 (KJV).
163. Bhagavad-Gita, trans. Juan Mascaro, p. 12.
164. 'Abdu'l-Bahá, *Promulgation of Universal Peace*, p. 52.
165. H.M. Balyuzi, *Muhammad and the Course of Islam*, p. 309.
166. Bahá'u'lláh, Kitáb-i-Aqdas, ¶51.
167. 'Abdu'l-Bahá, cited in "Music," *Compilation of Compilations*, vol. 2, p. 76.
168. Ibid.
169. Written on behalf of Shoghi Effendi, cited in "Music," *Compilation of Compilations*, vol. 2, p. 80.

170. Derrick Bell, *Gospel Choirs*, p. 1.

171. 'Abdu'l-Bahá, cited in "Music," *Compilation of Compilations*, vol. 2, p. 74.

Chapter 15

172. 'Abdu'l-Bahá, *Selections from the Writings of 'Abdu'l-Bahá*, no. 74.2.

173. 'Abdu'l-Bahá, *Tablets of the Divine Plan*, p. 6.

174. Bahá'u'lláh, *Gleanings*, no. 136.2.

175. Bahá'u'lláh, in *Bahá'í Prayers*, p. 4.

Chapter 16

176. 'Abdu'l-Bahá, *Promulgation of Universal Peace*, p. 86.

177. 'Abdu'l-Bahá, *Paris Talks*, no. 53.15–17.

178. Bahá'u'lláh, Hidden Words, Arabic, no. 5.

179. Bahá'u'lláh, Kitáb-i-Íqán, ¶8.

180. Bhagavad-Gita, trans. Edwin Arnold, 2:156–69.

181. Bhagavad-Gita, trans. Juan Mascaro, p. 53.

182. Edward Conze, *Buddhist Scriptures*, p. 100.

183. Dhammapada, 1:14.

184. Edward Conze, *Buddhist Scriptures*, p. 100.

185. Psalms, 1:2 (KJV).

186. 'Abdu'l-Bahá, *Paris Talks*, no. 54.13.

187. Ibid., no. 54.8.

188. Ibid., no. 54.12–16.

189. 'Abdu'l-Bahá, *Paris Talks*, p. 175.

190. Bahá'u'lláh, *Gleanings*, no. 29.1.

191. 'Abdu'l-Bahá, *Paris Talks*, no. 54.17–19.

192. Bahá'u'lláh, Hidden Words, Arabic, no. 31.

193. 'Abdu'l-Bahá, *Divine Philosophy*, pp. 117–8.

194. Ibid., p. 118.

Chapter 17

195. Bahá'u'lláh, *Tablets of Bahá'u'lláh*, p. 168.
196. Bahá'u'lláh, in "Consultation," *Compilation of Compilations*, vol. 1, p. 93.
197. Written on behalf of Shoghi Effendi, letter to an individual believer, in "The Importance of Prayer, Meditation, and the Devotional Attitude," *Compilation of Compilations*, vol. 2, p. 241.
198. 'Abdu'l-Bahá, *Promulgation of Universal Peace*, p. 72.
199. 'Abdu'l-Bahá, *Selections from the Writings of 'Abdu'l-Bahá*, p. 86.
200. 'Abdu'l-Bahá, *Promulgation of Universal Peace*, p. 72.
201. Ibid.
202. 'Abdu'l-Bahá, *Selections from the Writings of 'Abdu'l-Bahá*, no. 44.
203. Bahá'u'lláh, in *Bahá'í Prayers*, p. 238.

Chapter 18

204. 'Abdu'l-Bahá, in *Bahá'í Prayers*, pp. 215–6.
205. Bahá'u'lláh, cited in *The Importance of Obligatory Prayer and Fasting*, no. 16.
206. Bahá'u'lláh, *Gleanings*, no. 125.2.
207. Ibid., no. 125.3.
208. Bahá'u'lláh, Hidden Words, Arabic, no. 68.

Chapter 19

209. 'Abdu'l-Bahá, in *Bahá'í Prayers*, p. 28.
210. 'Abdu'l-Bahá, *Promulgation of Universal Peace*, p. 15.
211. Ibid., p. 180.
212. Bahá'u'lláh, *Epistle to the Son of the Wolf*, p. 14.
213. 'Abdu'l-Bahá, in *Bahá'í Prayers*, p. 29.

Chapter 20

214. 'Abdu'l-Bahá, *Selections from the Writings of 'Abdu'l-Bahá*, p. 147.

215. Shoghi Effendi, *Advent of Divine Justice*, p. 37.

216. Bahá'u'lláh, Hidden Words, Arabic, no. 22.

217. 'Abdu'l-Bahá, *Promulgation of Universal Peace*, p. 52.

218. The Universal House of Justice, Riḍván message to the Bahá'ís of the world, April 21, 2000.

219. 'Abdu'l-Bahá, *Selections from the Writings of 'Abdu'l-Bahá*, no. 98.2.

220. The Universal House of Justice, Riḍván message to the Bahá'ís of the world, April 21, 2000.

221. 'Abdu'l-Bahá, *Selections from the Writings of 'Abdu'l-Bahá*, no. 108.1.

222. Ibid., no. 96.1.

223. 'Abdu'l-Bahá, in *Bahá'í Prayers*, pp. 33–4.

224. Ibid., p. 29.

225. Ibid., pp. 28.

226. 'Abdu'l-Bahá, *Selections from the Writings of Abdu'l-Bahá*, no. 103.1.

227. Ibid., no. 111.1.

228. Ibid., no. 103.5.

229. Ibid., no. 110.2.

230. Bahá'u'lláh, cited in "Bahá'í Education," *Compilation of Compilations*, vol. 1, p. 248.

231. Ibid, p. 125.

232. 'Abdu'l-Bahá, *Promulgation of Universal Peace*, p. 174.

Chapter 21

233. Bahá'u'lláh, Hidden Words, Persian, no. 3.

234. Bahá'u'lláh, Kitáb-i-Aqdas, ¶51.

Chapter 22

235. 'Abdu'l-Bahá, *Memorials of the Faithful*, p. 191.

236. Ibid., p. 192.

237. Ibid., p. 193.

238. Nabíl-i-A'zam, *The Dawn-Breakers*, pp. 81–2.

239. 'Abdu'l-Bahá, *Memorials of the Faithful*, p. 194.

240. Ibid., p. 200.

241. The Báb, *Selections from the Writings of the Báb*, p. 78.

242. Nabíl-i-A'zam, *The Dawn-Breakers*, pp. 622–4.

243. Ibid., p. 625.

244. Ibid.

245. Shoghi Effendi, *God Passes By*, p. 75.

246. 'Abdu'l-Bahá, *Memorials of the Faithful*, p. 203.

247. Shoghi Effendi, *God Passes By*, p. 7.

248. Bahá'u'lláh, Hidden Words, Persian, no. 44.

249. Bahá'u'lláh, in *Bahá'í Prayers*, p. 4.

250. 'Abdu'l-Bahá, *Promulgation of Universal Peace*, p. 93.

251. Bahá'u'lláh, Kitáb-i-Íqán, ¶1–2.

252. Bahá'u'lláh, *The Seven Valleys and The Four Valleys*, pp. 11–12.

253. *Selections from the Writings of 'Abdu'l-Bahá*, no. 16.1.

254. Bahá'u'lláh, *Epistle to the Son of the Wolf*, p. 93.

255. Bahá'u'lláh, *Gleanings*, no. 153.5.

256. 'Abdu'l-Bahá, *Promulgation of Universal Peace*, pp. 231–2.

257. Ibid.

258. 'Abdu'l-Bahá, *Paris Talks*, no. 40.8–11.

259. Ibid., no. 41.8–9.

Epilogue

260. Bahá'u'lláh, *The Seven Valleys and The Four Valleys*, p. 5.

261. Bahá'u'lláh, *Prayers and Meditations*, pp. 195–6.

Bibliography

Works of Bahá'u'lláh

Epistle to the Son of the Wolf. 1st pocket-size ed. Translated by Shoghi Effendi. Wilmette, IL: Bahá'í Publishing Trust, 1988.

Gleanings from the Writings of Bahá'u'lláh. Translated by Shoghi Effendi. Wilmette, IL: Bahá'í Publishing, 2005.

The Hidden Words. Translated by Shoghi Effendi. Wilmette, IL: Bahá'í Publishing, 2002.

The Kitáb-i-Aqdas: The Most Holy Book. 1st pocket-size ed. Wilmette, IL: Bahá'í Publishing Trust, 1993.

The Kitáb-i-Íqán: The Book of Certitude. Translated by Shoghi Effendi. Wilmette, IL: Bahá'í Publishing, 2003.

Prayers and Meditations. Translated by Shoghi Effendi. 1st pocket-size ed. Wilmette, IL: Bahá'í Publishing Trust, 1987.

Seven Valleys and The Four Valleys. New ed. Translated by Ali-Kuli Khan and Marzieh Gail. Wilmette, IL: Bahá'í Publishing Trust, 1991.

The Summons of the Lord of Hosts: Tablets of Bahá'u'lláh. Haifa: Bahá'í World Centre, 2002.

Tablets of Bahá'u'lláh revealed after the Kitáb-i-Aqdas. Compiled by the Research Department of the Universal House of Justice. Translated by Habib Taherzadeh et al. Wilmette, IL: 1988.

Works of the Báb

Selections from the Writings of the Báb. Compiled by the Research Department of the Universal House of Justice. Translated by Habib Taherzadeh et al. Haifa: Bahá'í World Centre, 1976.

Works of 'Abdu'l-Bahá

Memorials of the Faithful. Translated by Marzieh Gail. Wilmette, IL: Bahá'í Publishing Trust, 1997.

Paris Talks: Addresses Given By 'Abdu'l-Bahá in Paris in 1911. 12th ed. London: Bahá'í Publishing Trust, 1995.

Promulgation of Universal Peace: Talks Delivered by 'Abdu'l-Bahá during His Visit to the United States and Canada in 1912. Compiled by Howard MacNutt. 2nd ed. Wilmette, IL: Bahá'í Publishing Trust, 1982.

Selections from the Writings of 'Abdu'l-Bahá. Compiled by the Research Department of the Universal House of Justice. Translated by a Committee at the Bahá'í World Center and Marzieh Gail. 1st pocket-size ed. Wilmette, IL: Bahá'í Publishing Trust, 1997.

Some Answered Questions. Compiled and translated by Laura Clifford Barney. 1st pocket-size ed. Wilmette, IL: Bahá'í Publishing Trust, 1984.

Works of Shoghi Effendi

Advent of Divine Justice. 1st pocket-size ed. Wilmette, IL: Bahá'í Publishing Trust, 1990.

Bahá'í Administration. Wilmette, IL: Bahá'í Publishing Trust, 1974.

Directives from the Guardian. Honolulu: Bahá'í Publishing Trust, 1973.

God Passes By. New ed. Wilmette, IL: Bahá'í Publishing Trust, 1974.

Compilations of Bahá'í Writings
Bahá'í Prayers: A Selection of Prayers Revealed by Bahá'u'lláh, the Báb, and 'Abdu'l-Bahá. Wilmette, IL: Bahá'í Publishing Trust, 2002.

The Compilation of Compilations. 2 vols. Inglewood, NSW: Bahá'í Publications Australia, 1991.

The Importance of Obligatory Prayer and Fasting. Haifa: Bahá'í World Center, 2000.

Lights of Guidance. Compiled by Helen Hornby. New ed. New Delhi: Bahá'í Publishing Trust, 1994.

Other Works
Babylonian Talmud. 18 vols. Edited by Rabbi Dr. Isidore Epstein. London: Soncino Press, 1935–48.

Bhagavad-Gita. Translated by Edwin Arnold. New York: P.F. Collier & Son Co., 1909–14.

Bhagavad-Gita. Translated by Juan Mascaro. London: Penguin Classics, 1962.

Bell, Derrick. *Gospel Choirs.* New York: BasicBooks, 1996.

Conze, Edward. *Buddhist Scriptures.* Middlesex, England: Penguin Books, Ltd., 1973.

Dhammapada. Translated by John Richards. Pembrokeshire, England: Electronic Buddhist Archives, 1993.

Esslemont, J. E., *Bahá'u'lláh and the New Era*, 5th rev. ed. Wilmette, IL: Bahá'í Publishing Trust, 1980.

Gail, Marzieh. *Summon Up Remembrance.* Oxford: George Ronald Publisher, Ltd., 1987.

Nabíl-i-'Aẓam [Muḥammad-i-Zarandí]. *The Dawn-Breakers: Nabil's Narrative of the Early Days of the Bahá'í Revelation.* Translated by Shoghi Effendi. Wilmette, IL: Bahá'í Publishing Trust, 1932.

For more information about the Bahá'í Faith,
or to contact the Bahá'ís near you, visit
http://www.us.bahai.org/
or call
1-800-22-UNITE

Bahá'í Publishing
and the Bahá'í Faith

Bahá'í Publishing produces books based on the teachings of the Bahá'í Faith. Founded nearly 160 years ago, the Bahá'í Faith has spread to some 235 nations and territories and is now accepted by more than five million people. The word "Bahá'í" means "follower of Bahá'u'lláh." Bahá'u'lláh, the founder of the Bahá'í Faith, asserted that he is the Messenger of God for all of humanity in this day. The cornerstone of his teachings is the establishment of the spiritual unity of humankind, which will be achieved by personal transformation and the application of clearly identified spiritual principles. Bahá'ís also believe that there is but one religion and that all the Messengers of God—among them Abraham, Zoroaster, Moses, Krishna, Buddha, Jesus, and Muḥammad—have progressively revealed its nature. Together, the world's great religions are expressions of a single, unfolding divine plan. Human beings, not God's Messengers, are the source of religious divisions, prejudices, and hatreds.

The Bahá'í Faith is not a sect or denomination of another religion, nor is it a cult or a social movement. Rather, it is a globally recognized independent world religion founded on new books of scripture revealed by Bahá'u'lláh.

Bahá'í Publishing is an imprint of the National Spiritual Assembly of the Bahá'ís of the United States.

Other Books Available from Bahá'í Publishing

Gleanings from the Writings of Bahá'u'lláh

BY BAHÁ'U'LLÁH

A selection of the most characteristic passages from the outstanding works of the Author of the Bahá'í Revelation

As the youngest of the world's independent religions, the Bahá'í Faith comprises several million adherents who can be found in virtually every part of the planet. Its members represent what may well be the most ethnically and culturally diverse association of people in the world. Its phenomenal expansion since its inception in Persia during the nineteenth century has been fueled by a body of teachings that its followers regard as the Revelation of God's guidance for the collective coming of age of humankind. The source of those teachings is Bahá'u'lláh, the Prophet and Founder of the religion, who left a voluminous body of writings.

Gleanings from the Writings of Bahá'u'lláh is an extremely important compilation that sets out the Bahá'í teachings on a myriad of subjects. Among the themes that fall within its compass are the greatness of the day in which we live, the spiritual requisites of peace and world order, the nature of God and His Prophets, the fulfillment of prophecy, the soul and its immortality, the renewal of civilization, the oneness of the Manifestations of God as agents of one civilizing process, the oneness of humanity, and the purpose of life, to name only a few.

To those who wish to acquire a deeper knowledge and understanding of the Bahá'í Faith, *Gleanings* is a priceless treasury. To the members of the Bahá'í Faith, it has been a familiar companion for many decades, bringing spiritual fulfillment to countless people throughout the world. This new edition includes paragraph numbering for easy reference and a revised and expanded glossary.

$12.00 / $15.00 CAN

ISBN 10: 1-931847-22-3
ISBN 13: 978-1-931847-22-3

Selected Writings of Bahá'u'lláh

Though most people see the world's religions as separate, unrelated entities, the Bahá'í Faith sees them as stages in a single process. Each represents a new stage in God's progressive revelation of His will for humanity. These successive revelations have always been the true source of moral values, ideals, and standards.

The revelation of Bahá'u'lláh (1817–1892) is the most recent stage in the process. It marks the collective "coming of age" of humanity and lays the moral foundation for a global society.

Bahá'u'lláh is the founder of the Bahá'í Faith, the youngest of the independent world religions. The cornerstone of his teachings is the establishment of the unity of humankind. Bahá'u'lláh taught that there is but one religion and that all the Messengers of God—among them Krishna, Abraham, Moses, Buddha, Jesus, Muḥammad—have progressively revealed its nature. Together, the world's great religions are expressions of a single, unfolding divine plan.

Selected Writings of Bahá'u'lláh provides an overview of the Prophet's teachings, including sections on God and His Messengers, the path to God, spiritual aspects of the world civilization described by Bahá'u'lláh, the nature of the human soul and its journey after death, and the renewal of God's covenant with humanity. This volume complements new Bahá'í Publishing editions of Bahá'u'lláh's major works that have appeared in recent years: *Gleanings from the Writings of Bahá'u'lláh* (2005), *The Book of Certitude* (2003), and *The Hidden Words* (2002).

$10.00 / $13.00 CAN

ISBN 10: 1-931847-24-X
ISBN 13: 978-1-931847-24-7

Healing the Wounded Soul

BY PHYLLIS K. PETERSON

A powerful story of courage, hope, and faith that offers encouragement to survivors of childhood sexual abuse and gives important information on prevention for everyone else.

A survivor of six years of childhood sexual abuse, Phyllis Peterson tells her intensely personal story of abuse and the lifelong quest to find healing and wholeness. Her incredible journey is marked by a series of traumas, ongoing therapy, misdiagnoses, reverses, and seemingly overwhelming obstacles to personal development.

Propelled by an unquenchable desire to investigate spiritual truths and bolstered by the discovery of the healing power of her faith, Peterson triumphs by achieving a lasting positive self-image and turning outward to help others. Today her spiritual journey continues to evolve through the teachings of the Bahá'í Faith, her service as a performing artist, and further study of issues of anger and codependency.

Includes comforting extracts from Bahá'í scripture for those who are suffering, dispels myths about child sexual abuse, and provides helpful information on prevention and treatment of childhood sexual abuse.
$14.00 / $17.00 CAN
ISBN 10: 1-931847-25-8
ISBN 13: 978-1-931847-25-4

Hope for a Global Ethic

BY BRIAN D. LEPARD

How can we look with confidence to the future in a world traumatized by terror, war, and human rights violations?

Terrorism. Wars and conflicts. Genocide. Ethnic cleansing. Torture. Oppression of women. Abuse of children. Debilitating poverty. Against this backdrop of the current world scene, Brian D. Lepard suggests that only a global ethic—a shared set of ethical principles—can meet the urgent needs of our troubled global community. But where is the evidence that such an ethic even exists? And where is it to be found?

In this provocative and engaging book, Lepard asserts that there is indeed hope for a global ethic. Surprisingly, the source of that hope is embedded in the scriptures of the various world religions. Reviewing selections from the sacred texts of seven world religions—Hinduism, Judaism, Buddhism, Confucianism, Christianity, Islam, and the Bahá'í Faith—Lepard identifies numerous common ethical principles found in the sacred writings of these faiths. He clearly demonstrates how these shared principles, when put into practice, will help us peacefully solve many problems facing the world that today seem so intractable.

This inspiring and uplifting book will be of interest to anyone who cares about global issues and seeks spiritual guidance from the world's religious traditions.

$14.00 / $17.00 CAN

ISBN 10: 1-931847-20-7
ISBN 13: 978-1-931847-20-9

The Purpose of Physical Reality

BY JOHN S. HATCHER

If human beings are essentially spiritual beings, then what is the purpose of our existence in this physical world?

John Hatcher examines this and other fundamental questions. According to Hatcher, the physical world is like a classroom designed by God to stimulate and nurture our spiritual growth. *The Purpose of Physical Reality* explores the classroom of physical existence and demonstrates how everyday life experiences can lead us to spiritual insights. By viewing this physical existence as a place to learn about spiritual realities, we come to appreciate the overall justice of God's plan and the divine assistance available to unleash human potential. Not only does this concept of physical reality enable us to gain spiritual and intellectual understanding while living on earth, it prepares us for further progress in the life hereafter.

$12.00 / $15.00 CAN

ISBN 10: 1-931847-23-1
ISBN 13: 978-1-931847-23-0